Child Psychotherapy
Homework Planner
Fifth Edition

Wiley Practice*Planners*® Series

Treatment Planners

The Complete Adult Psychotherapy Treatment Planner, Fifth Edition
The Child Psychotherapy Treatment Planner, Fifth Edition
The Adolescent Psychotherapy Treatment Planner, Fifth Edition
The Addiction Treatment Planner, Fifth Edition
The Continuum of Care Treatment Planner
The Couples Psychotherapy Treatment Planner, with DSM-5 Updates, Second Edition
The Employee Assistance Treatment Planner
The Pastoral Counseling Treatment Planner
The Older Adult Psychotherapy treatment Planner with DSM-5 Updates, Second Edition
The Behavioral Medicine Treatment Planner
The Group Therapy Treatment Planner
The Gay and Lesbian Psychotherapy Treatment Planner
The Family Therapy Treatment Planner, with DSM-5 Updates, Second Edition
The Severe and Persistent Mental Illness Treatment Planner, with DSM-5 Updates, Second Edition
The Mental Retardation and Developmental Disability Treatment Planner
The Social Work and Human Services Treatment Planner
The Crisis Counseling and Traumatic Events Treatments Planner, with DSM-5 Updates, Second Edition
The Personality Disorders Treatments Planner
The Rehabilitation Psychology Treatment Planner
The Special Education Treatment planner
The Juvenile Justice and Residential Care Treatment Planner
The School Counseling and School Social Work Treatment Planner, with DSM-5 Updates, Second Edition
The Sexual Abuse Victim and Sexual Offender Treatment Planner
The Probation and Parole Treatment Planner
The Psychopharmacology Treatment Planner
The Speech-Language Pathology Treatment Planner
The Suicide and Homicide Treatment Planner
The College Student Counseling Treatment Planner
The Parenting Skills Treatment Planner
The Early Childhood Intervention Treatment Planner
The Co-Occurring Disorders Treatment Planner
The Complete Women's Psychotherapy Treatment Planner
The Veterans and Active Duty Military Psychotherapy Treatment Planner, with DSM-5 Updates

Progress Notes Planners

The Child Psychotherapy Progress Notes Planner, Fifth Edition
The Adolescent Psychotherapy Progress Notes Planner, Fifth Edition
The Adult Psychotherapy Progress Notes Planner, Fifth Edition
The Addiction Progress Notes Planner, Fifth Edition
The Severe and Persistent Mental Illness Progress Notes Planner, Second Edition
The Couples Psychotherapy Progress Notes Planner, Second Edition
The Family Therapy Progress Notes Planner, Second Edition
The Veterans and Active Duty Military Psychotherapy Progress Notes Planner

Homework Planners

Couples Therapy Homework Planner, Second Edition
Family Therapy Homework Planner, Second Edition
Grief Counseling Homework Planner
Group Therapy Homework Planner
Divorce Counseling Homework Planner
School Counseling and School Social Work Homework Planner, Second Edition
Child Therapy Activity and Homework Planner
Addiction Treatment Homework Planner, Fifth Edition
Adolescent Psychotherapy Homework Planner, Fifth Edition
Adult Psychotherapy Homework Planner, Fifth Edition
Child Psychotherapy Homework Planner, Fifth Edition
Parenting Skills Homework Planner
Veterans and Active Duty Military Psychotherapy Homework Planner

Client Education Handout Planners

Adult Client Education Handout Planner
Child and Adolescent Client Education Handout Planner
Couples and Family Client Education Handout Planner

Complete Planners

The Complete Depression Treatment and Homework Planner
The Complete Anxiety Treatment and Homework Planner

Wiley Practice*Planners*®

Child Psychotherapy
Homework Planner

Fifth Edition

Arthur E. Jongsma, Jr.

L. Mark Peterson

William P. McInnis

WILEY

This book is dedicated to our fathers and fathers-in-law:

William "Muggs" McInnis
Robert Wieringa
Arthur E. Jongsma, Sr.
Frank Landis
Lloyd Peterson
James Shanks

They have blessed us in so many ways through
their love, laughter, guidance, and support.

CONTENTS

WILEY PRACTICE*PLANNERS*® SERIES PREFACE

Accountability is an important dimension of the practice of psychotherapy. Treatment programs, public agencies, clinics, and practitioners must justify and document their treatment plans to outside review entities in order to be reimbursed for services. The books and software in the Wiley Practice*Planners*® series are designed to help practitioners fulfill these documentation requirements efficiently and professionally.

The Wiley Practice*Planners*® series includes a wide array of treatment planning books including not only the original *Complete Adult Psychotherapy Treatment Planner*, *Child Psychotherapy Treatment Planner*, and *Adolescent Psychotherapy Treatment Planner*, all now in their fifth editions, but also *Treatment Planners* targeted to specialty areas of practice, including:

- Addictions
- Co-occurring disorders
- Behavioral medicine
- College students
- Couples therapy
- Crisis counseling
- Early childhood education
- Employee assistance
- Family therapy
- Gays and lesbians
- Group therapy
- Juvenile justice and residential care
- Mental retardation and developmental disability
- Neuropsychology
- Older adults
- Parenting skills
- Pastoral counseling
- Personality disorders
- Probation and parole
- Psychopharmacology
- Rehabilitation psychology
- School counseling and school social work
- Severe and persistent mental illness
- Sexual abuse victims and offenders

- Social work and human services
- Special education
- Speech-language pathology
- Suicide and homicide risk assessment
- Veterans and active military duty
- Women's issues

In addition, there are three branches of companion books that can be used in conjunction with the *Treatment Planners*, or on their own:

- *Progress Notes Planners* provide a menu of progress statements that elaborate on the client's symptom presentation and the provider's therapeutic intervention. Each *Progress Notes Planner* statement is directly integrated with the behavioral definitions and therapeutic interventions from its companion *Treatment Planner*.

- *Homework Planners* include homework assignments designed around each presenting problem (such as anxiety, depression, substance use, anger control problems, eating disorders, or panic disorder) that is the focus of a chapter in its corresponding *Treatment Planner*.

- *Client Education Handout Planners* provide brochures and handouts to help educate and inform clients on presenting problems and mental health issues, as well as life skills techniques. The handouts are included online for easy printing from your computer and are ideal for use in waiting rooms, at presentations, as newsletters, or as information for clients struggling with mental illness issues. The topics covered by these handouts correspond to the presenting problems in the *Treatment Planners*.

Adjunctive books, such as *The Psychotherapy Documentation Primer* and *The Clinical Documentation Sourcebook*, contain forms and resources to aid the clinician in mental health practice management.

The goal of our series is to provide practitioners with the resources they need in order to provide high quality care in the era of accountability. To put it simply: We seek to help you spend more time on patients, and less time on paperwork.

ARTHUR E. JONGSMA, JR.
Grand Rapids, Michigan

ACKNOWLEDGMENTS

We want to acknowledge and express appreciation to our wives—Judy, Cherry, and Lynn—who have supported us through the many years of the Practice*Planners* series. We appreciate their willingness to read the manuscripts and offer helpful suggestions. And, speaking of manuscript preparation, this project has had the benefit of many hours of perseverance by our dedicated typist, Sue Rhoda. She has organized our chaotic, scribbled details into a meaningful manuscript with a spirit of kindness and generosity. Thank you, Sue, for your loyalty and good work. Additionally, we would like to thank Blake Jurgens for his help with the artwork on the "Feelings and Faces" assignment.

A. E. J.
L. M. P.
W. P. M.

Child Psychotherapy
Homework Planner
Fifth Edition

INTRODUCTION

More and more therapists are assigning homework to their clients. Not only have short-term therapy models endorsed this practice, but the benefits are being recognized by many traditional therapists as well.

WHY HOMEWORK?

Assigning homework to psychotherapy clients is beneficial for several reasons. With the advent of managed care, which often requires shorter and fewer treatment sessions, therapists assign between-session homework to help maximize the effectiveness of briefer treatment. Homework is an extension of the treatment process, provides continuity, and allows the client to work between sessions on issues that are the focus of therapy. Homework can also be a tool for more fully engaging the client in the treatment process. Assignments place more responsibility on the client to resolve his or her presenting problems, counteracting the expectations that some clients may experience that it is the therapist alone who can cure him or her. For some, it even may bring a sense of self-empowerment.

Another added benefit of homework is that these assignments give the client the opportunity to implement and evaluate insights or coping behaviors that have been discussed in therapy sessions. Practice often heightens awareness of various issues. Furthermore, homework increases the expectation for the client to follow through with *making* changes rather than just *talking* about change. Exercises require participation, which creates a sense that the client is taking active steps toward change. Homework also allows the client to try new behaviors, bringing these experiences back to the next session for processing. Modifications can then be made to the client's thoughts, feelings, or behaviors as the homework is processed in the therapy session.

Occasionally treatment processes can become vague and abstract. By adding focus and structure, homework assignments can reenergize treatment. Moreover, homework can increase the client's motivation to change as it provides something specific to work on. Additionally, homework increases the involvement of family members and significant others in the client's treatment using assignments that call for their participation. Homework promotes more efficient treatment by encouraging the client to actively develop insights, positive self-talk, and coping behaviors between therapy sessions. Consequently, many clients express increased satisfaction with the treatment process when homework is given. They are empowered by doing something active that facilitates the change process, and it reinforces their sense of control over the problem. These advantages have made the assignment of therapeutic homework increasingly prevalent.

HOW TO USE THIS HOMEWORK PLANNER

Creating homework assignments and developing the printed forms for recording responses is a time-consuming process. This *Child Psychotherapy Homework Planner* provides a menu of homework assignments that can easily be photocopied. In addition to the printed format, the assignments in this *Planner* are provided online to allow the therapist to access them on a word processor and print them out as is or easily custom-tailor them to suit the client's individual needs and/or the therapist's style.

The assignments are grouped under presenting problems that are typical of those found in a child population. These presenting problems are cross-referenced to every presenting problem found in *The Child Psychotherapy Treatment Planner*, fifth edition. Although these assignments were created with a specific presenting problem in mind, don't feel locked in by a single problem-oriented chapter when searching for an appropriate assignment. Included with each exercise is a cross-referenced list of suggested presenting problems for which the assignment may be appropriate and useful called "Additional Problems for Which This Exercise May Be Most Useful." This cross-referenced list can assist you in applying the homework assignments to other situations that may be relevant to your client's particular presenting problem.

A broader cross-referenced list of assignments is found in the Appendix "Alternate Assignments for Presenting Problems." Review this Appendix to find relevant assignments beyond the two or three exercises found in any specific presenting problem chapter. For example, under the heading of Conduct Disorder/Delinquency in the Appendix, you will find 18 alternative assignments originally created for other presenting problems but relevant and easily adapted for use with a client struggling with conduct disorder issues. In this Appendix, every presenting problem is listed with relevant additional assignments from throughout the book. Remember, each assignment is available online and, therefore, can be quickly edited for use with a specific client. This modified assignment can be saved on your computer's hard disk for repeated later use.

This newest edition of the *Child Psychotherapy Homework Planner* includes some important changes. A number of the homework assignments from the previous edition of the *Child Psychotherapy Homework Planner* have been shortened and/or modified to make them more user-friendly for the child. A few of the old homework assignments were omitted, but several new assignments have been added. The improvements in the *Child Psychotherapy Homework Planner*, fifth edition, make it a valuable therapeutic tool/resource for the practicing clinician.

ABOUT THE ASSIGNMENTS

Some of the assignments are designed for the parents of a child who is in treatment; others are for the client; still others are designed for the parents and child to complete together. Therapists introduce the homework assignment with varying degrees of detail and client preparation. Recommendations regarding this preparation and post-exercise discussion are made on the title page of each assignment under the heading "Suggestions for Processing This Exercise With the Client."

Clinical judgment must be used to assess the appropriate developmental level necessary for a specific assignment, as well as choosing the homework assignments that focus on relevant issues for the client. The title page of each assignment contains a section on "Goals of the Exercise" to guide you in your selection of relevant homework for your client. Remember, all assignments can be modified as necessary for the individual client.

CARRYING OUT THE ASSIGNMENT

It is recommended that you review the entire book to familiarize yourself with the broad nature of the type and focus of the various homework exercises. Select a specific assignment from a chapter titled with your client's presenting problem or from the alternative list in the Appendix and then review the list of homework goals. Assigning therapy homework is just a beginning step in the therapy treatment process. Carrying out the assignment requires a follow-up exploration of the impact of the assignment on the client's thoughts, feelings, and behavior. What are the results? Was this assignment useful to the client? Can it be redesigned or altered for better results? Examine and search for new and creative ways to actively engage your client in participating in this homework process.

ARTHUR E. JONGSMA, JR.
L. MARK PETERSON
WILLIAM P. MCINNIS

ESTABLISH A HOMEWORK ROUTINE

GOALS OF THE EXERCISE

1. Assess the client's mood and attitude surrounding the completion of his/her homework.
2. Establish general guidelines and/or a routine to help the client complete his/her homework.
3. Complete school and homework assignments on a regular and consistent basis.

ADDITIONAL PROBLEMS FOR WHICH THIS EXERCISE MAY BE MOST USEFUL

- Attention-Deficit/Hyperactivity Disorder (ADHD)
- Oppositional Defiant

SUGGESTIONS FOR PROCESSING THIS EXERCISE WITH THE CLIENT

This assignment is given to the parents of the client who has trouble completing his/her homework in a regular or consistent manner. The parents' responses to the various questions will hopefully help the therapist gain greater insight into the factors contributing to the client's failure or resistance to regularly complete his/her homework. The parents are asked to identify the client's mood or attitude surrounding homework. After responding to several questions, the parents are also asked to list three to five guidelines, rules, or interventions that they can implement to help the child complete his/her homework. The therapist should review the parents' responses in a follow-up therapy session and then help the client and parents develop a regular routine for completing the homework.

ESTABLISH A HOMEWORK ROUTINE

Educators and therapists have found that providing structure and a routine for a child can help him/her complete his/her homework on a regular basis. Having a routine can also cut down on the number of arguments between the parents and the child. In this exercise, you are asked to answer several questions that will help your therapist understand your child's moods or attitudes about completing his/her homework. Your answers will hopefully also identify some of the problems that have contributed to your child's difficulty with completing his/her homework. The ultimate goal of this assignment is to establish a routine that will help your child regularly complete his/her homework in a timely manner.

1. On the average, how much time does your child spend on homework each night?

    _____ none   _____ 30 minutes to 1 hour

    _____ 1 to 15 minutes   _____ 1 to 2 hours

    _____ 15 to 30 minutes   _____ over 2 hours

2. What is your child's usual mood or attitude when completing his/her homework? Please review the following list and check all that apply.

    _____ Good attitude—willing to do homework without complaining

    _____ Indifferent or "I don't care" attitude

    _____ Bored and/or distracted

    _____ Makes up lies about not having homework

    _____ Often tries to avoid or procrastinate doing homework

    _____ Complains at first, but then settles down to do homework

    _____ Negative attitude—frequent complaints and expressions of anger about having to do homework

    _____ Frequent yelling, screaming, or crying when required to do homework

    _____ Nervous or unsure of self when doing homework

    _____ Gives up easily when encountering frustrating or difficult tasks

    _____ Sad and disappointed in self

    _____ Expects to fail or do poorly

    _____ Other _____

3. If your child has developed a negative attitude about his/her homework, what factors or stressors have contributed to your child's negative attitude? _____

_____

_____

_____

4. What is usually the best time of the day for your child to complete his/her homework?

_____ Immediately after getting home from school

_____ Allow child time to have snack, play, or watch TV for 30–45 minutes before doing homework

_____ Right before supper

_____ Right after supper

_____ Around 7:30 p.m.

_____ Right before bedtime

_____ In morning before going to school

_____ At recess

5. On the other hand, what is usually the worst time of the day for your child to complete his/her homework? _____

_____

6. What subject(s) does your child have the most ease in completing his/her homework? _____

_____

7. What subject(s) does your child have the most difficulty with completing his/her homework?

_____

_____

8. What interventions or strategies have you tried to get your child to complete his/her homework? Please review the list below and place a checkmark next to the interventions or strategies you have tried in the past.

_____ Regular communication with teachers and school officials (e.g., phone calls, emails, read home-to-school notes, etc.)

_____ Use of "homework hotlines" or school Internet services

_____ Daily/weekly progress notes sent home

_____ Teach test-taking skills

_____ Teach child to monitor his/her own behavior

_____	Attend after-school program or work with teacher after school hours	_____	Modify amount of homework
_____	Placement in resource room or study skills class	_____	Reward system
_____	Teach study skills	_____	Frequent praise
_____	Use of tutoring services	_____	Remove privileges for failure to complete homework
		_____	Establish regular homework time
		_____	Other

9. What interventions or approaches have you found to be effective in helping your child complete his/her homework? _____
_____
_____

10. What causes your child to lose focus and/or get out of a routine? _____
_____
_____

11. What kind of support would you like from the school in helping your child to complete his/her homework? _____
_____
_____
_____

12. Now look back over your responses and list three to five guidelines, rules, or interventions that would help your child to establish a routine and complete his/her homework on a regular basis.

    A. _____
    B. _____
    C. _____
    D. _____
    E. _____

Please bring your responses back to your next therapy session. Your therapist will review your responses and help your child and you to develop a routine surrounding his/her homework.

POSITIVE SELF-STATEMENTS

GOALS OF THE EXERCISE

1. Increase the frequency of positive statements about school experiences and confidence in the ability to succeed academically.
2. Replace negative and derogatory remarks about school experiences and/or academic performance with positive statements that help to build a healthy self-image.
3. Develop a positive coping strategy to effectively deal with frustrations or struggles surrounding learning.

ADDITIONAL PROBLEMS FOR WHICH THIS EXERCISE MAY BE MOST USEFUL

- Anxiety
- Depression
- Low Self-Esteem
- School Refusal

SUGGESTIONS FOR PROCESSING THIS EXERCISE WITH THE CLIENT

Clients with learning disabilities are often troubled by feelings of insecurity and self-esteem related to their frustrations and failures associated with learning. It is not uncommon for clients with a learning disability or academic weaknesses to verbalize negative remarks about their school experiences or academic performance. The purpose of this assignment is simply for the client to replace the recurrent negative remarks about his/her school experiences or performances with more frequent positive remarks. The client is instructed to verbalize at least one positive remark each day about his/her school experiences or performance. The client is encouraged to record the positive statement in a daily log. Emphasize that utilizing this coping strategy on a regular basis will help to improve his/her self-esteem and enable him/her to cope more effectively with any school stressors. The exercise can easily be used with clients struggling with depression, anxiety, low self-esteem, or related to other stressors in life.

POSITIVE SELF-STATEMENTS

Students who struggle with learning disabilities or weaknesses often express negative remarks about their school experiences or performance. The purpose of this exercise is for you to replace the negative remarks about school with positive statements. You are asked to express at least one positive remark each day about school or your academic performance. Record the comment below along with the date and place where you expressed the positive statement.

DAY 1   Date: _____   Class or Setting: _____

          Comment: _____

_____

DAY 2   Date: _____   Class or Setting: _____

          Comment: _____

_____

DAY 3   Date: _____   Class or Setting: _____

          Comment: _____

_____

DAY 4   Date: _____   Class or Setting: _____

          Comment: _____

_____

DAY 5   Date: _____   Class or Setting: _____

          Comment: _____

_____

READING ADVENTURE

GOALS OF THE EXERCISE

1. Increase the time spent in independent reading.
2. Demonstrate consistent interest, initiative, and motivation for reading.
3. Perform up to level of capability in area of reading.
4. Build self-esteem and increase enjoyment in reading to be more able to cope effectively with the frustrations associated with his/her learning disability in reading.

ADDITIONAL PROBLEMS FOR WHICH THIS EXERCISE MAY BE MOST USEFUL

*   Attention-Deficit/Hyperactivity Disorder (ADHD)
*   Intellectual Development Disorder
*   Low Self-Esteem
*   Speech/Language Disorders

SUGGESTIONS FOR PROCESSING THIS EXERCISE WITH THE CLIENT

This homework assignment is designed to increase the client's time spent in independent reading (or other academic subjects). The client is asked to read for a certain amount of time per day or week. The frequency and length of time spent reading can be adjusted to meet the individual needs of each client. Encourage the parents to consult with the teacher(s) to select appropriate reading materials for their child and to implement a reward system to reinforce their child for spending a specific amount of time in reading. The time spent in reading will provide the client with the opportunity to master or overcome his/her frustrations with reading. The reward system can also be easily modified to address weaknesses in the areas of mathematics or written expression. For example, the client may be reinforced for practicing with flashcards or spelling words for a certain period of time each day or week.

READING ADVENTURE

This homework assignment is designed to send you on a reading adventure in your very own home. You are asked to spend a certain amount of time per day or week reading. It is hoped that this program will not only improve your reading skills, but also help to build your confidence and increase your enjoyment of reading. You are encouraged to check out books from your school or public library that match your interests. You and your parents are also encouraged to meet with your teacher to select appropriate books for your reading level.

1. In this assignment, you will not only have the chance to go on a reading adventure, but you will also be rewarded for it. Sit down and talk with your parents, teacher(s), or therapist about what is an appropriate amount of time that you should be expected to read each day or week. Look upon your parents and teacher(s) as being part of your very own Reading Adventure Team. Your Reading Adventure Team will help you identify your goal of how much time you should spend reading each day or week. If you meet your goal, then you will receive a specific reward. Following is a list of suggested rewards that you may receive for meeting your reading goals:
    *   Purchase book(s) by your favorite author
    *   Rent a video or go see a movie
    *   Spend extra time playing video games
    *   Extended bedtime
    *   Spend one-on-one time with mother or father in an agreed-upon activity
    *   Invite friend over to spend the night at your house
    *   Help to fix and prepare your favorite meal
    *   Snacks
    *   Small toys
    *   Tokens or stickers that can be traded in to purchase toys, prizes, or privileges

2. Use the following Reading Log to track your reading adventures.

3. Use the following Reading Contract to formalize the agreement between you and your Reading Adventure Team on the amount of time you will spend reading each day or week.

READING LOG

Please record the date, book title, and time spent reading for the day. Ask your parents to initial the sheet each day.

Date	Book Title	Time Read (in minutes)	Parent's Initials

READING CONTRACT

If _____ spends _____ per _____ in reading,
   (Child's name)   (Time spent)   (Day or week)

then _____ will receive the following reward:
   (Child's name)

_____

_____

_____

_____

_____

_____

_____

_____

_____

_____

_____

_____ _____
Signature of Client   Signature of Parent

_____ _____
Signature of Parent   Signature of Teacher

_____ _____
Signature of Resource Room Teacher Signature of Therapist

QUESTIONS AND CONCERNS ABOUT BEING ADOPTED

GOALS OF THE EXERCISE

1. Identify key areas of concern around being adopted.
2. Become more open to sharing concerns about the adoption process.
3. Decrease the level of anxiety around being adopted.
4. Develop a nurturing relationship with parents.

ADDITIONAL PROBLEMS FOR WHICH THIS EXERCISE MAY BE MOST USEFUL

- None

SUGGESTIONS FOR PROCESSING THIS EXERCISE WITH THE CLIENT

This exercise is directed at the age range of 8 to 11 years old. It can be completed either by the client alone or you may ask the questions in session and record the responses. Three response options are offered to give the client a response other than "yes/no" to a question he/she has not thought about before and is hearing for the first time. Prior to starting the exercise and at appropriate intervals during the process, you should reinforce with the client that these are questions that most children who are adopted have. Point out that having questions answered can lessen nervousness and make the client a little more comfortable with the coming change. Even if the client gives all "no" responses, it opens the door for more processing.

QUESTIONS AND CONCERNS
ABOUT BEING ADOPTED

Place a checkmark in the YES, NO, or MAYBE column next to each question; then share your answers with your therapist.

YES   NO   MAYBE

_____ _____ _____   1. Will it be okay if I love both my adoptive parents and my "other parents"?

_____ _____ _____   2. What will my adoptive parents do or say if I lose it?

_____ _____ _____   3. Will I ever see my "other parents" again?

_____ _____ _____   4. Can I talk to my adoptive parents about my other family?

_____ _____ _____   5. If I mess up, will my adoptive parents send me back?

_____ _____ _____   6. What will happen if I don't do well in school?

_____ _____ _____   7. How will I know my adoptive parents' rules?

_____ _____ _____   8. How will I know when my adoptive parents are upset with me?

_____ _____ _____   9. Will I have my own room?

_____ _____ _____   10. Can I tell my adoptive parents I don't like something without them getting upset (their food, clothes, rules)?

_____ _____ _____   11. Will my adoptive parents like me?

_____ _____ _____   12. Will it be okay if I don't want to hug or kiss them?

_____ _____ _____   13. Will they ask a lot of questions about my other mom, dad, and family?

_____ _____ _____   14. Will I have to be good all the time?

_____ _____ _____   15. How will I be disciplined when I mess up?

_____ _____ _____   16. Will they tell people I'm adopted?

SOME THINGS I WOULD LIKE YOU TO KNOW ABOUT ME

GOALS OF THE EXERCISE

1. Develop an environment of openness that will build a bond with adoptive parents.
2. Increase ability to share personal information.
3. Learn to remove barriers to sharing personal information.
4. Build and maintain a healthy adoptive family.

ADDITIONAL PROBLEMS FOR WHICH THIS EXERCISE MAY BE MOST USEFUL

- Blended Family
- Low Self-Esteem

SUGGESTIONS FOR PROCESSING THIS EXERCISE WITH THE CLIENT

Process this exercise in a straightforward manner. Most likely, the client will need encouragement to disclose given the history of broken trust he/she has experienced. Emphasize that sharing thoughts, feelings, and information can be helpful and will not be used against him/her, as it may have been in the past. This will likely need to be reinforced in order for the client to believe it.

SOME THINGS I WOULD LIKE TO KNOW
ABOUT MY PARENTS

On the line provided, check the questions you would like answered.

_____ 1. How old are they?

_____ 2. How many other children do they have?

_____ 3. Why do they want to adopt?

_____ 4. What do they like to do for fun?

_____ 5. What are their rules?

_____ 6. What makes them upset?

_____ 7. What is their favorite thing to do as a family?

_____ 8. What are their favorite foods?

_____ 9. Do they attend church regularly?

_____ 10. Will they expect me to go to church?

_____ 11. What is their house like?

_____ 12. Would I have my own bedroom?

Other questions I have for my adoptive parents are:

1. _____

2. _____

3. _____

4. _____

5. _____

SOME THINGS I WOULD LIKE MY PARENTS TO KNOW ABOUT ME

Complete the following:

1. My favorite food is _____

2. One food I don't like is _____

3. Vegetables: Yes ____ No ____ Maybe ____

4. A TV show I like is _____

5. My favorite movie is _____

6. The color I like best is _____

7. A color I don't like is _____

8. The time I like to go to bed is _____

9. The worst punishment to get is _____

10. One thing that makes me upset is _____

11. One thing that makes me happy is _____

12. I feel loved when _____

13. Something that makes me sad is _____

14. Something I'm afraid of is _____

15. I like school (circle one)
    Not at all   A little   Sometimes   A lot

16. School is (circle one)
    Hard   Not too hard   Sort of easy   Easy

17. My favorite subject is _____

18. My least favorite subject is _____

19. I like to do my homework (circle one)
    Right after school   After dinner   At a set time   Not at all

20. What I like best about a family is _____

21. What I like doing with a dad is _____

22. What I like doing with a mom is _____

23. What I like doing as a family is _____

24. What I like about being adopted is _____

25. What I like least about being adopted is _____

26. Don't ask me about _____

27. One secret wish I have is _____

28. A thing that makes me have a meltdown is _____
    _____

ANGER CONTROL

GOALS OF THE EXERCISE

1. Express anger through appropriate verbalizations and healthy physical outlets on a consistent basis.
2. Reduce the frequency and severity of aggressive and destructive behaviors.
3. Increase the frequency of statements that reflect acceptance of responsibility for aggressive behaviors.
4. Identify the core conflicts that contribute to the emergence of anger control problems.

ADDITIONAL PROBLEMS FOR WHICH THIS EXERCISE MAY BE MOST USEFUL

- Attention-Deficit/Hyperactivity Disorder (ADHD)
- Conduct Disorder/Delinquency
- Fire Setting
- Oppositional Defiant

SUGGESTIONS FOR PROCESSING THIS EXERCISE WITH THE CLIENT

This homework assignment is designed for clients who demonstrate poor control of their anger. Instruct the client to use the positive and negative incident reports on the following pages to record times when he/she displays both good and poor control of his/her anger. Praise the client for occasions when he/she demonstrates good control of his/her anger. Reinforce the positive coping strategies that the client uses to control his/her anger. If, on the other hand, the client displays poor control of his/her anger, then assist the client in finding more effective ways to control his/her anger. In discussing the client's angry outbursts, be sensitive and attuned to any core issues that might precipitate the angry outbursts or acts of aggression. Identification of the core issues will hopefully lead to a discussion of ways that the client can more effectively manage his/her stress and meet his/her needs.

ANGER CONTROL

The goal of this assignment is to help you improve your control of your anger. Poor anger control can create a variety of problems in your life. Your angry outbursts or aggressive behaviors can place a strain on your relationships with parents, siblings, teachers, peers, and friends. Other people may grow tired of your angry outbursts and begin to pull away or respond with anger. If you have problems controlling your anger, then you will likely be punished more often. Anger control problems can affect your self-esteem and cause you to feel unhappy, insecure, or guilty. This program seeks to help you gain greater control over your emotions and behavior and, in turn, help you feel better about yourself.

1. The first step in solving any problem is to recognize that a problem exists and to identify it. Sit down with your parents and therapist and identify the specific aggressive behaviors that you want to learn to control more effectively. Following is a list of aggressive behaviors, both verbal and physical, that a person may exhibit. Circle or underline the aggressive behaviors that you have had in the past. Blank spaces have been provided to write any other aggressive behaviors that have not been included in this list.

   - Throwing things
   - Breaking things
   - Name calling
   - Cursing or swearing
   - Talking disrespectfully
   - Making critical remarks
   - _____
   - _____

   - Hitting
   - Kicking
   - Punching
   - Taunting
   - Pulling hair
   - Spitting
   - _____
   - _____

2. Now that your specific aggressive behaviors have been identified, you can join together with your parents and therapist as a team to find effective ways to control your anger. Remember, everyone becomes angry from time to time. The goal of this program is not to prevent you from ever experiencing any anger, but to help you learn to express your anger through talking and healthy physical outlets. Between therapy sessions, you and your parents are encouraged to record times when you show both good and poor control over your anger. Use the positive incident reports to identify times when you show good control. The positive incident reports can remind you of what you did right in controlling your anger. On the other hand, use the negative incident report when you display poor control over your anger. The negative incident reports can help you think of better ways to control your anger if you are faced with similar problems in the future. Bring the positive and negative incident reports to your next therapy session so the therapist can discuss the incidents with you and your parents.

3. A reward system can be set in place to reinforce you for showing good control of your anger. You will also receive a consequence if you show poor control. Use the contract form on the following pages to make the contract official. Talk with your parents and therapist about appropriate rewards that can be used to reinforce positive anger control. A list of potential rewards follows:
   - Extra time to spend watching television or playing video games
   - Spending one-on-one time with mother or father (e.g., attend a movie, exercise together, play a board game)
   - Extended bedtime
   - Extra time on telephone or computer
   - Invite a friend over or go over to a friend's house after school
   - Invite a friend to sleep over at your house
   - Outing to favorite fast-food restaurant
   - Money
   - Snacks
   - Tokens that can be cashed in for a larger reward or privilege at a later date

POSITIVE INCIDENT REPORT

1. Describe an incident where you showed good anger control. _____
    _____
    _____
    _____
    _____

2. How did you show your anger? _____
    _____
    _____
    _____
    _____

3. What strategies did you use to control your anger? _____
    _____
    _____
    _____
    _____

4. How did you feel about yourself after the incident? _____
    _____
    _____
    _____
    _____

5. How did other people respond to how you showed your anger? _____
    _____
    _____
    _____
    _____

6. What, if anything, would you do differently if you were faced with a similar problem in the future? _____

_____

_____

_____

_____

NEGATIVE INCIDENT REPORT

1. Describe an incident where you showed poor control of your anger. _____

    _____

    _____

    _____

    _____

2. What were you angry about? _____

    _____

    _____

    _____

    _____

3. How did other people respond to your anger? _____

    _____

    _____

    _____

    _____

4. What were the consequences of your angry outburst or aggressive behavior? _____

    _____

    _____

    _____

    _____

5. What would you do differently if you had to do it all over again? How would you
    handle your anger? _____

    _____

    _____

    _____

    _____

6. What can you do to solve the problem with the other person(s) in the future? _____

_____

_____

_____

_____

ANGER CONTROL CONTRACT

I, _____ , would like to work on controlling my aggressive behaviors.
(Name of child)
Aggressive behaviors are defined as the following: _____
(List specific behaviors)

_____

_____

_____

If _____ displays good control of his/her anger and demonstrates
(Name of child)
_____ aggressive behavior(s) or less per day/week (circle one), then
(Frequency)
_____ will receive the following reward: _____
(Name of child)

_____

_____

_____

_____

If _____ shows poor control of his/her anger and becomes aggressive
(Name of child)
_____ or more time(s) in the next day/week (circle one), then _____
(Frequency)   (Name of child)
will receive the following consequence: _____

_____

_____

_____

In witness of this contract, we have signed our names on this date: _____
(Month/Day/Year)

_____   _____
Signature of Child   Signature of Parent

_____   _____
Signature of Parent   Signature of Teacher or Therapist

CHILD ANGER CHECKLIST

GOALS OF THE EXERCISE

1. Identify precipitating events or core issues that contribute to the emergence of angry outbursts or aggressive behavior.
2. Take steps to control anger more effectively through appropriate verbalizations and healthy physical outlets.
3. Reduce the frequency and severity of angry outbursts and aggressive behavior.
4. Resolve the core conflicts that contribute to the emergence of anger control problems.

ADDITIONAL PROBLEMS FOR WHICH THIS EXERCISE MAY BE MOST USEFUL

- Conduct Disorder/Delinquency
- Disruptive/Attention-Seeking
- Oppositional Defiant
- Posttraumatic Stress Disorder (PTSD)

SUGGESTIONS FOR PROCESSING THIS EXERCISE WITH THE CLIENT

The client and parents should be given this homework assignment in the initial stages of treatment. The anger checklist helps the client and parents identify the precipitating events or core issues that contribute to the client's poor anger control. The client and parents are also asked to identify the three most common factors or events that cause him/her to become most angry. Identification of the core issues or precipitating events can help the client begin to learn more adaptive ways to control or express his/her anger. The checklist also helps the therapist identify the emotional issues or stressors that need to be explored more fully in future therapy sessions. The checklist is not all-inclusive. The client and parents are encouraged to identify other factors not on the list that may contribute to his/her poor anger control.

CHILD ANGER CHECKLIST
CHILD FORM

One of the first steps in learning to control your anger is to identify the issues or events that cause you to feel angry. Following is a list of things that may cause you to feel angry. Please review the list and place a checkmark next to the events or things that often cause you to feel angry. (Note—your parents can help you fill out this checklist if needed.) Next, circle the three most common events or things that cause you to be angry. If there are other issues that are not included in the list, please write them down in the spaces provided at the end of the list after Other.

_____ Death of family member or close friend

_____ Parents' separation/divorce

_____ Family move

_____ Change of schools

_____ Parents arguing or fighting a lot

_____ Parent(s) getting remarried

_____ Past abuse/neglect

_____ Parents working long hours

_____ Not a lot of time spent with mom doing fun things

_____ Not a lot of time spent with dad doing fun things

_____ Parents are too critical

_____ Mom does not give enough praise

_____ Dad does not give enough praise

_____ Parents put too much pressure on me to do well at school or sports

_____ Poor grades or failing school

_____ Losing or failing in sports

_____ Arguments over homework

_____ Arguments over chores

_____ Time spent on computer, playing video games, or watching TV

_____ Too early bedtime

_____ Arguments at dinner/mealtime

_____ Angry with parents telling me "no" to something I want to do

_____ Angry with parents telling me to do something I do not want to do

_____ Parents punish me unfairly

_____ Parents too strict or have too many rules

_____ Parents treat my brother/sister better

_____ Teasing or name-calling by brother/sister

_____ Teasing or name-calling by friends/peers

_____ Feeling ignored or unwanted by other kids

_____ Having little chance to play with friends

_____ Other _____

_____

CHILD ANGER CHECKLIST
PARENT FORM

One of the first steps in learning to control your anger is to identify the issues or events that cause you to feel angry. The following is a list of stressful events or issues that may cause your son or daughter to become angry. Please review the list and place a checkmark next to the issues or events that you feel cause your son/daughter to experience the most anger. Next, circle the three most common factors that cause him/her to become angry. If there are other key issues or factors that are not included in the list, please record them in the spaces provided at the end of the list after Other.

_____ Death of family member or close friend

_____ Parents' separation/divorce

_____ Family move

_____ Change of schools

_____ Parents arguing or fighting

_____ Past physical abuse/neglect

_____ Past sexual abuse

_____ Parents' long work hours

_____ Lack of quality time spent with mother

_____ Lack of quality time spent with father

_____ Complaints of parental criticism

_____ Complaints of receiving little parental praise

_____ Complaints of unrealistic expectations by parents or pressure to achieve

_____ Disagreements over homework

_____ Poor school grades or performance

_____ Failure in school

_____ Losing or failure in sports

_____ Complaints of having few chances to play with friends

_____ Time spent on computer, playing video games, or watching TV

_____ Arguments over chores

_____ Arguments over bedtime

_____ Arguments at dinner/mealtimes

_____ Arguments or disputes with teachers

_____ Complaints of being mistreated or unfairly punished

_____ Complaints of too many rules

_____ Difficulty accepting "no" to request to do something

_____ Being required to do something he/she does not want to do

_____ Teasing or name-calling by siblings

_____ Teasing or name-calling by peers

_____ Feeling rejected or unaccepted by friends/peers

_____ Feeling ignored

_____ Complaints of being bullied at school

_____ Other _____

_____ Other _____

_____

THE LESSON OF SALMON ROCK . . . FIGHTING LEADS TO LONELINESS

GOALS OF THE EXERCISE

1. Verbalize an understanding of how current acting-out and aggressive behaviors are associated with past separations, losses, or abandonment issues.
2. Identify and verbalize feelings associated with past separations, losses, or abandonment issues.
3. Reduce the frequency and severity of acting-out and aggressive behaviors.
4. Express anger through appropriate verbalizations and healthy physical outlets on a consistent basis.

ADDITIONAL PROBLEMS FOR WHICH THIS EXERCISE MAY BE MOST USEFUL

- Bullying/Intimidation Perpetrator
- Grief/Loss Unresolved
- Oppositional Defiant

SUGGESTIONS FOR PROCESSING THIS EXERCISE WITH THE CLIENT

The story, "The Lesson on Salmon Rock . . . Fighting Leads to Loneliness," is aimed at reaching the acting-out and aggressive child who has experienced separation, loss, or abandonment by a significant adult in his/her life. In this assignment, the remaining parent or caretaker is asked to read the story of an Alaskan brown bear, named Barkley, to the child between therapy sessions. It is hoped that the story will promote a discussion of the child's feelings surrounding the significant separation or loss in his/her life, either by allowing the child to spontaneously share his/her feelings during the story or afterward by asking the client several process questions. The process questions can be asked of the child during appropriate points in the story or after the entire story has been read. The specific questions are offered as guides to help the child express his/her feelings. The reader is encouraged to ask other questions that may be more appropriate for each individual client. It is not necessary for all the questions to be asked in one sitting. Likewise, the child should not be pressured to answer any questions that he/she does not feel ready to answer. The story is designed for children approximately 7 to 12 years of age. You also have the option of reading this story in the therapy session, particularly if the child has been removed from the home.

THE LESSON OF SALMON ROCK . . . FIGHTING LEADS TO LONELINESS
INTRODUCTION AND READER'S INSTRUCTIONS

"The Lesson of Salmon Rock . . . Fighting Leads to Loneliness" is a story about an Alaskan brown bear, Barkley, who responds to the abandonment by his father by becoming very aggressive. Barkley becomes the Lord of the Bears through his power and aggressiveness, but eventually realizes that he is all alone. In the end, Barkley realizes that he finds more happiness and power in being a good friend to other bears.

Storytelling can be an effective way to join with the child who has experienced separation, loss, or abandonment by a significant adult in his/her life. Before reading the story to the child, try to create a relaxed atmosphere. Spend a few minutes talking with the child. Feel free to sit on the floor with the child or have the child stretch on a couch. Familiarize yourself with the story by reading it in advance. This will help you be more animated or spontaneous in your expressions as you read the story.

The purpose of sharing this story about Barkley is to help the child understand and recognize how his/her anger and acting-out behaviors are associated with a past separation, loss, or abandonment. Hopefully, by creating a supportive environment, the child will feel comfortable in opening up and sharing his/her feelings about the significant separation or loss in his/her life. After reading the story, you are encouraged to ask the child some questions about his/her past separation or loss. It may be beneficial with some children to ask him/her some of the questions as you read through the story. If the child begins to spontaneously share his/her feelings about the past separation or loss, encourage this. Offer a listening ear and an understanding tone of voice.

Following is a list of questions that you may find helpful in allowing the child to open up and share his/her feelings. These questions are offered as a guide. Please feel free to ask other questions that you feel are more appropriate for each individual child. You are encouraged to be flexible in asking the questions. Do not feel that you need to ask all of the questions. Furthermore, it is very important that you be sensitive to how the child responds to the story or questions. Do not force or pressure a child into responding to any questions that he/she may not be ready or willing to answer. You are encouraged to record any noteworthy remarks that the child may make in the following spaces.

1. In the story, Barkley is angered and hurt by his father leaving. If you were Barkley, what would you say to Dugan? _____

_____

_____

2. If you have experienced loss or separation from your father (or other important adult), what would you like to say to him/her if you were free to say anything? _____

_____

_____

_____

3. What feelings did you have when you first experienced the loss of separation from your father (or other important adult)? _____

_____

_____

4. What feelings do you have at the present time about the loss or separation? _____

_____

_____

5. In the story, Barkley reacts with anger and fighting to the separation from his father and his defeat by Thor. How have you shown your feelings of anger? _____

_____

_____

6. Nikolai helps Barkley to realize that his fighting has caused him to feel lonely in the end. How has your fighting or aggressiveness affected your relationships with other family members, friends, or peers? _____

_____

_____

7. Identify three ways that you can express your anger that lets others know how you feel, but does not hurt them or yourself.
   A. _____
   B. _____
   C. _____

8. Nikolai helps Barkley discover the power of sharing and being a friend. Name three ways that you can share or be a friend to others.
   A. _____
   B. _____
   C. _____

THE LESSON OF SALMON ROCK . . . FIGHTING LEADS TO LONELINESS

Alaska, the great northern frontier, is a land like no other. It is a unique place, for nowhere on earth do the polar bear, Alaskan brown bear, and American black bear all live. These three different bears symbolize the beauty and power of the Alaskan wilderness.

Barkley, a brown bear, lived in Alaska. Barkley was born in the cold, sleepy winter months to his mother, Kiana, and father, Dugan. He snuggled close to his mother and father in their mountain cave as they hibernated during the winter months. He was awakened in the springtime to the sounds of buzzing insects, and he bounded out of his cave full of energy. His parents told him that they would leave their winter home in the mountains and travel down to the valley below.

While traveling down the mountainside, Barkley and his family found that many of the best fishing spots had already been claimed by the largest brown bears. When Dugan finally discovered a perfect place for his family to catch fish, a large 1,500-pound brown bear suddenly appeared out of the woods. He gruffly commanded Dugan and his family to leave his place on the river. The large bear became very angry and lunged at Dugan. Dugan fought bravely, but he was no match for the larger, stronger bear. Dugan ended up running away in defeat, with Kiana and Barkley following him. He was humiliated and ashamed in his family's presence. He did not say anything to them for the rest of the evening.

Barkley rose early the next morning and discovered that his father was gone. Barkley called out to his father in the wilderness, but received no answer. He explored the meadows and smaller streams looking for his father, but he could not find him. Barkley waited for his father to return that evening, but he never did. Barkley continued waiting all the next week. He felt hurt, sad, and confused. He wasn't sure whether his father had been hurt or he just left out of shame. Barkley told his mother that he wanted to set out and search for his father. Kiana could sense the hurt and anger in her son's voice and agreed to let him go. So, Barkley set out on his search.

The summer days passed and the busy streams were full of leaping salmon. Barkley was drawn to the river each day to see how many delicious fish he could catch. The salmon could be seen everywhere struggling to swim upstream to get to their final destination. Barkley was amazed by the number of fish. As he traveled upstream with them, he came to a six-foot-high waterfall. At the top of the waterfall, several small- and medium-sized rocks joined together to form a bridge that led out to a very large rock. Barkley climbed up the banks to get to the top of the waterfall and followed the path of stones out to the large rock. He climbed up and stood on top of the rock, ready to snag a leaping fish. A fish shot out of the water like a cannonball and Barkley was ready to grab it, but all of a sudden, he felt the rock trembling underneath his feet. Barkley's thoughts were no longer on the fish, but on the big bear that was before him. The other bear growled fiercely at Barkley, "What are you doing here on Salmon Rock? I am Thor, Lord of the Bears. Salmon Rock belongs to me!" Barkley felt both confused and frightened. He replied, "What's the problem? This rock seems big enough for both of us to fish on." Thor shouted back, "Get off my rock. I don't ever want to see you on this part of the river again," and with that, he smacked Barkley with his tremendous paw. Barkley tumbled into the water and crashed to the bottom of the waterfall. The weight of the rushing water pushed him downstream with such force that he was unable to come up for another 50 yards. Barkley struggled to make his way closer to the riverbank. Finally, he grabbed hold of a fallen tree and was just able to pull himself up on the riverbank.

Barkley shook the water out of his fur and wished that his father was there to stand up for him. Anger and shame swelled up inside of Barkley, to the point where he vowed to himself that he would never be treated like that again. He whispered to himself, "I will return next year and become the new Lord of the Bears. It will be me who stands atop Salmon Rock."

The fall season passed quickly. Barkley found a comfortable cave for his long winter nap and he laid down to hibernate. When the winter months passed, he made his way down the hills to the river, remembering his vow to return to Salmon Rock. As he journeyed to Salmon Rock, Barkley tested his strength by fighting other bears over their fishing spots. He battled 10 bears. He was the winner each time, but he did not stay to claim those spots on the river. He still wanted the most prized spot of all, Salmon Rock. Barkley finally reached Salmon Rock and growled to let Thor know of his presence. Thor immediately stood up and bellowed, "I thought I had warned you not to come back, and I see that you have ignored my warning. I will just have to give you more of the same medicine that I gave you last fall." Barkley responded, "I am no longer the same bear, which you will soon discover." Barkley jumped onto the rock, and a furious battle ensued. This time, Barkley grabbed Thor by his body and thrust him into the water. Thor was quickly swept downriver by the powerful waters. When he emerged from the water, Barkley roared, "I am the new Lord of the Bears. I have fulfilled my vow to myself. It is now you who must leave and never come back!" News of Barkley's victory spread throughout the nearby mountains and plains. Newcomers came to challenge Barkley for the title of Lord of the Bears. Each time, the challengers were defeated, and Barkley only grew more sure of himself.

Barkley left Salmon Rock one day to gather berries. While he was gone, a small, innocent bear, named Nikolai, climbed onto Salmon Rock to fish. The new Lord of the Bears became very angry when he saw the small bear on his throne and demanded that Nikolai leave. Barkley was shocked when Nikolai looked up at him and said, "I think there's enough room here for the two of us. I don't see any problem with me staying." Just as Thor did to him the previous year, Barkley struck Nikolai with his paw and sent him flying into the river. Barkley said, "See to it that you never set foot on Salmon Rock again, for I am Lord of the Bears. Go home to your family and stay put with them." Nikolai shouted over the sound of the rushing waters, "I will go home, and when I see the northern lights flashing in the sky tonight, I will feel happy being with my family, while you will feel lonely on this cold, hard rock with nothing but your title, Lord of the Bears. I don't think I'll need to ever come back."

That night, Barkley sat on Salmon Rock as the northern lights flashed in the sky. Nikolai's words came back to haunt him and he realized that he was truly alone. Barkley tried to ease his feelings of loneliness by telling himself that he was the most powerful bear around. However, Barkley's reassurances to himself did not work. He realized for the first time that he had scared away any possible friends with his anger and fury. Barkley broke down and wept. He cried over not having his father. He cried over leaving his mother. He cried over not having any friends and being all alone.

Barkley remained on the rock for 2 more days, barely moving. On the third day, Barkley decided to leave Salmon Rock and search for food elsewhere. During his travels, he came upon a bear family fishing in about a foot of water. Barkley was entertained by the youngest bear who was frustrated in his efforts to catch any fish. Barkley drew closer and was surprised to see that it was Nikolai. Barkley cried out, "What's the matter, little one, can't you catch any fish?" Nikolai then replied, "Oh, leave me alone. I haven't gone back to Salmon Rock to bother you anymore, so I don't need you teasing me here in my home."

An unfamiliar feeling came over Barkley. He looked at the young bear and admired his spunk. Barkley said, "Come with me to a place where you will surely catch fish. Come with me to Salmon Rock. There is more than enough room for the two of us." Nikolai hesitated before saying, "I thought you didn't let anyone else on your throne. How can I trust that you won't throw me back into the river?" Barkley shared, "I found out that what you said was true. I've found that Salmon Rock is a lonely place when you're the only one who stays there. I would like it if you would come back and fish with me." Nikolai reluctantly inquired, "Can I bring my family along with me?" Barkley softly replied, "Sure."

Barkley led Nikolai and his family back to Salmon Rock. The other neighboring bears were shocked to see Barkley sharing his space. The day passed and Barkley found more happiness in sharing Salmon Rock with Nikolai's family than in being selfish and alone. It felt so good to share. Barkley made sure from that day on that many other bears got their fair chance to fish from Salmon Rock. In sharing, Barkley learned the importance of making friends. He was no longer content in being Lord of the Bears. Rather, Barkley found happiness in knowing that he was a good friend. He also searched out and found his mother, Kiana. Barkley often invited her to visit him at Salmon Rock.

Barkley lived a good life sharing his place on Salmon Rock with many other bears. And, whenever the northern lights put on their dazzling display in the evening sky, Barkley made sure that Nikolai was by his side to enjoy the beauty. Ah, Alaska! There is no other place on earth quite like it.

AN ANXIOUS STORY

GOALS OF THE EXERCISE

1. Externalize the source of the anxiety by putting a face to the anxiety.
2. Reduce the overall frequency, intensity, and duration of the anxiety so that daily functioning is not impaired.
3. Increase sense of possibility and hope of dealing with the anxiety.
4. Develop unique outcomes that can be implemented to cope with or resolve the anxiety.

ADDITIONAL PROBLEMS FOR WHICH THIS EXERCISE MAY BE MOST USEFUL

- Obsessive-Compulsive Disorder
- School Refusal
- Separation Anxiety
- Social Anxiety
- Specific Phobia

SUGGESTIONS FOR PROCESSING THIS EXERCISE WITH THE CLIENT

This assignment is based on M. White's and D. Epston's approach of "Narrative Means to Therapeutic Ends." For centuries, stories have been a way, for children especially, to deal with difficult issues. It would be best to have the client do this assignment in the therapy session. Creating pictures to go along with the story is to be encouraged. If the client is younger than 8 years old, you should assist the child in writing the story by breaking it down and feeding the questions to him/her one by one in a style similar to Gardner's mutual storytelling technique. Allow the client to go where he/she needs to. Once the story is completed, have the client read the story to you. Act it out as much as the client directs you to. Then encourage the client to share the story with parents as a homework assignment.

AN ANXIOUS STORY

Write a short or long story about what makes you feel anxious or nervous. Begin by giving that "thing" that makes you anxious a name and then describe what it looks like and what it does. Next, tell all the things it does to get at you. (Be specific and use your imagination.) End the story with the way you beat, defeat, or outsmart that thing. You could begin with "Once upon a time," or "Just the other day," or "Every time I start to. . . ." To give you an example of how a story might begin, read the following.

Once upon a time, there was a young girl who lived with her parents, two brothers, one dog, and one cat in a big house in a quiet neighborhood. The girl was named Nicole. She was 7 years old and loved school and playing outside with her friends. However, for the last 3 months, every time she began playing with her friends outside, this ghostlike shadow, named Mr. Creep, would bother her and scare her by telling her she was going to get bit by a poisonous bug or kidnapped by a stranger. Nothing she tried could keep her from becoming frightened and running inside her house where she felt safe and where Mr. Creep left her alone. It was bad at home but worse at friends' houses. Since she stayed home all the time, her friends started to make fun of her and say she was weird. So Nicole tried. . . .

1.   Write your story in the following space.

_____
_____
_____
_____
_____
_____
_____
_____
_____
_____
_____
_____
_____
_____

_____

_____

_____

_____

_____

_____

_____

_____

_____

_____

_____

_____

_____

_____

_____

2. Now that you have completed the story, see if you can come up with another ending in which you beat, defeat, conquer, outsmart, or trick that "thing" again.

_____

_____

_____

_____

_____

_____

_____

_____

_____

_____

_____

_____

_____

Once you have finished the story, share it with your therapist and both of you act it out in your next meeting.

DEEP BREATHING EXERCISE

GOALS OF THE EXERCISE

1. Learn and practice deep breathing technique.
2. Identify specific situations to use this skill.
3. Demonstrate the ability to use the deep breathing technique in identified situations at home, school, and other social situations.
4. Enhance the ability to effectively cope with the full variety of life's anxieties.

ADDITIONAL PROBLEMS FOR WHICH THIS EXERCISE MAY BE MOST USEFUL

- Physical/Emotional Abuse Victim
- Posttraumatic Stress Disorder (PTSD)
- Separation Anxiety
- Sexual Abuse Victim
- Social Anxiety
- Specific Phobia

SUGGESTIONS FOR PROCESSING THIS EXERCISE WITH THE CLIENT

This is an important technique for many children who have heightened levels of anxiety due largely to adverse childhood experiences. As a result of these experiences, they have developed a shallow breathing pattern. Deep breathing helps slow their bodies down when they encounter situations that provoke anxiety, fear, or other threats and make it possible for them to use their skills to assess, process, and problem-solve the situation at hand. Obviously, the therapist is actively involved in this exercise, helping the client to learn, understand, master, and then implement this skill in his/her life situations. The practicing part should be made fun and appropriately competitive with the opportunity to praise the client for effort and the advancement of his/her skill level. Also, a parent or caregiver should learn this technique as well, in order to practice it with the child and to help him/her implement it in situations that arise at home.

DEEP BREATHING EXERCISE

It is important that when we become nervous, worried, or afraid, we learn to settle our bodies down first. By doing this, we can better handle situations, thus making things better for ourselves and making us feel better about ourselves. Learning deep breathing can help us to do this. Your therapist will help you learn this skill.

STEP 1 (Think 4–4–4)
- Take 4 deep breaths in.
- Hold these breaths for 4 counts.
- Then breathe out 4 counts.
- Repeat two times.

STEP 2
- Using a piece of paper, draw a slice of pizza, making sure that you put on it all of the toppings that are your favorites.
- Now, using the piece of pizza you have made, imagine it coming right out of the oven and how that smells. In order to smell it well, take in 4 deep breaths, holding that great smell for 4 counts.
- Next, cool the pizza off so you can eat it by blowing on it for 4 counts.
- Repeat two times.

STEP 3
- To further your skill at deep breathing, practice by using a pinwheel or bubbles.
- Remember the 4–4–4 technique, and using this, see either how long or fast you can make the pinwheel go or how big a bubble you can blow. You can also practice with the bubbles and pinwheel at home between appointments.

STEP 4
- Now to get this deeper breathing into our brains, teach this to your parent/caregiver. If they are not available, teach it back to your therapist.

STEP 5
- With the help of your parent and therapist, identify one situation at home and one at school that make you feel anxious/nervous, worried, or afraid.

At School: Situation _____

_____

_____

At Home: Situation _____

_____

_____

Now make a plan for how you will use your deep breathing skills the next time these two situations come up. Plan: _____

_____

_____

_____

_____

STEP 6

- Practice your deep breathing at home during the week by yourself using bubbles or a pinwheel or practice with your parent. Report to your therapist how you are doing and how you have used deep breathing in the situations you identified in Step 5.

DEEP BREATHING EXERCISE

GOALS OF THE EXERCISE

1. Identify what precipitates the feelings of anxiety.
2. Increase the ability to verbalize thoughts and feelings about what brings on anxiety.
3. Explore options for coping with or resolving the feelings of anxiety.
4. Enhance ability to effectively cope with the full variety of life's anxieties.

ADDITIONAL PROBLEMS FOR WHICH THIS EXERCISE MAY BE MOST USEFUL

- Separation Anxiety
- Social Anxiety
- Specific Phobia

SUGGESTIONS FOR PROCESSING THIS EXERCISE WITH THE CLIENT

Anxiety, or nervousness, can often be something that is hard to pin down. It can certainly be seen in children, but getting at the specific cause is difficult and often elusive. Different ages in children can bring different fears that vary in degree depending upon the individual child's makeup, family environment, and the situations life presents. The result is that most anxieties disappear and change with time. The important thing is for children to develop the ability to talk about their anxieties with someone they trust and someone who will take what they have to say seriously. Therefore, do not say that feelings do not make sense or offer some rational explanation as to why it cannot be; instead, it is essential to just listen, accept, and encourage. Acceptance and encouragement of sharing feelings can either help specifically identify what the source of the anxiety is or help reduce the anxiety through desensitization and extinction.

FINDING AND LOSING YOUR ANXIETY

There are many things that can make a person feel anxious or nervous. In order to feel better, it is important to identify exactly what makes you anxious. In the following word search, find the items that can make some of us feel anxious or nervous:

Monsters	Storms	Death	Mistakes	Fighting
Bugs	Dark	Yelling	Divorce	
Snakes	Strangers	Noises	Arguing	

Complete the following word search.

S	T	O	R	M	S	K	R	A	D
R	P	E	V	J	O	S	S	Y	I
E	R	L	K	F	E	N	T	G	V
T	D	E	A	T	H	A	R	N	O
S	L	U	K	W	R	K	A	I	R
N	P	S	R	G	N	E	N	T	C
O	I	B	U	G	S	S	G	H	E
M	T	I	A	C	E	D	E	G	B
C	N	O	I	S	E	S	R	I	U
G	N	I	L	L	E	Y	S	F	K
S	E	K	A	T	S	I	M	G	V

1. Name three things that make you feel anxious or nervous.

    A. _____

    B. _____

    C. _____

2. Which one of the three makes you feel the most anxious?

    _____

3. When you experience this anxious feeling, which of the following things happen to you? (Circle at least one.)

Hands sweat	Heart beats faster	Become short of breath
Get angry	Feel physically sick	Freeze and do nothing
Become fearful	Try to think or do something else quickly	Try not to let others know by acting okay
Call for help		
Run to a safe place	Start talking to anyone who is nearby	

    Other reactions to feeling anxious are: _____

4. What have you tried that helps you get over feeling nervous?

    _____

    _____

    _____

    _____

    _____

5. What has worked the best?

    _____

    _____

    _____

    _____

    _____

6. Now, ask two people whom you trust the following questions.

    A. Do you ever feel anxious?   1. Yes   No

                                       2. Yes   No

    B. What makes you anxious?   1. _____

                                       2. _____

C. How do you handle the anxiety
   you feel?

1. _____

   _____

2. _____

   _____

7. From the input you received from others or from an idea you have, create another
   possible way to handle your anxious feelings.

   _____

   _____

   _____

   _____

WORRY TIME

GOALS OF THE EXERCISE

1. Reduce overall frequency, intensity, and duration of the anxiety so that daily functioning is not impaired.
2. Learn and implement a strategy to limit the association between various environmental settings and worry, delaying the worry until designated "worry time."
3. Stabilize anxiety level while increasing ability to function on a daily basis.
4. Enhance ability to effectively cope with the full variety of life's anxieties.

ADDITIONAL PROBLEMS FOR WHICH THIS EXERCISE MAY BE MOST USEFUL

- Depression
- Low Self-Esteem
- Separation Anxiety
- Specific Phobia

SUGGESTIONS FOR PROCESSING THIS EXERCISE WITH THE CLIENT

Clients with a Generalized Anxiety Disorder often spend an excessive amount of time worrying. Furthermore, they have trouble "letting go" of their worries. The goal of this exercise is to decrease the amount of time spent in worrying by restricting worry to a specific time and place. It is important to sit down with the client and his/her parents to designate a specific time and place for him/her to worry. Younger children may find it beneficial to express their worries to a favorite stuffed animal or "worry rock." Teach the client how to recognize, stop, and delay worry to the agreed-upon "worry time" by using techniques such as deep breathing, deep muscle relaxation, thought-stopping, and refocusing. The client should be trained in the use of these various techniques before implementing the "worry time" intervention. The client, along with help from his/her parents(s), is asked to complete a daily Worry Time Log to identify how successful he/she was in restricting the amount of time spent in worrying each day.

WORRY TIME
PARENTS' AND CLIENT'S INSTRUCTIONS

Children dealing with anxiety spend a great deal of time worrying about different problems or things. They have trouble "letting go" of their worries. Excessive worrying can be tiring, both physically and emotionally. It can take away one's energy and interfere with the ability to relax and enjoy life. It is not uncommon for people who experience anxiety to have trouble with both falling and staying asleep. High levels of anxiety and excessive worrying can make it difficult to concentrate on one's schoolwork and other tasks in life. Furthermore, people who worry to excess often do not enjoy their time spent with family and friends because they are so focused on their problems.

The purpose of this exercise is to reduce the amount of time you spend each day worrying. The first step in this exercise is to recognize what it is that you are specifically worried about in your current life. Next, you will select a specific time and place where you can focus on your worries. You are asked to set aside a specific "worry time" for 15–20 minutes each day. Your therapist can help you select a specific time and place. The idea behind this exercise is to limit your worrying to a specific time and place. You have the option of sharing your worries with a parent, another family member, or a friend. You can also share your worries with your favorite stuffed animal or a "worry rock." After your "worry time" has ended, you are instructed to use the strategies or interventions (e.g., deep breathing, relaxation, thought-stopping, or refocusing) to help manage your anxiety and worries for the remainder of the day. Parents, you may find it helpful to encourage your child to play or do some leisure/recreational activity to take his/her mind off worries (this is called "refocusing"). Talk with your therapist about which specific strategy you feel is most helpful in limiting the amount of time you spend worrying outside of the "worry time." We realize that this is easier said than done, but with regular practice of these techniques (i.e., deep breathing, relaxation, thought-stopping, or refocusing), the hope is that you will be able to manage your anxiety more effectively. Please fill out the daily Worry Time Log at the end of each day to let your therapist know how successful you have been in limiting the amount of time you spent worrying each day. (Parents, you can help your child fill out the log.)

DAILY WORRY TIME LOG

Date and Time: _____ Place: _____

1. What you were worried about today: _____

   _____

   _____

2. Rate the degree of your anxiety and worry on a scale from 0 to 10 (place a checkmark above the appropriate number).

0	1	2	3	4	5	6	7	8	9	10

3. What strategy did you use to try and restrict the amount of time you spent worrying? (Please check all that apply.)

   _____ Deep breathing   _____ Relaxation   _____ Positive self-talk

   _____ Thought-stopping   _____ Refocusing   _____ Other (please list)

   _____

4. How successful was/were your strategy/strategies in limiting the amount of time you spent worrying?

   _____

   _____

   _____

   _____

5. If the strategies were not helpful in limiting the time you spent worrying today, what factors or stressful events interfered with your ability to let go of your worries? _____

   _____

   _____

   _____

   _____

ATTACHMENT SURVEY

GOALS OF THE EXERCISE

1. Decrease myths about attachment.
2. Identify and reinforce factors that promote attachment.
3. Reinforce the reality that there is hope for attachment, but it will be slow, hard work.
4. Establish and maintain a bond with primary caregivers.

ADDITIONAL PROBLEMS FOR WHICH THIS EXERCISE MAY BE MOST USEFUL

- Adoption
- Posttraumatic Stress Disorder (PTSD)

SUGGESTIONS FOR PROCESSING THIS EXERCISE WITH THE CLIENT

This exercise can be done with either a single parent, parental team, or as a group of parents. The process should encourage parents to be open about how they see attachment and how they would like it to occur. The survey offers the opportunity to dispel many myths and to focus on the key components and time frames of building attachment. It will be important to process the parents' feelings about the amount of work and time it may take for attachment to develop. The therapist needs to often reflect the hope that exists if parents stay committed to the relationship. Answers to the survey are: 1-T, 2-F, 3-T, 4-F, 5-T, 6-F, 7-T, 8-F, 9-T, 10-F, 11-T, 12-F, 13-T.

ATTACHMENT SURVEY

Check either TRUE or FALSE in response to the following statements about attachment and parenting children who have attachment difficulties.

TRUE   FALSE

_____ _____ 1. All human beings by nature want to attach.

_____ _____ 2. All children need is enough love.

_____ _____ 3. Attachment does not happen in a hurry (i.e., "Only bad things happen quickly").

_____ _____ 4. Children will show appreciation for what you do for them.

_____ _____ 5. Accepting the child's past and not hiding it contributes to healing.

_____ _____ 6. You'll naturally love any child.

_____ _____ 7. Establishing family traditions and rituals foster attachment.

_____ _____ 8. You will not think bad things about the child's biological parents.

_____ _____ 9. It is not helpful to be impressed or frightened by the child's emotions.

_____ _____ 10. Children's memories of abuse will fade in time if they are allowed to forget.

_____ _____ 11. Speak often and optimistically about the future.

_____ _____ 12. You'll be rewarded for caring for your children.

_____ _____ 13. Encouraging the right to feel and appropriately express feelings aids attachment.

14. What are two factors that indicate to me that a child is attached?

    _____

    _____

15. What are two factors that indicate to me that a child struggles with becoming attached?

    _____

    _____

16. Circle your response to the following statement: "Protecting, providing, and guiding are the three essential tasks of a primary caregiver that foster and nurture attachment."

    Strongly disagree   Disagree   Unsure   Agree   Strongly agree

    Explain your response: _____

    _____

    _____

BUILDING RELATIONSHIPS

GOALS OF THE EXERCISE

1. Identify specific activities that will encourage and promote connection to parents.
2. Increase activities that will further strengthen the bond with parents and others.
3. Resolve all barriers to forming healthy connections with others.

ADDITIONAL PROBLEMS FOR WHICH THIS EXERCISE MAY BE MOST USEFUL

- Physical/Emotional Abuse Victim
- Sexual Abuse Victim

SUGGESTIONS FOR PROCESSING THIS EXERCISE WITH THE CLIENT

Although the instructions indicate that the client could complete this exercise alone, it is recommended that the therapist and client work on it together. When it is completed with the therapist, the client's hesitations on certain questions can be observed to better assess the client's emotional state. The processing should be focused on looking for specific ways that the client is open to developing relationships. What is obtained through this exercise needs to be passed on to parents and others so they can do the identified activities together to build their relationship with the client.

BUILDING RELATIONSHIPS

Complete the following exercise by yourself or with your therapist.

1. Who are the people you trust? (Circle and fill in their name(s).)

    Mom   Teacher _____   Friend _____

    Dad   Grandparent _____   Brother/sister _____

2. Of all the people listed, whom do you *trust the most*? _____
    How much do you trust them? (circle)

    A little   It depends   Somewhat   Quite a bit   A whole lot

3. What makes you trust that person?

    _____

    _____

    _____

4. Whom do you *feel closest to*? (Circle and fill in the person's name.)

    Mom   Teacher _____   Friend _____

    Dad   Grandparent _____   Brother/sister _____

5. How much do you share with them about yourself (feelings, thoughts, dreams, and past)?

    Very little   Little   Some   Quite a bit   A whole lot

6. When someone special hugs me or sits close to me, I feel . . . (circle)

    Great   Good   Okay   A little uncomfortable   Unsure

7. Which two things from the following list would you like most to have a special person do either with you or for you? (circle)

    Read to me   Take a walk with me

    Buy me something I want   Talk just with me

    Fix my hair or nails   Hug me

    Compliment me   Play catch

8. Circle two things from the following list that you would like to hear from a person you trust and who is special to you.

You're likeable   You're safe here   You're needed/important

You're a good person   There's hope   You have great abilities

We love you   It's not your fault   We will always be here for you

GETTING IT DONE

GOALS OF THE EXERCISE

1. Complete school and homework assignments on a regular, consistent basis.
2. Develop positive study skills and work habits.
3. Increase frequency of on-task behaviors.
4. Parents maintain regular communication with the teacher(s) to increase the client's compliance with completion of school and homework assignments.
5. Parents develop and utilize an organized system to keep track of the client's school assignments.

ADDITIONAL PROBLEMS FOR WHICH THIS EXERCISE MAY BE MOST USEFUL

- Academic Underachievement
- Conduct Disorder/Delinquency
- Low Self-Esteem
- Oppositional Defiant

SUGGESTIONS FOR PROCESSING THIS EXERCISE WITH THE CLIENT

It is not uncommon for children with an attention-deficit/hyperactivity disorder (ADHD) to have difficulty completing their school or homework assignments on a regular basis. Many clients with ADHD require increased structure to complete their schoolwork regularly. The increased structure requires regular communication between home and school. In this program, the parents and teacher(s) are asked to maintain open lines of communication through the use of daily or weekly progress reports. The teacher(s) is asked to send home a daily or weekly progress report to the parents, informing them as to how well their son or daughter is doing at completing his/her school assignments. The frequency of the progress reports, either daily or weekly, should depend on several factors: the child's age, motivation, and how responsible he/she is about completing his/her school or homework assignments. Encourage the parents and teacher(s) to implement a reward system to reinforce the client for completing the work.

GETTING IT DONE
PARENTS' INSTRUCTIONS

Children who have been diagnosed as having ADHD often have difficulty completing school assignments on a regular basis. They frequently display problems with their organizational skills. The goal of this program is to help your child complete his/her school or homework assignments on a regular basis. In this program, parents and teachers are encouraged to maintain open lines of communication with one another. The teachers are asked to send home a daily or weekly progress report, informing you as to how well your child is doing at completing his/her school/homework assignments. Review this progress report at the end of each day or week. The frequency of the progress reports will depend on your child's degree of responsibility in completing the schoolwork.

In order for the program to be effective, cooperation among the parents, teacher(s), and child is important. Teachers are encouraged to fill out the Daily or Weekly School Report, which is provided on the following pages. They should check whether the child has completed his/her expected amount of work or note any uncompleted school assignments. A space is also provided for the teacher to record any additional homework. Parents should review the report with the child, initial the form, and send it back to the teacher. Space is provided on the Daily or Weekly School Report form for teachers or parents to record any additional comments. The child's cooperation is an important ingredient in the success of this program. He/she should be told that he/she will be responsible for bringing the progress report home at the end of each day or week. He/she will also be expected to bring home any books or materials necessary to complete his/her assignments. Failure to do so should result in a consequence or loss of reward.

Parents and teachers are encouraged to use a reward system to reinforce the child for completing his/her school/homework assignments. The child should be positively reinforced for completing all school or homework assignments at the end of each day or week. Use the following contract form as a means of formalizing the agreement with your child. Talk with your child about appropriate rewards that can be used to reinforce responsible behavior. The following rewards are offered as suggestions:

- Extra time to play video games
- Spend one-on-one time with parent
- Outing to favorite fast-food restaurant
- Money
- Snacks
- Tokens that can be cashed in for larger reward at a later date

DAILY SCHOOL REPORT

Name: _____   Date: _____

_____

School: _____   Grade: _____

_____

Subject	Teacher	Classroom Work Check if completed; note uncompleted assignments	Homework

Additional Comments:

_____

_____

_____

_____

_____

_____

_____

WEEKLY SCHOOL REPORT

Name: _____ Week from: _____ to: _____

Grade: _____

Subject	Teacher	Classroom Work Check if completed; note uncompleted assignments	Homework

Additional Comments:

_____

_____

_____

_____

_____

_____

_____

_____

SCHOOL CONTRACT

If ————————————, a student at ———————————, completes all of his/her
      (Name of client)   (School name)

school or homework assignments by the end of each day/week (circle one), then
————————————will receive the following reward:
(Name of client)

———————————————————————————————————————

———————————————————————————————————————

———————————————————————————————————————

———————————————————————————————————————

In witness of this contract, we have signed our names on this date: ————————————
         (Month/Day/Year)

———————————————————   ———————————————————

Signature of Client   Signature of Parent

———————————————————   ———————————————————

Signature of Parent   Signature of Primary Teacher

———————————————————   ———————————————————

Signature of Resource Room Teacher   Signature of Therapist

———————————————————

Other Signature

PROBLEM-SOLVING EXERCISE

GOALS OF THE EXERCISE

1. Improve problem-solving abilities.
2. Identify problem and explore alternative courses of action before making final decision to act.
3. Learn to evaluate own behavior and how it affects self and others.
4. Develop coping strategy to inhibit the tendency toward impulsive responding.
5. Demonstrate marked improvement in impulse control.

ADDITIONAL PROBLEMS FOR WHICH THIS EXERCISE MAY BE MOST USEFUL

- Anger Control Problems
- Conduct Disorder/Delinquency
- Depression
- Oppositional Defiant

SUGGESTIONS FOR PROCESSING THIS EXERCISE WITH THE CLIENT

Children with attention-deficit/hyperactivity disorder (ADHD) are characterized by their tendency to exercise poor judgment and act without considering the consequences of their actions. The ADHD client frequently finds himself/herself in trouble without realizing what caused him/her to get there, and fails to recognize the antecedents of his/her negative consequences. In this exercise, the client is taught a problem-solving strategy to inhibit his/her impulses and resolve conflict or problems more effectively. The client first identifies a problem and then works through the subsequent problem-solving stages. Younger children may need assistance from their parents or therapist in working through the problem-solving stages. This exercise can be used with other children who do not have ADHD, but are struggling with impulse control or other emotional problems.

PROBLEM-SOLVING EXERCISE

Children sometimes find themselves in trouble without realizing what caused them to get there. At times, children try to solve problems by quickly rushing into a situation without stopping and thinking about the possible consequences of his/her actions. Unfortunately, the failure to stop and think causes negative consequences for both self and others. If this sounds all too familiar and you are tired of finding yourself in trouble because of your failure to stop and think, then this problem-solving exercise is designed for you. In this exercise, you are taught to use basic problem-solving steps to deal with a stressful situation. Hopefully, by following these steps, you will find yourself in less trouble with others and feel better about yourself.

1. **Identify the Problem**: The first step in solving any problem is to realize that a problem exists. At this beginning stage, you are asked to identify either a major problem that you are currently facing or a common recurring problem that troubles you. Talk with your parents, teachers, friends, or peers if you have trouble selecting a problem that you would like to focus on solving.
    Identify the problem: _____
    _____

2. **Brainstorm Solutions (List Pros and Cons of Each Solution)**: After identifying the problem, consider three different possible courses of action to help you solve or deal with the problem. List the pros and cons of each possible course of action. Record at least three different pros and cons for each course of action.
    First possible course of action to be taken: _____

    Pros _____   **Cons** _____
    _____   _____
    _____   _____
    _____   _____

    Second possible course of action to be taken: _____

    Pros _____   **Cons** _____
    _____   _____
    _____   _____
    _____   _____

Third possible course of action to be taken: _____

_____

Pros _____   **Cons** _____

_____   _____

_____   _____

_____   _____

3. <u>**Select a Solution and Implement the Action:**</u> Next, review the pros and cons of each one of your possible courses of action. At this point, you are encouraged to talk with a teacher, parent, friend, or peer to help you choose a final plan of action. Identify the course of action that you plan to follow: _____

_____

_____

What factors influenced you to choose this course of action? _____

_____

_____

What advice or input did you receive from others that influenced your decision?

_____

_____

4. <u>**Evaluate the Outcome:**</u> Now it is time to follow through on your plan of action. In the space provided, describe the events that occurred when you followed through with your plan of action.

_____

_____

_____

_____

You are in the final stage of this exercise. You have identified the problem, considered different possible courses of action, made a decision, and followed through on your plan of action. Your final task is to evaluate the results or success of your plan of action. Please respond to the following questions.

What were the results of your plan of action? _____

_____

_____

_____

_____

How do you feel about the results? _____

_____

_____

How did your plan affect both you and others? _____

_____

_____

_____

What did you learn from this experience? _____

_____

_____

_____

_____

5. **<u>Modify the Action if Necessary</u>:** What, if anything, would you do differently if you were faced with the same or a similar problem in the future? _____

_____

_____

_____

_____

_____

What advice or input, if any, have others given you about what you should do differently in the future? What do you think of their advice? _____

_____

_____

_____

SOCIAL SKILLS EXERCISE

GOALS OF THE EXERCISE

1. Develop more appropriate social skills.
2. Increase the frequency of socially appropriate behaviors with siblings and peers.
3. Learn self-monitoring techniques to help assess social skills.
4. Identify and reinforce positive behaviors that will enable the establishment and maintenance of peer friendships.

ADDITIONAL PROBLEMS FOR WHICH THIS EXERCISE MAY BE MOST USEFUL

- Autism Spectrum Disorder
- Conduct Disorder/Delinquency
- Oppositional Defiant
- Peer/Sibling Conflict
- Social Anxiety

SUGGESTIONS FOR PROCESSING THIS EXERCISE WITH THE CLIENT

This exercise is designed to teach self-monitoring techniques to children with attention-deficit/hyperactivity disorder (ADHD) to improve their social skills. The parent(s), teacher(s), client, and therapist are encouraged to sit down as a team to identify specific social behaviors that the client needs to work on and improve. The client, with the assistance of his/her team, selects various social skills that he/she would like to practice each day or over the course of a week. Model the appropriate social behaviors for the client in the therapy sessions through the use of role-playing and behavioral rehearsal. Encourage the client to use a self-monitoring form as a reminder to practice the desired social skills and to assess his/her performance.

SOCIAL SKILLS EXERCISE
PARENT/TEACHER INSTRUCTIONS

Children with ADHD often experience problems in their interpersonal relationships with both peers and adults because of their poor social skills. In this exercise, the child will use a self-monitoring form to focus on improving specific social skills.

1. Meet with the child to identify and select the specific social skills that you would like him/her to practice each day or over the course of a week. Be specific in defining the desired social behaviors so that the child clearly understands what is expected of him/her. Model the positive social behaviors through the use of role-playing. The following is a list of suggested social skills that the child can practice:
    - Compliment peers or siblings
    - Express feelings in an appropriate and assertive manner
    - Apologize for misbehaviors
    - Respond to losing or failure by displaying good self-control
    - Perform a favor for someone without expecting anything in return
    - Demonstrate kindness to peers
    - Express thanks and appreciation
    - Ignore teasing or name-calling
    - Cooperate in a game or activity without arguing
    - Start conversations or introduce self to new peer

2. Instruct the child to use the Social Skills Self-Monitoring Form on the following page to help improve his/her social skills. Place the Self-Monitoring Form in a readily accessible place, such as in his/her notebook. Space is also provided on the form to record when and how effective the child was in practicing the skill.

3. Use a reward system to reinforce the child for his/her positive social behaviors. The reward system will help maintain his/her motivation for practicing the social skills. Please use the Social Skills Contract to identify the specific target behaviors.

SOCIAL SKILLS SELF-MONITORING FORM

Name:_____ Date:_____

Choose a social skill from the following list or write in one of your own ideas to practice.

Suggested Social Skills

- Compliment others
- Ignore teasing or name-calling
- Do a favor for someone
- Start a conversation
- Share your personal items
- Wait your turn patiently
- _____

- Express feelings in an appropriate manner
- Show kindness to peers
- Cooperate in a game or activity
- Introduce yourself to a new person
- Listen to others' concerns or problems
- _____
- _____

I will practice this skill today:

_____

_____

_____

Record incidents in which you practiced the social skill:

1. Name of person:_____ Location:_____

   Comments: _____

   _____

   _____

2. Name of person:_____ Location:_____

   Comments: _____

   _____

   _____

3. Name of person:_____ Location:_____

   Comments: _____

   _____

   _____

SOCIAL SKILLS CONTRACT

If _____ practices the following social skill _____
  (Child's name)   (Social skill)
_____ time(s) in the next day or week (circle one), then _____
  (Frequency)   (Child's name)
will receive the following reward:

_____

_____

_____

_____

_____

_____

_____

In witness of this contract, we have signed our names on this date: _____
                                                                   (Month/Day/Year)

_____   _____
Signature of Child   Signature of Parent

_____   _____
Signature of Parent   Signature of Teacher or Therapist

_____   _____
Signature of Therapist   Signature of School Official

INITIAL REACTION TO DIAGNOSIS OF AUTISM

GOALS OF THE EXERCISE

1. Provide parents with the opportunity to express their thoughts, feelings, and concerns soon after learning that the client has been diagnosed with autism.
2. Assist parents in addressing the challenges involved in raising a child with autism.
3. Increase the parents' awareness of their own fears and worries about raising a child with autism.
4. Eliminate parents' denial surrounding the client's autism.
5. Assist parents in gaining a healthy acceptance of the client's autism.
6. Parents increase social support network.

ADDITIONAL PROBLEMS FOR WHICH THIS EXERCISE MAY BE MOST USEFUL

- Attachment Disorder
- Intellectual Development Disorder

SUGGESTIONS FOR PROCESSING THIS EXERCISE WITH THE CLIENT

This assignment is designed for parents who have recently learned that their child has autism. One of the primary goals of the assignment is to provide parents with the opportunity to begin to open up and share their thoughts and feelings about raising a child with autism. The parents are also given the opportunity to share their fears, concerns, or worries about how the client's autism will impact not only themselves, but their other children as well. The parents' responses to the questions can help provide insight into whether they are experiencing any denial and/or have developed unrealistic expectations (either good or bad) regarding the client's future development. If the parents have developed any unrealistic expectations, then the therapist may need to educate the parents further about the diagnosis of autism. Ultimately, it is hoped that the parents will gain a healthy perspective and acceptance of the client's autism. The exercise concludes with the parents identifying the resources that they feel will help them cope with raising an autistic child.

INITIAL REACTION TO DIAGNOSIS OF AUTISM

When a parent learns that his/her child has been diagnosed with autism, this news can produce a mixture of emotions. Some parents may experience anger, fearfulness, or distress, while other parents may feel relieved because some of their questions have been answered. Please take a few minutes to answer the following questions. Your responses will help your therapist understand your thoughts and feelings about raising a child who has been diagnosed with autism.

1. When did you first begin to suspect that your child might have autism? _____
   _____
   _____

2. What signs or symptoms of autism does your child frequently exhibit? _____
   _____
   _____
   _____

3, What is the severity of your child's autistic symptoms? (Please check the appropriate space.)
   _____ borderline _____ mild _____ moderate _____ severe

4. What was your initial response after learning that your child has autism? _____
   _____
   _____
   _____

5. What was your spouse's initial response after learning that your child has autism?
   _____
   _____

6. How have your child's symptoms of autism affected your life? _____
   _____
   _____

7. How have your child's symptoms of autism affected your spouse? _____

_____

_____

8. How has your child's autism affected your other children? _____

_____

_____

_____

9. Before learning that your child had autism, how did you feel about your own parenting abilities?

_____

_____

_____

10. What are your greatest fears or worries about raising a child with autism? _____

_____

_____

_____

11. What do you perceive as being the biggest challenges in raising a child with autism? _____

_____

_____

_____

12. What services do you think your child will need in the future? _____

_____

_____

_____

13. In raising a child with autism, it helps for the family to receive support or help from other family members, friends, or agencies. Who can provide support for your family and you? What type of support would you like to receive for your family?

_____

_____

_____

_____

_____

REACTION TO CHANGE
AND EXCESSIVE STIMULATION

GOALS OF THE EXERCISE

1. Identify how the client copes with changes in routine or handles unstructured, large group settings with a significant amount of extraneous stimulation.
2. Assist parents in developing effective coping strategies to help client adapt to changes in routine or handle large group settings with excessive stimulation.
3. Stabilize mood and tolerate changes in routine or environment.

ADDITIONAL PROBLEMS FOR WHICH THIS EXERCISE MAY BE MOST USEFUL

- Attachment Disorder
- Attention-Deficit/Hyperactivity Disorder (ADHD)
- Intellectual Development Disorder

SUGGESTIONS FOR PROCESSING THIS EXERCISE WITH THE CLIENT

It is recommended that this assignment be given to the parents in the beginning stages of treatment to help the therapist gain a clearer picture of how the client copes with changes in his/her routine or environment. Likewise, the assignment provides insight into how the client adjusts to unstructured, large group settings where there is a significant amount of extraneous stimulation. The parents are first asked to identify how their son/daughter copes with changes in routine or his/her environment. The parents' responses provide insight into how the other siblings and they, themselves, react to the client's moods or behavior in these situations. The parents are asked to step back and reflect on what strategies or interventions have been useful in managing the client's negative reactions to changes in his/her routine or environment. It is hoped that they will also identify strategies or interventions that have not proven to be effective over time. The parents should be challenged to cease employing any strategies or interventions that have not been found to be helpful.

REACTION TO CHANGE AND EXCESSIVE STIMULATION

It is not uncommon for children with Autism Spectrum Disorder to have difficulty adapting to change, whether it be a major change in their lives or a smaller change in their everyday routines. Many times, these children also have difficulty adjusting to unstructured, large group settings where there is a great deal of stimulation (e.g., loud noises, bright or flashing lights, emotionally charged settings such as a packed gym for a basketball game). Please take the time to respond to the following questions to help your therapist gain a clearer picture of how your child reacts to change or unstructured, large group settings. Your responses to the following questions will also help your therapist understand what strategies or interventions have proven to be either helpful or not helpful. It is ultimately hoped that your responses will help your therapist and you to identify and use effective strategies.

1. How does your son/daughter typically adapt to changes in his/her routine or handle large group settings where there is a great deal of stimulation? Please review the following list and place a checkmark next to the signs, symptoms, or behaviors that your child frequently exhibits around these times.

_____ Becomes agitated or irritable

_____ Becomes oppositional or defiant

_____ Exhibits angry outbursts or emotional meltdowns

_____ Demanding of parent(s)' attention

_____ Frequent complaints of wanting to go home

_____ Crying or excessive whining

_____ Emotions become flat, constricted, or blunted

_____ Becomes quiet and withdrawn

_____ Tries to block out stimulation by focusing on small or minor details

_____ Becomes preoccupied with certain objects

_____ Engages in unusual motor movements (e.g., flapping or waving of arms, rocking back and forth, unusual gestures with fingers or hands)

_____ Exhibits oddities in speech (e.g., repeats certain words or phrases, talks in sing-song fashion, shouting loudly)

_____ Unable to shift response to meet demands of new situation

_____ Engages in self-harmful behaviors (e.g., banging head, biting or scratching self)

_____ Other _____

2. What percentage of the time does your child have trouble coping with change or handling large group settings?

____ 0–20%   ____ 20–40%   ____ 40–60%   ____ 60–80%   ____ 80–100%

3. How do you respond to your child's emotional or behavioral problems in these situations? _____

_____

_____

_____

4. How does your spouse respond to your child's moods or behavior in these situations?

_____

_____

_____

5. How do your other children react to your son/daughter's emotional problems in these situations? _____

_____

_____

_____

6. What strategies or approaches have you tried using to help your son/daughter cope with changes in routine or handle unstructured, large group settings? Please review the following list and place a checkmark next to all the strategies or approaches that you have tried.

_____ Ignore behavior

_____ Try to remove child from situation

_____ Redirect child to another activity

_____ Try to narrow child's focus onto smaller details

_____ Talk to child about topic of his/her interest

_____ Talk to child in advance about how to cope with change or group settings

_____ Yell at child or demand that he/she stop behavior

_____ Give time-outs

_____ Threaten to remove privilege or take away toy when he/she gets home

_____ Spank child

_____ Give child food to please him/her

_____ Promise to reward child with toy or desired object for behaving well in these situations

7. What other strategies or approaches have you tried that are not listed? _____
_____
_____
_____
_____

8. Which of the strategies listed above have proven to be helpful in allowing your child to adapt to changes in his/her routine or environment? _____
_____
_____
_____
_____
_____

9. Which of the strategies listed above have not been successful at all? _____
_____
_____
_____
_____
_____

10. What questions do you have for your therapist about how your child responds to changes in his/her routine or environment? _____
_____
_____
_____
_____

BLENDED FAMILY SENTENCE COMPLETION

GOALS OF THE EXERCISE

1. Promote identification and expression of thoughts, feelings, and beliefs about the client's nuclear and new blended family.
2. Identify the nature and quality of the relationship that the client would like to have with each new family member.
3. Establish a new family identity in which each family member feels he/she belongs and is valued.
4. Accept the new blended family system as not inferior to the nuclear family, just different.

ADDITIONAL PROBLEMS FOR WHICH THIS EXERCISE MAY BE MOST USEFUL

- Adoption
- Divorce Reaction
- Peer/Sibling Conflict

SUGGESTIONS FOR PROCESSING THIS EXERCISE WITH THE CLIENT

This, like many of the exercises, is one where the therapist is actively involved in order to assist the client in maximizing its benefits. At the start, it would be best to give some psychoeducation to the client around change and families and how that generally affects all of us (i.e., feelings, thoughts). It is helpful to have a safe place to express these thoughts and feelings in order to be able to work them out in a positive way. Further, it would be recommended that the starting paragraph be followed to not only introduce the exercise and set the mood, but to most importantly provide the client "choices" that give some sense of empowerment and control even as he/she is currently in this environment of a major change.

BLENDED FAMILY SENTENCE COMPLETION

Complete the following sentences with either one word or several. You can say the first thing that comes to your mind or take a minute and give a more thoughtful response. The exercise can be finished by you alone, or your therapist can read the questions and record your responses. The choice is yours. Have fun!

1. My mom is _____

2. My dad is _____

3. My stepmom's/stepdad's girlfriend is _____

4. My stepdad's/stepmom's boyfriend is _____

5. I like my mom when she _____

6. I like my dad when he _____

7. I like my stepmom's/stepdad's girlfriend when _____

8. I like my stepdad's/stepmom's boyfriend when _____

9. The thing that bugs me most about my family is _____
   _____

10. If I could change one thing about my family, it would be _____
    _____

11. If I could change one rule at my mom's house, it would be _____
    _____

12. If I could change one rule at my dad's house, it would be _____
    _____

13. One thing that I like about my family is _____
    _____

14. One thing that I like about my new family is _____

_____

15. The thing I miss the most about my old family is _____

_____

16. The biggest problem that I have at my mom's house is _____

_____

17. The biggest problem that I have at my dad's house is _____

_____

18. If one thing could be different at my mom's house, it would be _____

_____

19. If one thing could be different at my dad's house, it would be _____

_____

20. What makes me happiest at my mom's house is _____

_____

21. What makes me happiest at my dad's house is _____

_____

22. Something I like about my stepsister(s) is _____

_____

23. Something I like about my stepbrother(s) is _____

_____

24. A thing that bugs me about my mom is _____

_____

25. A thing that bugs me about my dad is _____

_____

26. A thing that bugs me about my stepdad's/stepmom's boyfriend is _____

_____

27. A thing that bugs me about my stepmom's/stepdad's girlfriend is _____

_____

28. I like it when _____

_____

29. I hate it when _____

_____

30. One wish that I have for my new family is _____

_____

31. I feel special when my mom _____

_____

32. I feel special when my dad _____

_____

33. The person in my family that I would like to spend more time with is _____

34. What I would like each family to do more of is _____

_____

_____

_____

INTERVIEWING MY NEW FAMILY MEMBER

GOALS OF THE EXERCISE

1. Increase dialogue among new family members.
2. Identify common likenesses and points of interest among members in order to establish and develop connections.
3. Decrease distance among members by the sharing of personal information.
4. Achieve a reasonable level of family connectedness and harmony whereby members support, help, and are concerned for each other.

ADDITIONAL PROBLEMS FOR WHICH THIS EXERCISE MAY BE MOST USEFUL

- Adoption
- Attachment Disorder
- Social Anxiety

SUGGESTIONS FOR PROCESSING THIS EXERCISE WITH THE CLIENT

This exercise can be completed in the office or given to the client to be completed at home and then processed at the client's next session. If the assignment is completed in a family session, the therapist must structure the interview with questions being answered one at a time by each member. During the interview process, it is hoped that the members will make connections on their own when they share common interests. However, if they do not see those points, the therapist will need to assist them in making these recognitions. Also, to maximize the sharing, the therapist should ask questions of members that encourage further elaboration of their responses. This process will model interchange for the family members and give permission for other members to ask their own probing questions.

INTERVIEWING MY NEW FAMILY MEMBER
ADULT TO CHILD

Interview your new family member and record his/her responses.

1. What is your favorite TV show? _____

2. What game do you like best to play with family? _____

3. What is one of your favorite foods? _____

4. What vegetable do you hate? _____

5. What time do you like to go to bed? _____

6. What is your favorite cartoon? _____

7. What do parents do to bug you? _____

8. What activity do you like to do with family? _____

9. What are your favorite movies? _____

10. What is your favorite subject in school? _____

11. What is your least favorite subject? _____

12. What is the best place to go on vacation? _____

13. What makes you feel really happy? _____

14. Who is more your hero, Superman or Batman? _____

15. What is your favorite sport? _____

16 How do you feel about attending church with the family? _____

INTERVIEWING MY NEW FAMILY MEMBER
CHILD TO ADULT

Interview your new family member and record his/her responses.

1. What is your favorite TV show? _____

2. What game do you like best to play with family? _____

3. What is one of your favorite foods? _____

4. What vegetable do you hate? _____

5. What time do you like to go to bed? _____

6. What is your favorite cartoon? _____

7. What do kids do to bug you? _____

8. What activity do you like to do with family? _____

9. What are your favorite movies? _____

10. What was your favorite subject in school? _____

11. What was your least favorite subject? _____

12. What is the best place to go on vacation? _____

13. What makes you feel really happy? _____

14. Who is more your hero, Superman or Batman? _____

15. What is your favorite sport? _____

16 How do you feel about attending church with the family? _____

THOUGHTS AND FEELINGS ABOUT PARENT'S LIVE-IN PARTNER

GOALS OF THE EXERCISE

1. Promote expression of thoughts and feelings about the parent's live-in partner residing in the home.
2. Assess the client's perception of the positive and negative aspects of the parent's boyfriend or girlfriend living in the home.
3. Identify the nature and quality of the relationship the client would like to establish with the parent's live-in partner.
4. Begin to take steps toward establishing a closer bond or more harmonious relationship between the client and his/her parent and live-in partner.
5. Attain a level of peaceful coexistence whereby daily issues can be negotiated without becoming ongoing conflicts.

ADDITIONAL PROBLEMS FOR WHICH THIS EXERCISE MAY BE MOST USEFUL

- Divorce Reaction
- Parenting
- Peer/Sibling Conflict

SUGGESTIONS FOR PROCESSING THIS EXERCISE WITH THE CLIENT

This exercise is designed for the client whose parent has recently had a boyfriend or girlfriend move into the home. (Note—the boyfriend or girlfriend will be referred to as the live-in partner or LIP.) The primary purpose of the exercise is to provide the client with the opportunity to share his/her thoughts and feelings about the LIP moving into the home. Many children, when faced with a new living arrangement, may be anxious or hesitant to share their thoughts and feelings. For this reason, the client may be reluctant to complete the exercise at home for fear that his/her responses may be read by the parent or LIP before he/she is ready to share them openly. The therapist may want to use this exercise in the therapy session. The questions can be asked in an interview format. The client may be more comfortable in confidentially sharing his/her thoughts and feelings in a therapy session. After processing the client's responses, the therapist should assess how comfortable the client would feel in sharing his/her thoughts and feelings with the parent and/or LIP. Before using the assignment, the therapist is also strongly encouraged to review the list of questions. The therapist may want to add, delete, or modify some of the questions depending on the client's unique living situation.

THOUGHTS AND FEELINGS ABOUT PARENT'S LIVE-IN PARTNER

Children often experience a variety of feelings when their parent has a boyfriend or girlfriend move into the home. You can have both good and bad feelings about the live-in boyfriend or girlfriend. This exercise gives you the chance to share your own thoughts and feelings about your parent having a boyfriend or girlfriend living in the home. Please answer the following questions. (Note—your parent's boyfriend or girlfriend will be referred to as the live-in partner or LIP in the questions.)

1. How long has the LIP been living in your home?

   _____

2. How did you first feel when the LIP moved into your home?

   _____

   _____

   _____

3. What do you like about the LIP as a person?

   _____

   _____

   _____

4. What do you dislike about the LIP as a person?

   _____

   _____

   _____

5. What do you like about the LIP living in your home?

   _____

   _____

   _____

6. What do you dislike about the LIP living in your home?

_____

_____

_____

7. Is your home or family life better, worse, or the same since the LIP moved into the house? If your family life is better or worse, please explain further.

_____

_____

_____

8. What are your worries or concerns about the LIP living in the home?

_____

_____

_____

9. How long do you think your parent's relationship with the LIP will last?

_____

_____

_____

10. How has your behavior been since the LIP moved into your home?

_____

_____

_____

_____

11. Since the LIP moved into your home, how do you get along with your parent?

_____

_____

_____

_____

12. Is your relationship with your parent better, worse, or the same since the LIP moved into the home? Please explain further if your relationship is better or worse.

_____

_____

_____

_____

13. What kind of relationship would you like to have with the LIP in the future?

_____

_____

_____

_____

14. How comfortable are you with sharing your thoughts and feelings about your home situation with your parent or LIP?

_____

_____

_____

_____

15. What would you be comfortable in sharing with your parent or LIP?

_____

_____

_____

_____

16. What thoughts and feelings would you not be comfortable in sharing with your parent or LIP?

_____

_____

_____

_____

APOLOGY LETTER FOR BULLYING

GOALS OF THE EXERCISE

1. Offer sincere and genuine apology to other children who have been victims of the bullying, threatening, or intimidating behavior.
2. Verbalize an acceptance of responsibility for the bullying or intimidating behavior.
3. Develop empathy and compassion for others.
4. Terminate intimidating behavior and treat others with respect and kindness.

ADDITIONAL PROBLEMS FOR WHICH THIS EXERCISE MAY BE MOST USEFUL

- Anger Control Problems
- Conduct Disorder/Delinquency
- Peer/Sibling Conflict

SUGGESTIONS FOR PROCESSING THIS EXERCISE WITH THE CLIENT

The purpose of this assignment is to prepare the client to offer a sincere, genuine apology to the other child (or children) who has been a victim of his/her bullying, threatening, or intimidating behavior. The client is first required to respond to a series of questions or items that will help him/her offer a well-thought-out apology. After responding to the questions, the client is encouraged to write a rough draft on a separate piece of paper. The client should share and process the contents of the rough draft with the therapist before giving a sincere apology to the victim(s). The therapist should explore whether the client should give either a verbal or a written apology. One of the primary goals of the exercise is to increase the client's empathy and sensitivity to how his/her aggressive and threatening behavior may negatively impact others. The therapist should challenge or confront any statements in which the client projects the blame for his/her bullying or threatening behavior onto other people or outside circumstances and refuses to accept full responsibility.

APOLOGY LETTER FOR BULLYING

You are being asked to apologize to _____
(Name of child/other children)
who you have either bullied, threatened, or frightened in some way. Before giving your apology, please respond to the following questions or items. Your answers or responses will help you give a well-thought-out apology and show that you are truly sorry for your bullying or threatening behavior.

1. Please describe your bullying or threatening behavior. _____
   _____
   _____
   _____

2. What were the reasons or factors that caused you to either bully or threaten the other child or children? _____
   _____
   _____
   _____

3. Tell in your own words why you are responsible or at fault for your bullying or threatening behavior. _____
   _____
   _____
   _____

4. Now tell the reasons why the other child or children are not responsible or to blame for your bullying or threatening behavior. _____
   _____
   _____
   _____

5. What bad things happened to the other child or children as a result of your bullying or threatening behavior? Was the other child physically hurt or emotionally upset? Please describe. _____
   _____
   _____
   _____

6. What punishment did you receive, either at home or school, because of your bullying or threatening behavior? _____

    _____

    _____

    _____

7. How has your bullying or threatening behavior affected your relationship with the other child or children involved in the incident? _____

    _____

    _____

    _____

8. What lessons have you learned about how your bullying behavior affects others?

    _____

    _____

    _____

9. What can you say to the other child or children to show that you have accepted your punishment? _____

    _____

    _____

    _____

10. What can you say to the other child or children that will help them feel better or safer in the future? _____

    _____

    _____

    _____

On a separate piece of paper, write a rough draft of your apology to the other child or children. Look back over your responses or answers to the previous questions to help write your letter. Do not send the rough draft or give an apology to the other child or children without first talking to your therapist. Please bring your responses and rough draft to the next therapy session.

BULLYING INCIDENT REPORT

GOALS OF THE EXERCISE

1. Identify contributing factors and sequence of events that led up to the bullying or threatening behavior at home, at school, or in the community.
2. Explore underlying emotions that contributed to the bullying or intimidating behavior at home, at school, or in the community.
3. Express hurt and anger in nonviolent ways.
4. Terminate intimidating behavior and treat others with respect and kindness.

ADDITIONAL PROBLEMS FOR WHICH THIS EXERCISE MAY BE MOST USEFUL

- Anger Control Problems
- Depression
- Oppositional Defiant

SUGGESTIONS FOR PROCESSING THIS EXERCISE WITH THE CLIENT

The incident report in this assignment should be completed by the client shortly after engaging in an act of bullying or intimidation at home, at school, or in the neighborhood. Hopefully, the client's responses to the questionnaire will provide insight into the factors or sequence of events that led up to his/her bullying or intimidating behavior. The client is asked to identify the underlying emotions that he/she was experiencing prior to the bullying incident. It is hoped that the client will learn more adaptive ways to express and/or manage his/her anger other than behaving in an intimidating or bullying manner. It is acceptable for teachers or other school officials to help the client complete the questionnaire if this behavior occurred at school.

BULLYING INCIDENT REPORT

1. Date of incident: _____
    Approximate time: _____
    Place or setting: _____

2. Please describe the incident when you either bullied or threatened someone. _____
    _____
    _____
    _____

3. What events led up to you bullying or threatening the other child or children? ____
    _____
    _____
    _____

4. What had your mood and behavior been like on the day before the incident
    occurred? (Check all that apply.)

    ___ Angry or mad   ___ Fearful   ___ Quiet and withdrawn
    ___ Irritable or grouchy ___ Guilt   ___ Disappointed
    ___ Frustrated   ___ Happy   ___ Bored
    ___ Lonely   ___ Content or satisfied ___ Embarrassed
    ___ Felt unwanted   ___ Hyperactive   ___ Other (please identify)
    ___ Nervous   ___ Sad   _____
    ___ Worried

5. What thoughts did you experience before you made the threats or bullied the other
    child or children? _____
    _____
    _____

6. What were the consequences of your behavior for the other child or children? What
    bad things happened to them? _____
    _____
    _____

7. How did other kids react to your threatening or bullying behavior? _____
   _____
   _____

8. How did the teachers, school officials, or parents of the other child or children react to your threatening or bullying behavior? _____
   _____
   _____

9. How did your parents react to your threatening or bullying behavior? _____
   _____
   _____

10. What punishment did you receive at home or school because of your threatening or bullying behavior? _____
    _____

11. What other things could you do in the future to control your anger and stop acting like a bully? (Please check all that apply.)

    ____ Walk away before bullying others

    ____ Ignore teasing, name-calling, or mean remarks

    ____ Talk calmly to other kid(s) about the problem

    ____ Listen better to other kid(s) with whom I am angry

    ____ Find appropriate physical ways to express anger (e.g., play sports, run)

    ____ Express anger by writing in journal

    ____ Express anger through drawings

    ____ Talk to friends or other kids about the problem

    ____ Talk to parents, school counselor, or teacher

    ____ Meet with other kids involved in incident and grown-ups to talk about the problem

    ____ Other (please identify) _____

12. If you had to do it all over again, how would you have handled the incident differently? _____
    _____
    _____
    _____

BUILDING EMPATHY

GOALS OF THE EXERCISE

1. Increase awareness of how hurtful words, acting out, and aggressive behaviors negatively impact other people.
2. Begin to show empathy, concern, and sensitivity for the thoughts, feelings, and needs of other people.
3. Increase verbalizations of empathy and concern for other people.
4. Increase frequency of actions that reflect empathy, concern, and kindness for others.

ADDITIONAL PROBLEMS FOR WHICH THIS EXERCISE MAY BE MOST USEFUL

- Anger Control Problems
- Bullying/Intimidation Perpetrator
- Lying/Manipulative
- Oppositional Defiant

SUGGESTIONS FOR PROCESSING THIS EXERCISE WITH THE CLIENT

The primary goal of this assignment is to help the client begin to demonstrate empathy for the thoughts, feelings, and needs of other people. The assignment has three parts and does not have to be done all at once. The different parts of the assignment can be assigned across two to three sessions or weeks. The first part of the assignment asks the client to reflect on times when he/she has been hurt by the words and actions of other people. The second part requires the client to think about times when his/her hurtful words or actions negatively impacted other people. The final part of the assignment seeks to increase the client's empathy by reflecting on how one of his/her behaviors adversely affects others. The therapist may need to take time to define empathy. Likewise, the therapist and parents may need to illustrate how empathy is shown. The assignment concludes with the child identifying a specific way that he/she can demonstrate empathy and kindness in the next week.

BUILDING EMPATHY

Most of us have heard of the *Golden Rule*, which states, "Do unto others as you would have them do unto you." Following the *Golden Rule* helps one to build strong family relationships and close friendships. A person demonstrates kindness, respect, and caring for others when they regularly follow the *Golden Rule*.

The Silver Rule is not as well known as the *Golden Rule*. The *Silver Rule* states, "If you don't want it done to you, then don't do it to others." All of us have been hurt by the hurtful words and actions of other people. At the same time, we, ourselves, have likely said or done things to others that have caused them hurt. In this assignment, you will have the chance to follow both the *Silver Rule* and *Golden Rule*.

This assignment has three parts and one main goal. First of all, you will be asked to write about times when you were hurt by the words or actions of other people. Second, you will then be asked to identify times when other people were negatively affected by your hurtful words, actions, or behaviors. By realizing how you have been hurt by others and how you sometimes hurt others through your words and actions, you will be encouraged to follow the *Silver Rule* and not seek to hurt others as much. The main goal of this assignment is to increase your empathy for other people. We show empathy for other people's thoughts, feelings, and needs when we try to "put ourselves in their shoes" and really try to understand their thoughts and feelings. Empathy is one of the basic building blocks for establishing close relationships. By showing empathy, we also show kindness and concern for others (which is following the *Golden Rule*).

PART ONE

Before you are asked to consider how your words or actions may hurt other people, you are first asked to think about times when you have been hurt by others. Take a few moments to think about when you have been hurt by other people's words, actions, or misbehaviors, either physically or emotionally. After thinking about these experiences, please write about some of them below.

1. When was a time when your parent(s), brother(s), or sister(s) said or did something to you that you did not like? _____

   _____

   _____

   _____

2. How did the words or actions make you feel? _____
    _____

3. How did you show your feelings? _____
    _____

4. If you expressed your feelings to your family member(s), how did they respond to
    your feelings? _____
    _____
    _____

5. How did their words or actions affect your life? _____
    _____
    _____

6. When was a time that your teacher(s) or peer(s) said or did something to you that
    you did not like? _____
    _____
    _____

7. How did the words or actions make you feel? _____
    _____

8. How did you show your feelings? _____
    _____

9. If you expressed your feelings, how did your teacher(s) or peer(s) respond to your
    feelings? _____
    _____
    _____

10. How did their words or actions affect your life? _____
    _____
    _____

PART TWO

Now that you have thought about times when you were hurt by the words, actions, or
misbehaviors of other people, do the reverse and think about times when your words,
actions, or misbehaviors hurt other people in some way, either physically or emotionally.
Write about some of these incidents below.

1. When was a time that your parent(s), brother(s), or sister(s) were hurt by your words, actions, or misbehaviors? _____

    _____

    _____

2. How did your parent(s), brothers(s), or sister(s) feel about your words or actions?

    _____

3. How did they show their feelings? _____

    _____

4. How did your words, actions, or misbehaviors affect their life? _____

    _____

    _____

5. When was a time that your teacher(s) or peer(s) were hurt by your words, actions, or misbehaviors? _____

    _____

    _____

6. How did your teacher(s) or peer(s) feel about your words, actions, or misbehavior?

    _____

7. How did they show their feelings? _____

    _____

8. How did your words, actions, or misbehaviors affect their life? _____

    _____

    _____

PART THREE

You are now asked to think about a specific behavior that you regularly do that hurts other people either physically or emotionally. If you are having a hard time thinking of a specific behavior, then please ask your parents, teachers, or therapist for help.

1. After you have given this some thought, what is a specific behavior that you regularly do that irritates, annoys, or negatively affects other people in some way?

    _____

    _____

    _____

2. How can you "undo" your hurtful words or actions? In other words, what can you say or do that shows the other person(s) that you realize you are aware of how your words or actions have hurt them? _____

_____

_____

_____

3. What changes can you make that will show the other person(s) that you care about their thoughts and feelings? _____

_____

_____

_____

4. How can you show empathy for the other person(s) thoughts and feelings? Be specific.

_____

_____

_____

_____

5. Finally, you are asked to show empathy and kindness to others. Share one incident where you showed empathy and kindness and how that person(s) reacted to your words or action. _____

_____

_____

_____

Remember, showing empathy on a regular basis helps to make and keep friends!

CHILDHOOD PATTERNS OF STEALING

GOALS OF THE EXERCISE

1. Identify frequency, duration, and severity of stealing behavior.
2. Assess factors or core issues contributing to the problem with stealing.
3. Develop and utilize effective coping strategies to resist urge to steal.
4. Demonstrate marked improvement in impulse control.
5. Eliminate all acts of stealing.

ADDITIONAL PROBLEMS FOR WHICH THIS EXERCISE MAY BE MOST USEFUL

- Anger Control Problems
- Attention-Deficit/Hyperactivity Disorder (ADHD)
- Lying/Manipulative
- Oppositional Defiant

SUGGESTIONS FOR PROCESSING THIS EXERCISE WITH THE CLIENT

It is recommended that the client and parents complete the questionnaire in the beginning stages of treatment. There are two parts to the assignment. In Part I, the parents and child work together in answering the various questions. The parents alone are asked to answer some questions in Part II. The client's and parents' responses will help provide useful diagnostic information about the frequency, duration, and severity of the problem with stealing. It is further hoped that the exercise will help identify the external factors or underlying dynamics contributing to the emergence of the stealing behavior. After reviewing the responses in the follow-up therapy session, the therapist can assist the client in developing effective coping strategies to resist the urge to steal. The therapist can also counsel the parents on how to respond to any incidents of stealing.

CHILDHOOD PATTERNS OF STEALING

There are two parts to this assignment. The parents and child are encouraged to work together on Part I to answer the different questions. In Part II, the parents alone are asked to answer the questions. Your responses to the various questions or items will help your therapist learn more about your child's problem with stealing.

PART I—PARENT AND CHILD

1. At what age did you first steal something? ____ years old

2. What did you first steal and from where or whom? _____
_____

3. Approximately how often did you steal something before the age of 8?

    _____ none   _____ 1–5 times   _____ 6–10 times

    _____ 11–15 times   _____ 16–20 times   _____ over 20 times

4. Approximately how often did you steal something after turning 8 years old?

    _____ none   _____ 1–5 times   _____ 6–10 times

    _____ 11–15 times   _____ 16–20 times   _____ over 20 times

5. Please check the people or places from whom you have stolen in the past. (Check all that apply.)

    _____ Parents   _____ School

    _____ Brother(s) or sister(s)   _____ Car/vehicle

    _____ Friends   _____ Small store

    _____ Kids at school   _____ Large store

    _____ Neighbors   _____ Other (please identify)

    _____ Neighbor's home   _____

    _____ Unknown people in neighborhood   _____

6. Have you ever bullied or threatened someone when stealing? _____ yes ____ no

7. What type of things have you stolen? (Check all that apply.)

___ Money   ___ Art supplies

___ Food/snacks   ___ Computer or video games

___ Toys   ___ Cell phone

___ Bike   ___ Clothes

___ Sports equipment   ___ Other (please identify)

___ School supplies

_____

8. Have you stolen mostly by yourself or with other people?

____ I have stolen mostly by myself.

____ I have stolen mostly when I have been with other people.

9. What have been the main reasons why you have stolen things in the past? Please review the following list and check all that apply. (Parents, you may need to take time to explain some of these possible reasons to your child.)

___ Desire to have toy, item, or snack   ___ Desire to be accepted by other kids

___ Greedy or selfish (i.e., "I wanted it")   ___ Bullied, pressured, or threatened by other kids to steal

___ Did not think of consequences or getting punished

___ Pressured or encouraged by other family members to steal

___ Did not think how stealing would affect other people

___ Feelings of sadness or loneliness

___ Anger   ___ Feelings of being unloved or unwanted

___ Desire to get revenge or get back at someone   ___ Other (please identify)

_____

PART II—PARENTS ALONE

1. In your opinion, what are some of the stressful events or factors that have contributed to your child's problem with stealing? (Note—you may want to elaborate on some of the reasons listed in Part I.) _____

_____

_____

_____

_____

2. How did you react emotionally to your child's past incidents of stealing? _____
    _____
    _____
    _____

3. What consequences did you give your child for stealing? _____
    _____
    _____
    _____

4. How did your child react to the consequences? _____
    _____
    _____
    _____

5. What has been the longest period of time that your child has gone without stealing
    after the first incident? (Please identify how long the child went without stealing
    and at what age.) _____
    _____
    _____

6. What do you think your child can do to resist the urge to steal in the future? _____
    _____
    _____
    _____
    _____

7. What questions do you have for the therapist about your child's problem with
    stealing? _____
    _____
    _____
    _____
    _____

CONCERNS ABOUT PARENT'S DRUG OR ALCOHOL PROBLEM

GOALS OF THE EXERCISE

1. Express thoughts and feelings connected to the parent's substance abuse problem.
2. Assess impact that the parent's substance abuse problem has had on the client's mood and behavior.
3. Explore whether the client is willing to share his/her thoughts, feelings, and concerns with the parent or other family members.
4. Refer parent for a substance abuse assessment and/or treatment.
5. Parents participate in marital therapy.

ADDITIONAL PROBLEMS FOR WHICH THIS EXERCISE MAY BE MOST USEFUL

- Anxiety
- Disruptive/Attention-Seeking
- Lying/Manipulative
- Oppositional Defiant

SUGGESTIONS FOR PROCESSING THIS EXERCISE WITH THE CLIENT

This exercise is designed for the client who has a parent with a serious substance abuse problem. The client's responses to the questions or items will provide him/her with the opportunity to express his/her thoughts, feelings, and concerns about this issue. On several of the items, the client also has the option of drawing a picture that reflects his/her thoughts, feelings, or concerns. Some clients may be hesitant to complete this assignment at home because of their worry or concern that their parent may review their responses. In this case, the therapist may want to consider using the assignment in a therapy session. The client can be asked the questions in an interview format or be allowed to draw the pictures in the session. After processing the client's responses and/or feelings reflected in the drawings, the therapist should explore whether the client is willing to share his/her thoughts, feelings, and concerns with the parent or other family members. In the best-case scenario, the parent with the problem would be willing to seek a substance abuse assessment and/or treatment. Even if the client chooses not to share his/her concerns openly with the parent or other family members, then he/she at least has had the opportunity to share his/her thoughts and feelings in the context of a trusting therapeutic relationship.

CONCERNS ABOUT PARENT'S DRUG OR ALCOHOL PROBLEM

When a parent has a serious drug or alcohol problem, it can create many different thoughts and feelings for the children. This exercise gives you the opportunity to express your thoughts and feelings about your parent's drug or alcohol problem. It will also help your therapist to better understand your feelings. Most of the items require you to answer questions and write your answers in the space provided. However, there are several items that give you a chance to draw a picture that reflects your thoughts and feelings. If you choose to draw a picture that shows your feelings and concerns, please use a separate piece of paper.

1. How does your parent act when he/she has been drinking or using drugs? _____
   _____
   _____
   _____

2. How do you feel while your parent is using drugs or alcohol? On this item, you may also choose to draw a picture that shows how you feel when your parent is drinking or using drugs._____
   _____
   _____
   _____

3. How do you behave at home or at school soon after your parent has been drinking or using drugs? _____
   _____
   _____
   _____

4. What is your biggest fear, worry, or concern about your parent's drug or alcohol problem? You may choose to draw a picture that reflects your biggest fear, worry, or concern about your parent's drug or alcohol problem. _____

_____

_____

_____

_____

5. How has your parent's drug or alcohol problem affected his/her life or health? _____

_____

_____

_____

_____

6. How has your parent's drug or alcohol problem affected other family members and you? _____

_____

_____

_____

_____

7. What bad things have happened to your family or you as a result of your parent's drug or alcohol problem? You may also choose to draw a picture that shows something bad that has happened to your family as a result of your parent's drug or alcohol problem. _____

_____

_____

_____

_____

8. If you were free to say anything to your parent about his/her drug or alcohol problem, what would you tell him/her? _____

_____

_____

_____

_____

9. What do you think will happen in the future to your parent, family members, and you if he/she continues to drink or use drugs? You may also draw a picture that shows what you think might happen in the future if your parent continues to drink or use drugs. _____

_____

_____

_____

_____

Please bring your responses or drawings to your next therapy session to go over with your therapist.

RISK FACTORS LEADING TO CHILD BEHAVIOR PROBLEMS

GOALS OF THE EXERCISE

1. Identify risk factors contributing to early delinquent behavior.
2. Identify social supports that will help facilitate the implementation of new skills.
3. Develop coping strategies to effectively deal with psychosocial stressors or personal problems.
4. Decrease frequency and severity of acting-out and delinquent behaviors.

ADDITIONAL PROBLEMS FOR WHICH THIS EXERCISE MAY BE MOST USEFUL

- Anger Control Problems
- Disruptive/Attention-Seeking
- Fire Setting
- Oppositional Defiant

SUGGESTIONS FOR PROCESSING THIS EXERCISE WITH THE CLIENT

The primary purpose of this exercise is to identify the risk factors that have contributed to the client's early delinquent behaviors. The parents are asked to identify the stressful events or problems that the client has had to deal with or endure in his/her life. It is hoped that the exercise will be useful in identifying social supports or resources that the client and family can draw upon to effectively deal with the stressors or problems. In addition, the exercise can be used as a springboard in the therapy sessions to discuss what changes need to occur in the family system to help bring the client's behavior under control.

RISK FACTORS LEADING TO CHILD BEHAVIOR PROBLEMS

Many times when a child acts out or gets into trouble at a young age, that child has also experienced some very stressful events or has had to deal with some difficult problems. The purpose of this exercise is to identify the risk factors that have contributed to your child's behavioral problems. Please respond to the following questions or items.

1. What stressful or traumatic events has your child experienced in his/her life? Review the following list and place a checkmark next to all the items that apply.

_____ Death of a parent or loved one

_____ Parents' separation/divorce

_____ Infrequent contact or abandonment by a parent

_____ Multiple relationships and/or breakups by parent(s)

_____ Past history of neglect

_____ Emotional abuse

_____ Physical abuse

_____ Sexual abuse

_____ Growing up in violent neighborhood

_____ Witnessing acts of violence

_____ Family financial problems

_____ Parent's unemployment

_____ Parent's long work hours

_____ Parent works evening hours

_____ Client often left alone at night or unsupervised

_____ Parent incarceration or involvement with court

_____ Sibling involvement with court

_____ Client socializes with negative peer group

_____ Serious emotional problems of parent or family member

_____ Alcohol or drug abuse by parent or family member

_____ Chronic health problems of parent or family member

_____ Other (please list)

_____

_____

_____

2. What other types of problems (e.g., physical, emotional, social, learning) has your child had to deal with while growing up? Please check all that apply.

    ____ Learning disability
        ____ Reading
        ____ Math
        ____ Writing
    ____ Speech/language delays
    ____ Serious or chronic health problem
    ____ Fetal alcohol syndrome
    ____ Sleep problems

    ____ Attention-deficit/hyperactivity disorder (ADHD)
    ____ Depression
    ____ Bipolar disorder
    ____ Anxiety and fearfulness
    ____ Separation anxiety
    ____ Other (please list)
    _____

3. How does your child react emotionally to these stressful events or problems? _____

_____

_____

_____

4. How do the other family members and you manage or deal with these stressful events or problems? _____

_____

_____

5. What support have you received in dealing with these problems? _____

_____

_____

6. What support would you like to receive for your family to help cope with the stressful events? Please be specific. For example, would you like to receive support from outside family members, school, church, community, or mental health agencies?

_____

_____

_____

_____

7. What changes need to occur in the family to help your child behave better? _____

_____

_____

_____

_____

CHILDHOOD DEPRESSION SURVEY

GOALS OF THE EXERCISE

1. Verbally identify, if possible, the source of depressed mood.
2. Identify unmet needs that contribute to the emergence of depressed mood.
3. Specify what in the past or present life contributes to sadness.
4. Begin to express feelings of sadness about painful or stressful event(s) in the context of a supportive therapeutic relationship.
5. Develop effective coping strategies to help reduce feelings of depression.

ADDITIONAL PROBLEMS FOR WHICH THIS EXERCISE MAY BE MOST USEFUL

- Anger Control Problems
- Divorce Reaction
- Grief/Loss Unresolved
- Low Self-Esteem

SUGGESTIONS FOR PROCESSING THIS EXERCISE WITH THE CLIENT

The therapist is encouraged to use this assignment in the initial stages of treatment to identify the core issues or stressful events that contribute to the emergence of the client's depression. The client's responses to the survey will help the therapist identify the factors or stressors that need to be explored more fully in future therapy sessions. Identification of the core issues or factors will allow the client to begin to express his/her feelings of sadness more openly. After providing the client with the opportunity to express his/her feelings, the therapist can then begin to teach the client effective coping strategies to reduce his/her depression and meet his/her needs. The survey is not all-inclusive. At the end of the survey, space is provided for the client to identify other factors that may be contributing to his/her depression. The survey can also be very useful when conducting psychological evaluations.

CHILDHOOD DEPRESSION SURVEY

Please check the appropriate box to help your therapist understand what you may be feeling sad about in the present or from your past. Complete the survey and remember to bring it to your next therapy session so you can review it with your therapist.

Statement	True	False	Some-times	Not True at Present, but True in Past
I feel sad about the death of an important person (e.g., parent, sibling, grandparent, friend).				
I feel sad about the death of a family pet.				
I feel sad about my family's financial problems.				
I feel sad about my parents getting a divorce.				
I feel sad about hardly ever seeing my father or mother.				
I feel unhappy about not spending more time with Mom.				
I feel unhappy about not spending more time with Dad.				
I'm upset about my mother or father not sticking with his/her promise(s) to do something special with me.				

Statement	True	False	Some-times	Not True at Present, but True in Past
I often feel that Mom or Dad pay more attention to my brother(s) or sister(s).				
I feel guilty about my bad behavior at home or school.				
I feel upset about receiving poor grades at school.				
I feel down about losing or failing in sports.				
I am unhappy with my looks.				
I often feel lonely because I have no friends or very few friends.				
I often feel ignored or left out by the other kids at school or in the neighborhood.				
I often feel let down by my family members or friends.				
I feel sad about bad things that have happened to my friends.				
I often feel sad about . . . (please list other things that often make you feel sad). _____ _____ _____				

REPLACE NEGATIVE THOUGHTS WITH POSITIVE SELF-TALK

GOALS OF THE EXERCISE

1. Decrease frequency of negative thoughts or verbalizations and replace with positive self-talk or statements on a more consistent basis.
2. Identify and replace negative thinking that leads to depression.
3. Develop healthy cognitive patterns and beliefs about self and the world that lead to alleviation and help prevent the relapse of depression symptoms.

ADDITIONAL PROBLEMS FOR WHICH THIS EXERCISE MAY BE MOST USEFUL

- Anxiety
- Low Self-Esteem
- Separation Anxiety
- Social Anxiety

SUGGESTIONS FOR PROCESSING THIS EXERCISE WITH THE CLIENT

Clients who suffer with depression, anxiety, and low self-esteem often experience many negative thoughts about themselves. Likewise, they may verbalize many negative remarks around other people. The purpose of this assignment is to simply teach the client to replace the negative thoughts or expressions about himself/herself with positive self-statements or remarks. The client is instructed to record times when he/she has experienced a negative thought or verbalized a derogatory remark about himself/herself in the presence of others. The client is instructed to record the statement on the assignment sheet and replace it with a positive self-statement. Emphasize that practicing this coping strategy on a regular basis will help to improve the client's self-esteem and elevate his/her mood. The exercise can easily be used with clients who are struggling not only with depression, but with anxiety, low self-esteem, separation anxiety, or shyness.

REPLACE NEGATIVE THOUGHTS WITH POSITIVE SELF-TALK

Children who struggle with depression, anxiety, or feelings of low self-esteem often experience negative thoughts or express negative statements about themselves around other people. The purpose of this exercise is for you to replace your negative thoughts or self-statements with positive thoughts or statements. You are asked to record times when you either experienced or expressed negative thoughts about yourself. After recording the negative thought or remark, you are asked to then replace it with a positive thought or statement. For example, let's say you are having a tough day and are struggling to learn how to do some new math problems. When frustrated you may say something like, "I'm so stupid. I'll never be able to learn how to do these problems." With this exercise, you are asked to replace such negative thoughts with more positive statements like, "Everybody makes mistakes. Just keep trying. I'll ask my parents or teacher for help if I can't figure them out." Below, please record the date and place where you experienced or expressed the negative thought, and then write a positive statement. Your parents and teachers can help you identify a more positive self-statement if you are struggling to come up with one on your own. Make as many copies of this assignment sheet as needed and bring them back to your next therapy session to review with your therapist.

1. Date:_____ Setting: _____
   Negative thought or remark: _____

   _____

   Positive thought or remark: _____

   _____

2. Date:_____ Setting: _____
   Negative thought or remark: _____

   _____

   Positive thought or remark: _____

   _____

SURFACE BEHAVIOR/INNER FEELINGS

GOALS OF THE EXERCISE

1. State the connection between rebellion, self-destruction, or withdrawal and the underlying depression.
2. Identify own feelings of hurt and sadness that have led to acting out.
3. Identify trusted resource people with whom feelings can be shared.
4. Reduce irritability and increase normal social interaction with family and friends.

ADDITIONAL PROBLEMS FOR WHICH THIS EXERCISE MAY BE MOST USEFUL

- Anger Control Problems
- Conduct Disorder/Delinquency
- Divorce Reaction
- Obsessive-Compulsive Disorder
- Oppositional Defiant

SUGGESTIONS FOR PROCESSING THIS EXERCISE WITH THE CLIENT

Children often camouflage their depressed feelings in a cloak of anger or irritability. This exercise, designed for clients over 10 years old, helps the client recognize this common dynamic by asking him/her to analyze a character in a story who covers his pain of rejection and lack of nurturing with self-defeating anger. The client may need help making the transition from recognizing this dynamic in the story character and seeing it in himself/herself. Process the questions with the client in a session if additional help is needed to bring this insight home.

SURFACE BEHAVIOR/INNER FEELINGS

Sometimes the feelings you show on the outside may not be an accurate reflection of the struggle that is going on inside. You may show anger when you really feel depressed. You may show a lack of interest in friends, schoolwork, and family when you actually feel rejected, hopeless, and helpless. Your behavior may be getting you in trouble because the feelings under the surface are all jumbled up, confusing, and painful. If you could just share your feelings and sort them out, life would be easier.

1. Read this story of a confused boy named Jack who showed one feeling, anger, on the surface when he felt so many different emotions on the inside.

    Sadness Looks Like Anger

    "Shut up and leave me alone!" shouted Jack to Mrs. Lewis, his sixth-grade teacher. "I'm sick of you always bugging me about keeping my head up and having to listen to you. It's none of your business if I put my head down. I'm not bothering anyone. Nobody cares about what I do anyway," he snarled. Mrs. Lewis was shocked by Jack's disrespectful outburst toward her. He usually was polite and cooperative but lately he was withdrawn and his mind seemed to be on something other than schoolwork. Because of his angry refusal to obey her, she had to send him to the principal's office to discuss his lack of respect for authority.

    Jack rose out of his seat in the classroom slowly and shuffled toward the door to the hall. Other students whispered and moved restlessly in their seats. They hadn't seen Jack act like this before. Jack kept his head and eyes toward the floor as he made his way down the aisle of desks and out the door to the hallway leading to the principal's office.

    Jack was feeling sad and angry at the same time. Lately, he often felt confused; he would come close to tears but then force them back in anger. He was not sure why he had lashed out at Mrs. Lewis, either. She had always been kind and fair to him. But he felt so tired lately and not interested in school as much as he used to be. He even felt that the other kids didn't like him as much or include him as often as they used to.

    As he turned the corner and headed down the long corridor leading to the front entrance of Hillbrook Middle School, he thought about the principal having to call his mother at work to discuss this incident. Jack didn't want his mother to know about his problems. She had enough to deal with herself since the divorce between her and Dad a year ago. She had to switch to full-time work at the hospital cafeteria where she served food to employees and visitors until 6 p.m. every night. She also worked every other Saturday to help pay the bills. Jack hated it that she was gone so much and hated it even more that he had to go to the latchkey daycare program after school every day because she didn't get home until 6:20 p.m. She was always so tired that she often fell asleep on the couch watching a video with him at night.

Now Jack could see the principal's office door as he rounded the last corner. Mr. Clarkson was a big man who spoke in a firm, deep voice that forced you to pay attention to every word. Jack entered the office slowly and sheepishly said to the secretary, "Mrs. Lewis sent me to see Mr. Clarkson." He was embarrassed but also felt somewhat numb and sad. "Have a seat by his door, young man," replied the secretary.

Jack sat down outside Mr. Clarkson's office and stared off into space with his face pointed toward the window, though he wasn't seeing anything outside. He was thinking about yesterday when Dad was supposed to come and pick him up and take him over to Grandma's for supper. "I'll be there at 3:00 tomorrow to get you," Dad had said on the phone on Saturday. Jack had called him to ask why he had not come to see him for 5 weeks in a row. "Been working a lot of hours and had to spend some time with Nancy," Dad explained. Nancy was his new girlfriend, whom Jack did not like because she ordered Dad around so much and acted like Jack was an interference in their relationship.

On Sunday, as 3:00 approached, Jack was lying in his bedroom where he spent most of his time alone. He had a sick feeling in his stomach as 3:15 came and went. Then it was 3:30, and no Dad. When 4:00 arrived, Jack had begun to cry in spite of his angry efforts to fight back the tears. He sobbed into his pillow for a few minutes and then took a deep breath and tried to think of what he could have done to make Dad not want to be with him. His eyes burned and his heart pounded because he felt sad and angry at the same time. He began to think about running away. Perhaps he would go to his mother's parents' place in Chicago, 150 miles away.

Just then his thoughts of yesterday were interrupted when Mr. Clarkson opened his office door. "Jack, I'm surprised to see you at my office," Mr. Clarkson said with kindness and concern. "Something must be very wrong in your life to cause you to be sent to my office. Come on in and let's talk about it." As Jack rose to enter the principal's office, tears came to his eyes as his sadness replaced his anger.

2. Answer the following questions.

A. What was Jack really feeling inside when he showed anger toward Mrs. Lewis? _____

_____

_____

B. Why was Jack feeling sad? _____

_____

_____

C.   What are the causes for your own sadness and hurt? _____

_____

_____

_____

D.   Tell about a time when you showed one feeling when you actually felt something different inside. _____

_____

_____

_____

_____

E.   Whom can you trust enough to tell your *real* feelings to?

_____

_____

F.   Sometimes we do things that hurt ourselves and get ourselves into trouble (such as disobey rules, run away, fight with someone) when we are actually feeling hurt and sad.

Write down an example of a time or times when you have done this.

_____

_____

_____

_____

_____

_____

_____

_____

THREE WAYS TO CHANGE THE WORLD

GOALS OF THE EXERCISE

1. Elevate mood by identifying steps that can be taken to cope with stress or to overcome life's problems.
2. Identify stressors or unmet needs that contribute to feelings of depression.
3. Specify what in past or present life contributes to sadness.
4. Establish rapport with the therapist in the beginning stages of therapy.

ADDITIONAL PROBLEMS FOR WHICH THIS EXERCISE MAY BE MOST USEFUL

- Anxiety
- Low Self-Esteem
- Physical/Emotional Abuse Victim
- Sexual Abuse Victim

SUGGESTIONS FOR PROCESSING THIS EXERCISE WITH THE CLIENT

This activity can be used with children with a variety of problems, but it has been included in this section because of its potential for identifying unmet needs and core sources of the client's depression. In this activity, the client is requested to draw three separate pictures between therapy sessions that symbolize how he/she would like to change the world. Instruct the client to bring the drawings to his/her next therapy session, along with the form containing his/her responses to several questions. The drawings and the client's responses to the questions will provide you with the opportunity to assess whether the desired changes are directly or indirectly related to his/her depression. If the desired changes are directly related to the client's problems, then you can help him/her develop coping strategies to manage stress or overcome problems. Furthermore, the drawings may reflect some of the client's unmet needs, which can facilitate a discussion on what steps he/she can take to meet his/her needs. This activity can also be helpful in identifying clear-cut therapy goals. It is recommended that this assignment be used in the beginning stages of therapy with clients who are over 10 years old.

THREE WAYS TO CHANGE THE WORLD

In this activity, you are invited to be an artist and create three separate drawings that show how you would like to change the world. Before you actually sit down to draw the pictures, spend a few minutes thinking about what it is you would like to express in your drawing. Find a quiet place where you can reflect on how you'd like to change the world. Be yourself and express what is important to you, but also remember to have fun.

1. Just pretend for the sake of having fun that you have been granted the power to make any three changes in this world that you so desire. There are a number of ways that you could change the world. Perhaps you would like to produce a change in your world that directly affects you. On the other hand, you may like to see some change that would benefit another person, such as a family member, friend, peer, or teacher. Another option is to express a desire for change in your school, community, state, or country. You may even wish to change something about the whole world.

2. There are only a couple of rules in this activity. First, at least two of your three desired changes must have something to do directly with your life. Second, we ask that you draw a picture of something that symbolizes or represents the desired change. Do not use any words in your drawings. The reason for this is so that your therapist can guess what you are trying to express in your drawing.

3. In the following space, list the three changes you would like to see happen in the world and your reasons for selecting each one of them. Please respond to the other questions that are appropriate to your desired change. Do not show this list to your therapist until he or she has seen your drawings and attempted to guess what your desired changes are.

    The first change I would like to see happen in the world is: _____

    _____

    _____

    Reasons why I would like to see this change happen: _____

    _____

    _____

    If this change is realistic or possible, what can I do to help bring about this change?

    _____

    _____

If this change is not likely to occur, what can I do to cope with this problem or issue?

_____

_____

Who can help me cope with this problem or issue? _____

_____

The second change I would like to see happen in the world is: _____

_____

Reasons why I would like to see this change happen: _____

_____

_____

If this change is realistic or possible, what can I do to help bring about this change?

_____

_____

If this change is not likely to occur, what can I do to cope with this problem or issue?

_____

_____

Who can help me cope with this problem or issue? _____

_____

The third change I would like to see happen in the world is: _____

_____

Reasons why I would like to see this change happen: _____

_____

_____

If this change is realistic or possible, what can I do to help bring about this change?

_____

_____

If this change is not likely to occur, what can I do to cope with this problem or issue? _____

_____

_____

Who can help me cope with this problem or issue? _____

_____

_____

FINDING WAYS TO GET POSITIVE ATTENTION

GOALS OF THE EXERCISE

1. Identify and implement appropriate ways to elicit attention from family members, authority figures, and/or peers.
2. Gain attention, approval, and acceptance from other people through appropriate verbalizations and positive social behaviors.
3. Reduce the frequency and severity of disruptive or negative attention-seeking behaviors at home and/or school.

ADDITIONAL PROBLEMS FOR WHICH THIS EXERCISE MAY BE MOST USEFUL

- Bullying/Intimidation Perpetrator
- Gender Identity Disorder
- Lying/Manipulative
- Oppositional Defiant
- Peer/Sibling Conflict

SUGGESTIONS FOR PROCESSING THIS EXERCISE WITH THE CLIENT

This assignment is to be given as a follow-up to the other homework assignment in this section, "Reasons for Negative Attention-Seeking Behaviors." There are two parts to this assignment. The client is first asked to list positive and appropriate ways to gain attention from his/her parents, teachers, and peers. After identifying the positive behaviors, the client is instructed to practice or try out at least three of these behaviors before the next therapy session. The therapist should counsel or warn the client that other people may not respond in ways that he/she hopes they will. The client is encouraged to use the Positive Attention Form to describe his/her attempts to gain positive attention from others. Parents and teachers are allowed to assist the client in filling out this form.

FINDING WAYS TO GET POSITIVE ATTENTION

Now that you and your therapist have identified and talked about some of the reasons why you behaved in ways to get negative attention, it is time to identify ways that you can get positive or good attention from other people. These are called "positive attention-seeking behaviors." There are two parts to this assignment. Please respond to the following items.

PART 1

What are three to five ways to get positive attention from your . . .
Parents?

_____

_____

_____

Teachers?

_____

_____

_____

Peers or other kids?

_____

_____

_____

PART 2

Next, you will be asked to practice or try out some of these positive behaviors at least three times before the next therapy session. You are certainly encouraged to try and get positive attention from others more than just three times. However, you will be required to write about only three of your experiences. Please use the Positive Attention Form to write about your experiences. It is hoped that other people will recognize your good behavior and respond in a positive way. You should remember, though, that not all people will recognize that you are trying to be good. Your parents and teachers can help you fill out the Positive Attention Form.

POSITIVE ATTENTION FORM

Please answer the following questions.

1. What was the positive attention-seeking behavior? _____
    _____
    _____
    _____

2. Whose positive attention did you try to get? _____
    _____

3. How did you expect the person(s) to respond to your positive behavior? _____
    _____
    _____
    _____

4. How did the other person(s) react to your positive or good behavior?
    _____
    _____
    _____

5. How did you feel about the way the other person(s) responded to your positive behavior?

    ___ Happy   ___ Depressed   ___ Angry
    ___ Excited   ___ Ignored   ___ Disappointed
    ___ Content   ___ Unsure   ___ Other _____

6. What are some other positive ways that you can get this person's attention in the future?

    _____
    _____
    _____

7. Would you be willing to try and get this person's or other people's positive attention by behaving in the same way in the future? ___ yes ___ no
   If no, please explain why you would not want to try this behavior again in the future.

   _____

   _____

REASONS FOR NEGATIVE ATTENTION-SEEKING BEHAVIORS

GOALS OF THE EXERCISE

1. Identify specific nature of negative attention-seeking behaviors.
2. Explore underlying factors or reasons contributing to the emergence of negative attention-seeking behaviors.
3. Verbalize an awareness of how disruptive behaviors negatively affect self and others.
4. Reduce the frequency and severity of disruptive or negative attention-seeking behaviors at home and/or school.

ADDITIONAL PROBLEMS FOR WHICH THIS EXERCISE MAY BE MOST USEFUL

- Bullying/Intimidation Perpetrator
- Lying/Manipulative
- Oppositional Defiant
- Peer/Sibling Conflict

SUGGESTIONS FOR PROCESSING THIS EXERCISE WITH THE CLIENT

The purpose of this assignment is threefold. First, the assignment seeks to identify the specific nature of the client's negative attention-seeking behaviors. Second, the assignment seeks to uncover the underlying factors or reasons contributing to the emergence of the negative attention-seeking behaviors. Finally, the client is encouraged to consider how his/her negative attention-seeking behaviors affect both self and others. Parents and teachers are encouraged to help the client respond to the various questions or items. The assignment was designed to be used in conjunction with the other homework assignment, "Finding Ways to Get Positive Attention," in this section. This assignment should be given first, and then followed up with "Finding Ways to Get Positive Attention."

REASONS FOR NEGATIVE ATTENTION-SEEKING BEHAVIORS

At some time or another, all children act in ways that bring them either positive (good) or negative (bad) attention. Unfortunately, some children often find themselves in trouble at home or school because they behave in ways that bring them negative attention. These are called "negative attention-seeking behaviors." The purpose of this assignment is to help your therapist understand the ways that you often get negative attention from other people. The assignment will also help your therapist and you identify the reasons why you often behave in ways that bring you negative attention instead of positive attention. Please respond to the following questions or items. Feel free to ask your parents and teachers to help you complete this assignment.

1. What are the negative attention-seeking behaviors that often cause you to get in trouble with your parents, teachers, or other adults? Please review the following list and check all that apply.

    ____ Talking too much or blurting out remarks at inappropriate times

    ____ Talking loudly in class

    ____ Making inappropriate or silly noises

    ____ Laughing or joking around at wrong time

    ____ Acting silly or younger than your age

    ____ Interrupting parents or teachers

    ____ Refusing to share or cooperate in games with peers

    ____ Teasing, mocking, or "bugging" other kids or brothers/sisters

    ____ Calling other kids or brothers/sisters names

    ____ Annoying others by touching or hitting them

    ____ Acting tough, bullying, or threatening other kids

    ____ Refusing to follow directions from parents or teachers

    ____ Frequent arguing

    ____ Refusing to cooperate in games or demanding that things go your way

    ____ Other (please list)

    _____

    _____

2. How do your parents, teachers, or other adults react to your negative attention-seeking behaviors? _____
_____
_____

3. How do other kids or your brothers/sisters react to your negative attention-seeking behaviors?

_____
_____
_____

4. What consequences or types of punishment do you receive for your negative attention-seeking behaviors? _____
_____
_____
_____

5. Next, it is important to look at the reasons why you often get in trouble for the negative attention-seeking behaviors. Another way to look at this is to ask yourself: "What do I get out of behaving in ways that bring me negative attention?" Following is a list of reasons why some kids behave in negative attention-seeking ways. Please review this list and check all that may apply to you.

____ Feel ignored—negative attention is better than no attention at all

____ Get attention from Mom/Dad

____ Get attention from teacher/other adults

____ To be liked or accepted by other kids

____ Make other kids laugh or be seen as funny

____ Act silly because of boredom

____ Act out when feeling sad or nervous

____ Act out when feeling afraid

____ Act out after losing or failing in sports

____ Act out or get negative attention when struggling to do schoolwork or homework

____ Act out because of anger toward Mom/Dad

____ Act out because of anger toward teachers

____ Act out to get back at parents/teachers for punishing me

____ Make other kids mad

____ Make other kids feel weak, small, or embarrassed

____ Make myself look better than others

6. The previous list does not give all the reasons why kids act out to get negative attention. What are some other reasons why you may act out to get negative attention?

_____

_____

_____

_____

FEELINGS AND FACES GAME

GOALS OF THE EXERCISE

1. Identify and express feelings related to parents' separation and/or divorce.
2. Begin to work through the grieving and letting go process associated with parents' separation or divorce.
3. Enlist the support and cooperation of parent(s) or significant others in helping the child to identify and express feelings.
4. Work through feelings so energy can be channeled or invested in other healthy or adaptive activities.

ADDITIONAL PROBLEMS FOR WHICH THIS EXERCISE MAY BE MOST USEFUL

- Anxiety
- Blended Family
- Depression
- Grief/Loss Unresolved

SUGGESTIONS FOR PROCESSING THIS EXERCISE WITH THE CLIENT

The purpose of this activity is to help the child identify and express his/her feelings about his/her parents' separation or divorce. It is recommended that this activity be utilized in the beginning stages of therapy with children ranging in age from 5 to 12 years. It is a fun activity that helps you establish rapport with the child through the medium of art. This game-like activity can easily be incorporated into a therapy session, but it can also be given as an assignment to be performed at home with the parent(s) or significant other(s). It provides the child with an opportunity to share his/her feelings with the parent(s) or significant other(s) in the home environment. In this manner, the child learns some healthy ways to express feelings, instead of suppressing or acting them out. This assignment can also be modified to assist the child who is coping with the death of a parent or significant other.

FEELINGS AND FACES GAME

It is important for you to be able to express your feelings when your parents get separated or divorced instead of keeping them inside or showing them in negative ways (such as hitting or kicking someone or crying over small, unrelated things). The purpose of this exercise is to help you express your feelings in a fun-filled way with someone you care about and can trust. You are asked to identify your feelings and then to draw a picture of a face with that feeling.

1. Review the following list of feelings. These are some of the feelings children may have when their parents get separated or divorced. Place a checkmark next to five different feelings that you have had since your parents first separated. Feel free to add any other feelings that you have had.

_____ Sad	_____ Relieved	_____ _____
_____ Angry	_____ Frustrated	_____ _____
_____ Lonely	_____ Guilty	_____ _____
_____ Embarrassed	_____ Content	_____ _____
_____ Nervous	_____ Unwanted	_____ _____
_____ Unsure	_____ Ignored	_____ _____
_____ Happy	_____ _____	_____ _____

2. After you have picked the different feelings you have experienced, please draw a picture of those feelings on the blank faces on the following pages. Your therapist will give you copies of five blank faces. Label or identify the feeling you are drawing at the top of each page. After you have finished your drawing of each face, write down or share a time when you felt that way (that is, sad, angry, lonely, and so on) about your parents' separation or divorce. Share these feelings or experiences with a parent, relative, teacher, friend, or somebody else you can trust. Bring the pictures with you to your next therapy session.

FEELINGS AND FACES GAME

Boy

Feeling _____

Write about a time when you felt _____ about your parents' separation/divorce.

_____

_____

_____

FEELINGS AND FACES GAME

Girl

Feeling _____

Write about a time when you felt _____ about your parents' separation/divorce.

_____

_____

_____

MY THOUGHTS AND FEELINGS ABOUT MY PARENTS' DIVORCE

GOALS OF THE EXERCISE

1. Identify and express feelings related to parents' separation and/or divorce.
2. Identify and change any irrational beliefs about parents' divorce.
3. Eliminate feelings of guilt and statements that reflect self-blame about parents' divorce.
4. Recognize and affirm self as not being responsible for the parents' separation or divorce.
5. Accept parents' divorce with consequent understanding and control of feelings and behavior.

ADDITIONAL PROBLEMS FOR WHICH THIS EXERCISE MAY BE MOST USEFUL

- Anxiety
- Blended Family
- Depression
- Grief/Loss Unresolved

SUGGESTIONS FOR PROCESSING THIS EXERCISE WITH THE CLIENT

This homework assignment is designed to help the client express his/her thoughts and feelings about the parents' divorce. The client's responses can provide insight into whether he/she has developed any irrational thoughts or beliefs about the parents' separation or divorce. For example, the therapist can assess whether the client blames himself/herself for the divorce. Likewise, the client may indicate that he/she feels it is in his/her power to reunite the parents. After completing the survey, the client should bring it to the follow-up therapy session for review with the therapist. The client's response to each statement need not be processed or reviewed; the therapist may choose to discuss only a few of the items. For younger children or those with learning problems, the therapist may choose to read the items and complete the survey in the therapy session.

MY THOUGHTS AND FEELINGS ABOUT MY PARENTS' DIVORCE

Please check the appropriate box to express your real thoughts, feelings, and beliefs about your parents' divorce. Complete the survey and remember to bring it to your next therapy session to review with your therapist.

Statement	True	False	Sometimes	Does Not Apply
I wish my parents had never separated.				
I believe that divorce is wrong and unfair to the children.				
Parents should stay married for the sake of the children.				
My parents should have tried harder to work things out before the separation.				
I have felt very angry about my parents' divorce.				
I have felt very sad and hurt by my parents' divorce				
I have felt unloved since my parents' divorce.				
I do not believe that my parents understand my feelings.				
I blame myself for my parents' divorce.				
I blame my mother for the divorce.				
I blame my father for the divorce.				
I wish my parents would get back together.				

Statement	True	False	Sometimes	Does Not Apply
I believe that there is a good chance my parents will get back together.				
I believe that I can say or do something to help my parents reunite.				
My parents should have separated a long time ago.				
I believe that it is better that my parents remain separated.				
I often wish my parents would stop arguing or fighting, even after the separation.				
I wish I could spend more time with the noncustodial parent (i.e., parent you don't live with).				
I find it difficult to "fit in" time to visit with my noncustodial parent.				
I worry about being rejected or abandoned by one or both of my parents.				
There is a good chance that I will get a divorce when I am an adult.				

BLADDER RETENTION TRAINING PROGRAM

GOALS OF THE EXERCISE

1. Increase awareness of the sensation or need to urinate.
2. Eliminate all diurnal and/or nocturnal episodes of enuresis.
3. Assume greater responsibility in developing bladder control.
4. Increase disengaged parent's role in client's toilet-training practices.

ADDITIONAL PROBLEMS FOR WHICH THIS EXERCISE MAY BE MOST USEFUL

- Attention-Deficit/Hyperactivity Disorder (ADHD)
- Fire Setting
- Low Self-Esteem

SUGGESTIONS FOR PROCESSING THIS EXERCISE WITH THE CLIENT

This bladder retention training program involves teaching the child to retain his/her urine for increasingly longer periods of time. The client is expected to follow through with the retention exercise on a daily basis. The client is initially instructed to hold in his/her urine for approximately 2 minutes after he/she reports the urge to urinate. The length of the retention interval is gradually increased when it becomes clear that the child is easily able to retain his/her urine for that specified period of time. It is suggested that the time be increased by 2- to 3-minute intervals. Many children can quickly increase their period of retention up to 30 minutes. It is strongly recommended that the child be rewarded for being able to retain his/her urine for the specified period of time. Using a reward system will help to maintain the child's interest and motivation for following through with the program. If one of the child's parents is disengaged, then enlist the support and involvement of this parent in implementing the program, provided it is practical or feasible and therapeutically indicated. The retention program can easily be used in combination with medication and other therapeutic interventions, such as the use of a bell and pad apparatus.

BLADDER RETENTION TRAINING PROGRAM
PARENTS' INSTRUCTIONS

Children who have problems with enuresis (that is, bed-wetting or wetting their pants or undergarments during the day) often fail to notice their bodily signals until it is too late. This program is designed to increase your child's bladder control by increasing his/her awareness of the sensation or need to urinate. The child's increased awareness of the need to urinate will hopefully lead to an elimination of both daytime and nighttime accidents. Your involvement and support in this program is important because it will help your child stay interested and motivated to follow through with the program. This program can be used in conjunction with other interventions, such as medication, classic bell and pad apparatus, and a reward system.

1. Before you begin this program, it is strongly recommended that your child receive a physical examination by his/her physician to rule out any possible medical or biological factors that may be contributing to his/her bladder control problems. If the examination shows that there is a medical basis for your child's bladder control problems, then you should talk with the physician about appropriate medical interventions. Even if the examination shows that there are no medical factors contributing to your child's enuresis, you are still encouraged to talk with the physician about the possible need for medication. There are medications (e.g., Imipramine pamoate, Desmopressin acetate) available that can help your child develop greater bladder control. If your child is indeed placed on medication, then it is important to monitor the effectiveness of the medication. It is also very important that your child take the medication as recommended. Inquire about any possible side effects and promptly inform your physician if any of the side effects appear.

2. This program can also be used in combination with other interventions such as the bell and pad apparatus. Talk with your child's therapist about how to use the bell and pad apparatus. Your therapist will be able to provide information about where you can obtain it. Read the instructions carefully after obtaining the apparatus.

3. In this program, your child is required to practice retaining his/her urine on a daily basis for a specified period of time. The retention exercises will help increase your child's awareness of the sensation or need to urinate.

    It is recommended that on the first day of this program, your child hold his/her urine for 2 minutes after he/she first informs you of the need to urinate. Use a timer with younger children to signal when the time is up. Increase the time of the retention interval gradually when it becomes clear that the child is able to easily hold in his/her urine for the specified period of time. It is recommended that the interval be increased by 2 to 3 minutes. Do not increase the time by more than 5 minutes because the child may refuse to cooperate with the program if he/she experiences too much discomfort. You also do not want to risk causing the child embarrassment if he/she has an accident. Many children are able to gradually increase their retention period up to 30 minutes.

Your child will be able to drink fluids freely at any time with this program. Do not withhold liquids because the intake of fluids will help him/her practice his/her retention.

Keep in mind that one of the first signs that this program is working is that your child will experience a reduction in the frequency of times that he/she has to urinate during the day. The child's increased bladder control will typically lead to a later decrease in the amount of bed-wetting that occurs overnight.

4. Use a reward system with this program. Use the Bladder Retention Training Contract on the following page to formalize the agreement. Your child should receive a specific reward for being able to successfully retain his/her urine. Talk with your child about an appropriate reward for his/her success. With some children, it may be necessary to increase the size or amount of the reward as their retention increases. Following is a list of suggested rewards that you may use to reinforce your child for being successful.
    - Snacks
    - Soda
    - Small toys
    - Tokens or stickers that can be exchanged for toys, prizes, or privileges
    - Prepare a favorite meal
    - Allow child to invite a friend over to house after school
    - Spend one-on-one time with child in agreed-upon activity
    - Extended bedtime
    - Extra time to play video games or use computer
    - Rent a video or go see a movie
    - Have a story read to him/her

BLADDER RETENTION TRAINING CONTRACT

If_____is able to successfully hold in his/her urine for _____
　　　(Name of child)　　　　　　　　　　　　　　　　　　　　　　(Amount of time)

without having an accident, then _____will receive the following
　　　　　　　　　　　　　　　　　(Name of child)

reward:

_____

_____

_____

_____

_____

_____

_____

_____　　_____
Signature of Child　　　　　　　　　　Signature of Parent

_____　　_____
Signature of Parent　　　　　　　　　　Signature of Teacher or Therapist

BOWEL CONTROL TRAINING PROGRAM

GOALS OF THE EXERCISE

1. Eliminate all episodes of encopresis, whether voluntary or involuntary.
2. Assume greater responsibility in developing bowel control.
3. Recognize negative social consequences that occur as a result of encopretic incidents.
4. Identify emotional and psychosocial factors that contribute to the encopresis.

ADDITIONAL PROBLEMS FOR WHICH THIS EXERCISE MAY BE MOST USEFUL

- Low Self-Esteem
- Oppositional Defiant
- Physical/Emotional Abuse Victim
- Sexual Abuse Victim

SUGGESTIONS FOR PROCESSING THIS EXERCISE WITH THE CLIENT

This program addresses the problem of encopresis by utilizing principles of operant conditioning. Before starting the program, it is important to refer the client to his/her physician to rule out any organic or medical factors that may be contributing to the encopresis. If the medical examination does not reveal the presence of any organic causes, then meet with the parents and client to identify (1) specific rewards to use to reinforce the client each time he/she has a successful bowel movement without soiling his/her undergarments or clothes, and (2) a negative consequence if the client does indeed soil his/her undergarments or clothes. Instruct the client to fill out an incident report if he/she has an encopretic incident. The client's responses to this form will help provide some insight into the factors that contribute to the encopresis. The form will also help the client realize how others react to his/her encopresis. Discourage the parents from making hostile or critical remarks to the client after a soiling incident. Finally, the client's role and responsibility in managing the encopresis should be clearly spelled out in the therapy sessions. The program can easily be combined with the use of glycerine suppositories and enemas.

Note: This assignment is based on a program developed by L. Wright and C. E. Walker (Wright, L., and C. E. Walker, "Case Histories and Shorter Communications: A Simple Behavioral Treatment Program for Psychogenic Encopresis", *Behavioral Research & Therapy,* 1978, pp. 16, 209–212).

BOWEL CONTROL TRAINING PROGRAM
PARENTS' INSTRUCTIONS

Children who struggle with encopresis, or soiling, as it is more commonly called, often experience feelings of low self-esteem and inadequacy. Many times, the child is very reluctant to talk about the problem of soiling because of the sense of shame or embarrassment that the subject produces. The child's self-esteem may further decrease if his/her peers detect a problem with encopresis. Peers may tease or ridicule the child upon realizing the problem. The parents of the child often feel confused, frustrated, and angry about how to deal with the problem. In frustration, parents sometimes make hostile, critical remarks to the child after a soiling incident. Yet, the hostile, critical remarks rarely help the situation. Indeed, severely judgmental remarks may only serve to reinforce the problem because the child may strike back at the parents' anger by soiling his/her pants again. However, there is good news. Encopresis, or soiling, can be successfully treated by a number of different approaches. In this program, rewards and negative consequences are used to help the child develop appropriate bowel control.

1. Before starting the program, it is very important that your child receive a physical examination by his/her physician to rule out any possible medical or organic factors that may be contributing to the encopresis. If the examination shows that there is a medical reason for your child's encopresis, then you should talk with the physician about appropriate medical interventions. You are encouraged to cooperate fully with the recommended medical interventions.

2. This program can be combined with the use of glycerine suppositories and enemas. Carefully consult with your therapist and/or physician about this option. Your therapist or physician can instruct you on the appropriate use of the suppositories or enemas. Furthermore, they can inform you as to when and how often the suppositories or enemas should be used with your child. The glycerine suppositories, which are used before the enemas, usually produce the desired results so that the enema is not necessary. The enemas are seldom used with such frequency that they create a problem for your child. Nonetheless, caution is recommended if the enemas are used on a regular basis. Here again, consult with your physician or therapist. Use the suppositories or enemas every other day to every third day if the child does not voluntarily produce a bowel movement. It is also important to remember to give the child enough time to have a bowel movement after a suppository or enema has been administered, so that the child does not have an untimely soiling incident in a public place (e.g., school).

3. Encourage your child to take an active role in this program to develop his/her bowel control. It is recommended that your child attempt to have a bowel movement at a specified time each day. In the morning, shortly after the child wakes up, is usually the best time for the child to attempt to have a bowel movement. Other times of the day may be used if they are more practical or feasible for your family.

    Encourage the child to try and voluntarily have a bowel movement within a specified period of time (such as 5 to 10 minutes). The suppositories or enemas can be used if the child has not gone after 5 to 10 minutes. If the child has a successful bowel movement and produces a reasonable amount (approximately 1/4 to 1/2 cup), then reward the child for his/her success.

    It is important to select a reward that will motivate the child. Talk with your child and the therapist about appropriate rewards. Following is a list of suggested rewards that may be used to reinforce your child for having a successful bowel movement.
    *   Snacks
    *   Soda
    *   Small toys
    *   Tokens or stickers that can be exchanged for toys, prizes, or privileges
    *   Extended bedtime
    *   Extra time to play video games or use computer
    *   One-on-one time with child in activity of child's choice
    *   Rent a video or go see a movie
    *   Have a story read to him/her
    *   Free pass that allows the child to skip a chore
    *   Allow child to invite a friend over to the house after school

4. Your child should receive a negative consequence if he/she soils his/her undergarments or clothes. The choice of the negative consequence or punishment should be carefully considered. The consequence should be sufficient to have an impact on the child and motivate him/her to defecate in the toilet. Yet, at the same time, don't use a negative consequence that is overly punitive or harsh. Likewise, do not make any hostile or critical remarks, which only serve to weaken your child's self-esteem. Rather, the negative consequence should be dispensed in a matter-of-fact fashion. Following is a list of negative consequences that you may use if your child soils his/her undergarments or clothes.
    *   Time-out (such as sitting in a chair or staying in the bedroom) for a specified period of time
    *   Loss of computer or TV time (recommended length—1 day)
    *   Loss of privilege to play video games or use computer
    *   Must complete one extra chore
    *   Must remain in house and not be allowed to play with friends outside for specified period of time (such as a couple of hours or the rest of the day)

Your child should be encouraged to assume responsibility for his/her soiling. Instruct your child as to how you want him/her to clean or take care of the soiled undergarments, clothing, or linens.

5. It is strongly recommended that your child sign a contract to formalize the agreement. Use the Bowel Control Contract on the following pages, which spells out the rewards and negative consequences that will be used.

   Keep a record of times when your child experiences success and when he/she soils his/her underwear or clothes. Keeping a record will help your therapist obtain accurate information on the success of the program.

6. It is further suggested that your child complete an incident report each time he/she has an accident. Use the Bowel Control Incident Report on the following page. The child's responses will help provide insight into the factors that contribute to the soiling problem. The child will also be asked to reflect on how others react to his/her problem with soiling. Bring the incident reports to the next therapy session.

BOWEL CONTROL INCIDENT REPORT

Date: _____ Approximate time of incident: _____

1. What factors contributed to the soiling incident? What were you doing around the time that you soiled your clothes? Why didn't you use the toilet?

   _____

   _____

   _____

2. How were you feeling just before the soiling incident? _____

   _____

   _____

   _____

3. How did you feel about yourself after the soiling incident? _____

   _____

   _____

   _____

4. How did your parents and family members react after they discovered that you soiled your clothes? _____

   _____

   _____

   _____

5. How did your peers react to the soiling incident? _____

   _____

   _____

   _____

6. What responsible action(s) did you fail to take to prevent the soiling incident? _____

   _____

   _____

   _____

7. What responsible action(s) can you take in the future to avoid another soiling incident? _____

    _____

    _____

    _____

BOWEL CONTROL CONTRACT

If _____is successful in voluntarily having a bowel movement without
                 (Name of child)

soiling his/her undergarments or clothes, then _____will receive the
                                                            (Name of child)

following reward:

_____

_____

_____

_____

On the other hand, if _____ soils his/her undergarments or clothes, then
                                    (Name of child)

_____ will receive the following consequences:
      (Name of child)

_____

_____

_____

_____

_____   _____

Signature of Child   Signature of Parent

_____   _____

Signature of Parent   Signature of Teacher or Therapist

DRY BED TRAINING PROGRAM

GOALS OF THE EXERCISE

1. Eliminate all nocturnal episodes of enuresis.
2. Take greater responsibility in managing nocturnal enuresis.
3. Decrease the frequency and severity of hostile, critical remarks by parent(s) regarding the client's toilet-training practices.

ADDITIONAL PROBLEMS FOR WHICH THIS EXERCISE MAY BE MOST USEFUL

- Attention-Deficit/Hyperactivity Disorder (ADHD)
- Fire Setting
- Low Self-Esteem

SUGGESTIONS FOR PROCESSING THIS EXERCISE WITH THE CLIENT

In this program, the parent(s) and child address the problem of nocturnal enuresis by combining principles of operant conditioning with the use of medication and a bell and pad apparatus. Before implementing the program, refer the client to his/her physician for a medical examination to rule out any organic or medical factors that may be contributing to the enuresis. Encourage the parents to talk to the physician about the possible use of medication to aid in the control of nocturnal enuresis. Instruct the parents to purchase a bell and pad apparatus and train them in its use. The client's role and responsibility in managing the enuresis should also be clearly spelled out during the therapy session. The parents are strongly discouraged from making any hostile or critical remarks toward the client about his/her enuresis. If the parents have been overly critical or hostile in the past, then this issue needs to be addressed in the family therapy sessions. Finally, it is strongly recommended that a reward system be implemented to reinforce the client for having a dry night.

DRY BED TRAINING PROGRAM
PARENTS' INSTRUCTIONS

Children who experience problems with nocturnal enuresis, or bed-wetting, as it is more commonly known, often feel embarrassed and ashamed. The problem of bed-wetting can cause feelings of low self-esteem. Many times, children are very reluctant to talk about the problem because of the embarrassment that they feel. The parents of the child often feel angry, frustrated, or confused about how to treat the problem. Yet, there is good news. Bed-wetting can be successfully treated by a number of different approaches. In this program, three separate interventions will be used to help deal with your child's bed-wetting.

1. First, contact your child's physician, if you have not already done so. It is important that your child receive a medical examination to rule out any possible organic or medical factors that could be contributing to the problem of bed-wetting. If it is discovered that there is a medical basis for the problem, then talk with your doctor about appropriate medical interventions or forms of treatment.

    Also, talk with your physician about the option of using medication (e.g., Imipramine pamoate, Desmopresin acetate) to help manage the bed-wetting. Medication can be a beneficial supplement to the other aspects of this training program. If your child is placed on medication, then it is important that he/she take the medication as prescribed. Closely monitor the effectiveness of the medication. Inquire about any possible side effects and promptly inform your physician if any of the side effects appear.

2. Second, purchase a classic bell and pad enuresis treatment apparatus from your local pharmacy or medical supply store. If you have any difficulty finding the bell and pad apparatus, talk with your therapist or physician about where you may be able to purchase one. The bell and pad apparatus may go by different names in different parts of the country, but your therapist or physician will be able to help you locate the product. Read the instructions carefully. Your therapist will provide additional instruction or training on the use of the bell and pad apparatus. The classic bell and pad apparatus consists of a pad with electrodes embedded in it. The pad is activated and placed under the child's sheet at night. When the child urinates and causes the pad to be moistened, then either a loud bell, buzzer, or alarm is activated. The child is awakened and instructed to go to the toilet to finish voiding. Newer, updated versions of the classic bell and pad apparatus include a small alarm that is attached to the shoulder of the child's pajamas. A smaller pad,

which is connected to the alarm, is placed into the child's snug-fitting underwear. (*Note:* Some children may sleep so soundly that they do not wake up to the sound of the alarm. Please consult your therapist and physician if your child consistently does not wake up when the alarm is activated.)

3. If a bed-wetting incident has occurred, your child (or you) should disconnect the alarm. You are encouraged to approach your child in a matter-of-fact manner if he/she has had an accident at night. Refrain from making any hostile or overly critical remarks to your child. Belittling your child only hurts his/her self-esteem and does not help solve the problem.

   It is recommended that your child assume some responsibility for his/her bed-wetting if he/she is 6 years of age or older. Teach your child about proper cleanliness. Your child should be expected to change his/her pajamas or clothes. Instruct the child to remove the wet bedsheet and place the sheet and wet pajamas into the dirty laundry or in another identified place. It is further recommended that your child assist in remaking the bed.

4. Depending on the child's rate of success, the use of the bell and pad apparatus can be reduced gradually over time. It is recommended that you begin to taper off on the use of the bell and pad apparatus if the child has been dry for 2 consecutive weeks. Gradually reduce the frequency of the use of the bell and pad apparatus to every other night, then every 3 nights, and so on. The frequency can be increased again if the child regresses and begins to wet the bed. Talk with your therapist about how you should begin to taper off on the use of the bell and pad apparatus.

5. Use a reward system to reinforce your child for having a dry night. Before using the bell and pad apparatus, sit down with your child and identify specific rewards to reinforce the child for meeting his/her goal. Your therapist can also help you identify specific rewards. It is recommended that the child, parent(s), and therapist sign a contract to formalize the agreement. Use the following Dry Night Training Contract, which spells out the terms of the agreement. Simply put, if the client experiences a dry night, then he/she will receive a specific, identified reward. Following is a list of rewards that you might use when your child has a dry night.
   - Extended bedtime
   - Allow child to invite a friend over to spend the night at house
   - Purchase a book (by child's favorite author)
   - Rent or go see a movie
   - Extra time to play video games or use computer
   - One-on-one time with child in an agreed-upon activity
   - Prepare a favorite meal
   - Snacks
   - Small toys
   - Tokens or stickers that can be exchanged for toys, prizes, or privileges

DRY NIGHT TRAINING CONTRACT

If _____ has a dry night and does not wet the bed,
(Name of child)

then _____ will receive the following reward:
(Name of child)

_____

_____

_____

_____

_____

_____

_____

_____

_____

_____   _____
Signature of Child   Signature of Parent

_____   _____
Signature of Parent   Signature of Teacher or Therapist

FIREPROOFING YOUR HOME AND FAMILY

GOALS OF THE EXERCISE

1. Decrease preoccupation with fire and its trappings.
2. Develop ability to handle fire in an appropriate, safe, and respectful way.
3. Eliminate the impulse to play with fire.
4. Increase parents' nurturing, training, and supervision of the client and other siblings.
5. Establish safety of self, the family, and the community.

ADDITIONAL PROBLEMS FOR WHICH THIS EXERCISE MAY BE MOST USEFUL

- Attention-Deficit/Hyperactivity Disorder (ADHD)
- Conduct Disorder/Delinquency
- Oppositional Defiant

SUGGESTIONS FOR PROCESSING THIS EXERCISE WITH THE CLIENT

Fire setting by a child is very alarming to all parents and to the people who live in the community. Because of the possible danger, therapists must respond in a very proactive manner. With rare exception, fire setters are boys and, if they are not borderline psychotic or do not have a conduct disorder, this activity can be successfully stopped in a short period of time. The child does not need to be present in treatment because the parents can be guided in how to intervene. Using the following three-step assignment, guide and monitor the parents' follow-through and the child's progress. If parents have a difficult time following through, step one can be completed with the therapist nearby as support.

FIREPROOFING YOUR HOME AND FAMILY
PARENTS' INSTRUCTIONS

THREE-STEP PLAN FOR PARENTS

Step 1 Dad will gather a large coffee can (3-lb size); some medium-size twigs, tongue depressors, or fire-starter sticks; paper; several blue-tip safety matches; and some water and/or sand. Set a time with the child and go to a quiet, safe area to teach him/her how to safely and effectively build a fire and how to put it out. After you have done this, allow your child to do it step by step on his/her own under your guidance and encouragement. When done, give positive verbal reinforcement for the safe, careful way he/she did the task. Then follow this up with a conversation about the constructive and destructive aspects of fire (*Constructive:* Gives light, heat, it makes our lives easier when under control. *Destructive:* It destroys, kills, and burns when out of control). Ask questions in an open-ended manner that encourages dialogue between the two of you. (*Example:* How do you see fire helping us?)

Step 2 Mom and Dad confer and establish a monetary reward for when the child turns in any matches, lighters, and so on that he/she has or finds (e.g., $.50 per item); for not having any matches, lighters, and the like on his/her person or in his/her room at the end of the day (ask your child to turn pockets inside out and to allow his/her room to be looked over); and for no reports from other children or adults concerning fire-related activities. Mom will take the lead and explain the system to the child. Mom will also purposely leave matches around the house that the child can find and turn in. Keep a chart of how much money the child earns each day. Set the reward amount high enough ($.50 to a $1.00), bearing in mind that it is a small price when compared to your belongings or life.

Step 3 Mom or Dad take 40 matches and a can of either sand or water to a safe place where the child is encouraged to light as many of the matches as he/she desires. Tell the child that he/she will be given $.10 to $.25 for every match that is not used. Again, as before, guide the child step by step in how to light and dispose of each match properly. Allow the child to do this guilt-free, and he/she may use all the matches the first time. While he/she is doing the lighting, talk about the safety required when using fire and about fire's positive and negative effects. Repeat this exercise no fewer than three times a week and use the chart on the following page to track results. Remember to give brief verbal acknowledgment to the progress you see your child making.

STEP 3 CHART

Date	Total Number of Matches	Total Number Lit	Total Number Not Lit	Money Received
Week 1				
Week 2				
Week 3				
Week 4				

WHEN A FIRE HAS NO FUEL

GOALS OF THE EXERCISE

1. Diminish the setting of inappropriate fires and playing with fire-setting materials.
2. Increase the family's communication among all members.
3. Develop the time and environment within the family where grievances can be aired and resolved.
4. Parents responsibly monitor and supervise the client's behavior and whereabouts.

ADDITIONAL PROBLEMS FOR WHICH THIS EXERCISE MAY BE MOST USEFUL

- Anxiety
- Grief/Loss Unresolved
- Peer/Sibling Conflict
- Sexual Abuse Victim

SUGGESTIONS FOR PROCESSING THIS EXERCISE WITH THE CLIENT

This is essentially a family systems approach to the issue of fire setting. The assignment is most appropriate for an older child or early adolescent who just recently had an incident or two of fire setting as opposed to a longer history of playing with fire-setting materials and setting fires. To emphasize the importance of using fire safely and appropriately, the first step of the previous exercise, "Fireproofing Your Home and Family," could be used either prior to the first family session or at the beginning of the first family session. The first questions are designed to help family members feel comfortable and begin to be open about themselves. It also affords you the opportunity to engage each in the process and to help each person see things he/she has in common and what he/she has been taking for granted in being part of the family. This should make a good basis for moving on to the issues of grievances.

WHEN A FIRE HAS NO FUEL

When we live in a family day in and day out, there is a lot that we just naturally take for granted. In order to keep a family running well, from time to time it is important that the family members stop to identify what is good about the family so everyone can express appreciation for these special things. Following are several questions about your family. Answer them as honestly as you can, but do not allow any other family member to see the answers until you share them at the next family session.

THE GOOD THINGS ABOUT MY FAMILY

1. What are the things you like about your family? List them in the following spaces.

    _____   _____   _____

    _____   _____   _____

    _____   _____   _____

2. Of the things you identified in the previous question, which two do you like the best and why?

    _____   _____

3. To whom in the family do you feel the closest? Why do you feel close to that person?

    _____

    _____

    _____

4. What is your favorite family memory? (Explain.)

    _____

    _____

5. What is missing in your family that you wish were present?

    _____

    _____

    _____

IDENTIFYING GRIEVANCES

Another important thing that happens when we live in a family is that we build up resentments or grievances against other members. This is something that happens in all families or in other situations where people work or live close together. To keep resentments or grievances from becoming unhealthy and hurting the whole system, family members need to get them out in the open by expressing them to each other. The following questions are designed to help you do this. Answer them honestly and completely, but do not share them with other family members until your next family session. Here are brief definitions of a resentment and a grievance:

Resentment   Indignation or ill will felt as a result of a real or imagined offense.

Grievance   Indignation stemming from a feeling of having been wronged.

1. List the most significant grievances you have toward members of your immediate family:

    Grievance   **Person**

    _____   _____

    _____   _____

    _____   _____

    _____   _____

2. Now choose two from the preceding list that you would most like to see resolved. Explain what you think could be done to make that happen.

    _____

    _____

    _____

3. If these two grievances were resolved, what difference would it make for you and your family?

    _____

    _____

    _____

4. What are the chances of the grievances being resolved?

    |_____|_____|_____|_____|

    No chance   Slight chance   50/50 chance   Good chance   Sure thing

5. Why do you feel this way about it?

    _____

    _____

    _____

I WANT TO BE LIKE . . .

GOALS OF THE EXERCISE

1. List positive role models of either sex and tell why they are admired or respected.
2. Express comfort with or even pride in sexual identity.
3. Identify positive aspects of desired sex role.

ADDITIONAL PROBLEMS FOR WHICH THIS EXERCISE MAY BE MOST USEFUL

- Low Self-Esteem
- Separation Anxiety
- Social Anxiety

SUGGESTIONS FOR PROCESSING THIS EXERCISE WITH THE CLIENT

The purpose of this assignment is to help the client feel comfortable and accepting of his/her desired sexual identity. In this assignment, the client is required to identify three positive role models of either sex. The client is asked to identify his/her reasons for selecting those persons as positive role models. The client is then asked to identify ways that he/she can act or be like the positive role models in some way. Encourage the client to engage in activities that help him/her to identify with the positive role model. Likewise, the client can be encouraged to engage in these activities with his/her peers. (Note: Provide the child with three copies of the two-page form to allow him/her to complete the assignment.)

I WANT TO BE LIKE . . .

While growing up, it is important to have positive role models. Positive role models, through their words and actions, can teach us many valuable lessons about how to be successful in life. We can learn a lot from positive role models by listening to them and watching them in action. Many times it is fun, exciting, and interesting to watch our role models in action. Sometimes, we make decisions about what we want to do or be in the future by modeling or following in the footsteps of the role model. Having positive role models can also help us fit in and feel accepted by our peers.

In this assignment, you are asked to list three positive role models that are of the sex you desire to be. Take a few minutes now to think about who you consider to be positive role models and choose three. Think about your reasons for choosing these people as positive role models. You can choose role models who you know personally or have never met in your life. These people may be famous and well known, or they may be individuals in your everyday life who you like and respect.

After deciding on three positive role models, please respond to the following items or questions. Fill out a separate form for each role model. (Note—your therapist will give you three copies of this form.) Remember to bring the forms to your next therapy session.

1. Identify the name of a positive role model: _____

2. What do you admire or respect about this person? _____
    _____
    _____
    _____
    _____
    _____

3. What did this person do to make you choose him/her as a positive role model? _____
    _____
    _____
    _____
    _____
    _____

4. In what ways would you like to act or be like this positive role model? _____

    _____

    _____

    _____

    _____

    _____

5. What tasks can you do that will help you to be like the positive role model? _____

    _____

    _____

    _____

    _____

    _____

6. What fears or worries, if any, would hold you back from doing this task? _____

    _____

    _____

    _____

7. Perform an activity that is like that of the positive role model and then write about
    how you felt during and after this experience. _____

    _____

    _____

    _____

    _____

    _____

    _____

    _____

    _____

    _____

    _____

    _____

    _____

    _____

    _____

    _____

ONE-ON-ONE

GOALS OF THE EXERCISE

1. Same-sex parent (or parent substitute) and the client agree to increase time spent together in activities.
2. Facilitate a closer relationship with same-sex adult.
3. Promote the possible acceptance and comfort with birth-sex identity.

ADDITIONAL PROBLEMS FOR WHICH THIS EXERCISE MAY BE MOST USEFUL

- Depression
- Low Self-Esteem
- School Refusal
- Separation Anxiety

SUGGESTIONS FOR PROCESSING THIS EXERCISE WITH THE CLIENT

In this assignment, the client and a same-sex adult are instructed to spend more time together to help develop a closer relationship. The development of a closer relationship may help the client feel more comfortable and accepting of his/her sexual identity. The client and same-sex adult are told to engage in three activities for a minimum of 1 hour. The frequency and duration of the three activities can be modified, depending on the needs of the client, same-sex adult, or other family members. The activity may be either passive or active. If the client and same-sex adult have difficulty reaching an agreement on what activities to perform, then the client should have the greater say in making the final decision. Instruct the client and same-sex adult to respond to several process questions after each activity. The responses to these questions can provide useful information into the nature of the adult-child relationship.

ONE-ON-ONE

In this assignment you are asked to spend one-on-one time together with an adult of your same sex on three separate 1-hour occasions before your next therapy session. The idea behind this assignment is to explore whether you feel more comfortable and accepting of yourself as either a boy or girl by spending quality time with a same-sex adult. The activities with a same-sex adult can be active ones that require a lot of energy or can be more peaceful and quiet tasks.

1. First, sit down with the adult and decide what activities you would like to do or what outings you would like to go on. Look at the calendar and plan in advance when you will spend time together. Hopefully, you can both agree on three mutual activities or outings, but if you cannot reach an agreement, then you may make the final decision. There are a number of activities that you can do together. Following is a list of ideas that may help you decide what to do:

    - Bike ride or rollerblade
    - Go fishing
    - Play catch with a baseball or softball
    - Play basketball at local park or in driveway
    - Go swimming
    - Hike in the woods
    - Go to the movies
    - Watch a sporting event on TV
    - Watch a favorite video together
    - Read stories together
    - Spend time talking about adult's childhood experiences
    - Prepare a meal together
    - Bake cookies or a cake
    - Sew
    - Change the oil in the car
    - Build shelves in a garage or closet
    - Go sledding
    - Build a snowman
    - Visit a local museum
    - Pick wildflowers
    - Go shopping

2. After you have finished each activity, please sit down with the adult and respond to the items or questions on the One-on-One Activity Form, which is on the following page. Your therapist will give you three separate copies. Bring the responses to your next therapy session.

ONE-ON-ONE ACTIVITY FORM

1. Briefly describe the activity or outing. _____
    _____
    _____
    _____

2. What did you like about this activity or outing? _____
    _____
    _____
    _____

3. What did you dislike about this activity or outing? _____
    _____
    _____
    _____

4. How did you get along with the adult during the activity or outing? _____
    _____
    _____
    _____

5. Would you be interested in doing this activity in the future? Please explain your reasons for why you would or would not like to do this activity in the future.
    _____
    _____
    _____
    _____

6. What activities would you like to do with the same-sex adult in the future? _____
    _____
    _____
    _____
    _____

CREATE A MEMORY ALBUM

GOALS OF THE EXERCISE

1. Tell the story of the loss through drawings or artwork.
2. Express feelings surrounding the loss of a significant person through the modality of art therapy.
3. Begin a healthy grieving process around the loss.
4. Successfully grieve the loss within a supportive emotional environment.
5. Create a personal memory album that will serve as a keepsake and reminder of the relationship with the deceased person.

ADDITIONAL PROBLEMS FOR WHICH THIS EXERCISE MAY BE MOST USEFUL

- Anxiety
- Depression
- Low Self-Esteem
- Separation Anxiety

SUGGESTIONS FOR PROCESSING THIS EXERCISE WITH THE CLIENT

In this homework assignment, the child is given a list of suggested ideas for drawings and then is asked to draw a series of pictures between therapy sessions that can be collected and made into a personal memory album. The child's drawings can be used as valuable therapeutic tools to facilitate a discussion about his/her feelings or grief experiences in the context of a supportive environment. After all the pictures have been completed and gathered together, they can be made into a personal memory album during one of the therapy sessions. The child may choose to include some actual photographs of the deceased person in the album. Likewise, he/she may want to add a letter to the deceased person (please see the following homework assignment, "Grief Letter"). This therapeutic intervention can become a valuable keepsake for the child in later years.

CREATE A MEMORY ALBUM

This homework assignment gives you the opportunity to be an artist and create your own personal memory album of ―――――――― You are asked to draw several
(Name of Person)
pictures having to do with your relationship with ――――――――and how you felt
(Name of Person)
after he or she died. You are asked to draw these pictures between therapy sessions and then to share them with your therapist in the following therapy sessions. These pictures will be collected and then made into your own personal memory album.

1. The purpose of this homework assignment is to help you share your feelings and experiences about your loss through pictures and artwork. After you have completed each picture and brought it to the therapy session, you will discuss your drawings with the therapist. This will give you the opportunity to share your feelings and experiences with the therapist. Feel free to also share your pictures with other family members, friends, or peers.

2. Following is a list of suggested ideas or topics that you can draw about. Some of the pictures will allow you to identify what ―――――――― was like before
(Name of Person)
he/she passed away. You may choose to draw pictures of what you enjoyed doing with ――――――――in the past. You also have a choice of drawing what your
(Name of Person)
experiences have been like after ―――――――― died. Please feel free to draw
(Name of Person)
other pictures that you feel are important. Give each picture a title when you have finished your drawing.

Suggested ideas for drawings:
- The entire family, including the deceased person, doing an activity together
- Three activities that you enjoyed doing with the deceased person
- A time when you felt proud of the deceased person or when he/she felt proud of you
- A time when you felt especially sad or angry with the deceased person while he/she was living
- How you felt when you first found out that the deceased person was seriously ill or dying
- How you felt on the day that the person died
- The funeral
- Three activities that help you feel less sad about the loss

GRIEF LETTER

GOALS OF THE EXERCISE

1. Begin a healthy grieving process around the loss of a significant other.
2. Identify and express feelings connected with the loss.
3. Successfully grieve the loss within a supportive emotional environment.
4. Start reinvesting time and energy into relationships with others and age-appropriate activities.

ADDITIONAL PROBLEMS FOR WHICH THIS EXERCISE MAY BE MOST USEFUL

- Anxiety
- Depression

SUGGESTIONS FOR PROCESSING THIS EXERCISE WITH THE CLIENT

Therapists have found letter-writing to be an effective intervention to assist the client in working through the grief process. In this assignment, the client is asked to first respond to a series of questions before actually writing the letter to the deceased person in order to help him/her organize his/her thoughts. The questions listed on the following pages are offered as guides to help write the letter. Some of the questions may not be relevant to your particular client. Encourage the client to express other thoughts and feelings that may be unique to his/her grieving process. After the client responds to the questions, he/she can then begin writing the actual letter. Instruct the client to bring the letter to the following therapy session for processing. Be sensitive and do not assign this task to clients who dislike writing or have a learning disability in written expression.

GRIEF LETTER

Writing letters can be a way to help you identify and express your thoughts and feelings. This is especially true when you need to work through your feelings surrounding the death of an important person in your life. In this homework assignment, you are asked to write a letter to the deceased person to help you identify and express your own feelings about the significant loss in your life. First, find a quiet or relaxing place where you can write the letter. After finding a quiet or relaxing place, please respond to the following questions. These questions will help you organize your thoughts and feelings before you begin to actually write the letter. Feel free to write down whatever thoughts come into your mind at this stage of the assignment. You can decide later whether you want to include these thoughts in your final letter.

1. What thoughts and feelings did you experience around the time of the death or as soon as you learned of _____'s death? _____
   (Name of Person)

   _____

   _____

   _____

2. What are some of the positive things you miss about _____?
   (Name of Person)

   _____

   _____

3. What are some of the problems or disappointments that you had in your relationship with _____? _____
   (Name of Person)

   _____

   _____

4. It is not uncommon for some people to experience guilt or remorse about not having said or done something with a person before that person died. What, if anything, do you wish you could have said or done with _____ before he/she died?
   (Name of Person)

   _____

   _____

5. Do you experience any feelings that _____'s death was your fault? If
    (Name of Person)
    so, please describe why you feel responsible. _____

    _____

    _____

6. Are you sorry about some of the things that happened between you _____?
    (Name of Person)
    Describe. _____

    _____

    _____

7. Did _____ hurt you in some ways? Explain._____
    (Name of Person)

    _____

    _____

8. How has the death affected your present life? _____

    _____

    _____

9. What are some of the important events that are occurring in your present life that
    you would like to share with _____? _____
    (Name of Person)

    _____

    _____

10. What dreams or goals do you have for yourself in the future because you knew
    _____? _____
    (Name of Person)

    _____

    _____

11. What would _____want you to do with your life now? _____
    (Name of Person)

    _____

    _____

12. Please use the following space to express any other thoughts or feelings that you
    would like to include in the letter.

    _____

    _____

    _____

13. Next, review your responses and begin to write the letter on a separate sheet of paper. Bring the completed letter to your next therapy session to go over with your therapist. After discussing the letter, please consider what you would like to do with the letter—do you want to throw the letter away or share it with someone? Your therapist can help you decide what to do with your letter.

PETEY'S JOURNEY THROUGH SADNESS

GOALS OF THE EXERCISE

1. Successfully grieve the loss within a supportive emotional environment.
2. Tell own story about the loss of the significant person.
3. Identify and verbalize feelings pertaining to the loss.
4. Verbalize positive memories of the past and hopeful statements about the future.
5. Reinvest energy and talents into age-appropriate activities and other relationships.

ADDITIONAL PROBLEMS FOR WHICH THIS EXERCISE MAY BE MOST USEFUL

- Anxiety
- Depression
- Low Self-Esteem
- Separation Anxiety

SUGGESTIONS FOR PROCESSING THIS EXERCISE WITH THE CLIENT

Storytelling is an effective therapeutic tool to help children work through their feelings surrounding the death of a significant person. In this assignment, the surviving parent or a significant other is asked to read the story of a young pelican, Petey, who experiences the loss of his father. It is hoped that the story will promote a discussion of the child's own grief experience, either by allowing the child to spontaneously share his/her feelings about the loss or by asking him/her specific questions. Several process questions that can be asked of the client are included. The specific questions are offered as guides to help the child share his/her feelings. It is not necessary that all of the questions be asked at one sitting. Likewise, the child should not be pressured to answer any questions that he/she does not feel ready or willing to answer. The story is designed for children approximately 6 to 11 years of age. The therapist may consider using the story with younger children who are more verbal and mature or with older children who are less verbal and mature.

PETEY'S JOURNEY THROUGH SADNESS
INTRODUCTION AND READER'S INSTRUCTIONS

"Petey's Journey Through Sadness" is a story about a young pelican who experiences the loss of his father. Petey struggles to work through the grieving process and tries to escape his emotional pain by flying away. Eventually, the young pelican's journey takes him back home where he starts a new life.

Before reading "Petey's Journey Through Sadness" to the child, try to create a relaxed atmosphere. Spend a few minutes talking gently with the child. Feel free to sit on the floor with the child or have the child stretch out on a couch. Familiarize yourself with the story by reading it in advance; this will help you to be more animated and spontaneous in your expressions as you read the story.

The purpose of sharing this story of Petey's journey is to help the child identify and verbalize his/her own feelings about the significant loss or death in his/her life. It is hoped that by creating a supportive environment, the child will feel comfortable in opening up and sharing his/her feelings and experiences. After reading the story, ask the child some questions about his/her own loss or grief experience. For some children, it may be beneficial to ask them some of the questions as you read the story. If the child begins to spontaneously share his/her feelings about the grief experience, encourage this. Offer a listening ear and empathetic tone of voice.

Following is a list of questions that you may find helpful in getting the child to open up and share his/her feelings and experiences. These questions are offered as a guide. Please feel free to ask other questions that you feel are more appropriate for each individual child. Do not feel that you have to ask all of the questions. Furthermore, it is very important that you be sensitive to how the child responds to the story or questions. Do not force or pressure the child into responding to any questions that he/she may not be ready to answer. Record any noteworthy remarks that the child may make in response to the questions in the following spaces.

1. What feelings did you experience when ⸺⸺⸺⸺ died?
    (Name of Person)

⸺⸺⸺⸺⸺⸺⸺⸺⸺⸺⸺⸺⸺⸺⸺⸺⸺⸺⸺⸺⸺⸺⸺⸺⸺⸺⸺⸺

⸺⸺⸺⸺⸺⸺⸺⸺⸺⸺⸺⸺⸺⸺⸺⸺⸺⸺⸺⸺⸺⸺⸺⸺⸺⸺⸺⸺

⸺⸺⸺⸺⸺⸺⸺⸺⸺⸺⸺⸺⸺⸺⸺⸺⸺⸺⸺⸺⸺⸺⸺⸺⸺⸺⸺⸺

⸺⸺⸺⸺⸺⸺⸺⸺⸺⸺⸺⸺⸺⸺⸺⸺⸺⸺⸺⸺⸺⸺⸺⸺⸺⸺⸺⸺

2. Tell your story about the events leading up to the death of _____.
    (Name of Person)

    _____

    _____

    _____

    _____

3. What are the strongest feelings that you have at this time, and when do you experience them?_____

    _____

    _____

    _____

4. In the story, Petey is thankful that his father taught him how to fly and catch fish. What things are you thankful for that _____ taught you?
    (Name of Person)

    _____

    _____

    _____

5. Petey found himself acting very irritable and grumpy around the other pelicans after his father died. How did you get along with your other family members, friends, and peers after _____ passed away?
    (Name of Person)

    _____

    _____

    _____

6. Petey left Terra Island because he came in touch with so many painful reminders about his father's death. What painful reminders do you have of _____?
    (Name of Person)

    _____

    _____

    _____

7. At the end of the story, Petey returns home and remembers his father in a kind way by teaching other young or small pelicans how to fly and catch fish. What positive things can you do that will help you to remember ——————?
(Name of Person)

_____

_____

_____

_____

8. What are some of the positive things that you remember about _____ and have good feelings about?
(Name of Person)

_____

_____

_____

_____

_____

_____

_____

PETEY'S JOURNEY THROUGH SADNESS

Just imagine a tropical island lying in the warm Caribbean Sea. Perhaps you or a relative have visited such a place; but if you haven't, that's okay. Just sit back, relax, and let your imagination take you on a journey to Terra Island, a place where the sun warms the friendly creatures and the gentle trade winds offer cool refreshment. It's a wonderful place to live for creatures of all sorts, especially if you're a pelican. Pelicans live a very good life on Terra Island. The beaches are neatly brushed with white sand, and the friendly waters are teeming with a variety of fish, such as mackerel, bluefish, red snapper, and tuna.

One January, Terra Island was hit by some very strong winds. The rough winds of El Niño came in from the west and collided with the gentle trade winds. The collision created swirling winds and made flying difficult for even the strongest of pelicans. Imagine what it would be like to learn to fly in such swirling winds. Indeed, it was a difficult task for most of the young pelicans, but it was even more difficult for one small pelican named Peter Samuel Pelican. Peter, who was nicknamed Petey, had a much shorter wingspan than the average pelican. Petey tried so hard to learn how to fly, but it seemed that the harder he tried, the more difficult it was to stay in the air. One time, Petey was swept up by a strong wind and flew 27 yards before crashing into a huge palm tree. He tumbled to the ground, and two coconuts were shaken loose and plopped right on his head.

A group of pelicans, including his five brothers and sisters, watched Petey's bumpy landing and burst out in laughter. Now, Petey's father, Jonathon Christopher Pelican, also happened to be watching his son's efforts. Taking his son under his enormous wings, Jonathon Christopher quietly instructed his son in the art of flying. His father told him that he needed to let the air glide under his wings. He also told Petey that he was fighting the air by flapping his wings so hard. Petey listened to the gentleness of his father's voice and was encouraged to try again. And, what do you know?! It wasn't long before Petey was soaring through the air as he let the air glide under his feathers. He cried out to his father, "Look, Father, I'm flying!" His father smiled and nodded his approval.

Petey quickly learned that flying made him hungry. It was now time for his second lesson—finding and catching fish. His father taught him to locate the fish by noticing changes in the color of the water. Jonathon Christopher taught his son to look for the darker shades in the water that were moving, because they most likely would be a school of fish. Locating a school of fish usually was easy enough, but catching a fish was another matter. Petey observed other pelicans dive-bombing into the water to catch the fish. After listening to his father's advice and watching several other pelicans, Petey decided to give it his best shot. Gathering up his courage, Petey soared high above the water and then dramatically dropped straight down like a missile. Petey was screaming toward the water at a high speed when, at the last moment, he felt a little bit of fear and pulled up ever so slightly. This caused Petey to do a belly flop right on the water. Smack! The water splashed around him and all of the fish escaped. Petey cried out, "Ouch!" and then had a terrible bellyache. Jonathon Christopher flew down to comfort his son, saying, "You must dive straight down into the water. If you pull up even just a little, you'll do a belly flop every time." At that moment, Petey felt like quitting, but he decided to keep trying. His father showed him the proper way to dive-bomb for fish. Petey failed two more times, but at least he didn't do any more belly flops. Finally, on his third attempt, Petey dove straight through the water and came up with two little fish. His father squawked with joy and Petey felt very proud.

Petey grew stronger with each passing day, and he became quite good at catching fish. He enjoyed soaring high above the water and then dive-bombing to catch his daily meals. Most of all, however, he loved listening to his father's stories about his ancestors. His father would gather Petey and his brothers and sisters around him when the sun was sinking into the sea each night. Petey listened closely to his father's stories as the reflection of the sinking sun danced on the water like sparkling diamonds. This was his favorite time of the day and he loved his father very much.

As time went on, Petey's journeys took him further and further out to sea. His father would tell Petey that he could not go on these journeys with Petey because he was getting older. Petey noticed that his father also seemed to be growing weaker as well. At first, Petey thought that his father would snap out of it and join him again, but after a couple of weeks, his father only seemed more tired and weak. Petey finally asked his father, "What's wrong?" His father, with sadness in his eyes, told him that he had Pelican's Disease. Petey felt afraid, but boldly stated, "I know you, Father. You're so tough, you'll be up in no time, flying around with the rest of us." But, his father did not recover; he only grew weaker.

Jonathon Christopher gathered his children around him and told them that his days on Terra Island were drawing to a close. Sadly, he told his children that he would die soon, and that he would be going to a more peaceful place called Paradise Island. Petey cried and said, "No, Father, please don't leave us." His father quietly replied, "I have lived a good life, but my life is coming to an end. I will be going to a more peaceful place. Try not to worry, Petey, for my voice will always be with you. Remember our heritage as pelicans. It is our heritage to teach the younger and smaller pelicans how to fly and fish. Just as I taught you, you must teach others." With that, Jonathan Christopher closed his eyes and breathed his last breath.

Petey cried hard. He did not understand why his father had to die. He missed his father so much that he ached inside. Petey started getting bellyaches. His heart was filled with sadness and loneliness. Petey was not his usual happy self and he cried when he was alone and thought of his father. He found himself becoming irritable and grumpy with the other pelicans. He was quick to squawk at them if they even came close to invading his airspace. Terra Island no longer seemed like a tropical paradise to him; the island held too many reminders of his father. Petey felt especially sad in the evening when the sun began to sink in the sky and the diamonds danced on the water. These moments painfully reminded Petey of his father's death.

In his sadness, Petey decided to leave Terra Island, the place where he had learned to fly and catch fish. He said good-bye to his family and flew off to the east. He flew for a day and a half before coming to a solitary island called Pergos Island. The beaches were not as white, nor did the waters teem with as many fish. Petey decided it was a good enough place to call his new home.

Petey stayed a week on Pergos Island. He thought he would be able to get away from all the painful reminders of his father's death, but he couldn't. He found himself thinking of his father as he explored the island or ate his meals. However, Petey discovered that he did not think about his father as much when he was flying. So, he decided to fly and just keep on flying. He allowed the gentle trade winds to carry him away. Petey flew and he continued flying until he spotted a curious sight on the horizon. He decided to check it out and swooped down for a closer look. When he landed, he discovered a very small pelican trying to catch his evening meal. Petey called out to the small pelican, "What are you doing?" The small pelican replied in frustration, "I'm trying to catch some fish; but as you can see, I'm not very good at it."

Petey suddenly heard his father's voice stir within him. His father's gentle voice was saying, "Remember your heritage. Take care of the younger and smaller pelicans." Responding to this voice within him, Petey flew over to this small, young pelican and taught him about the art of catching fish. The small pelican listened closely to Petey and after three tries he caught his first meal. He thanked Petey very much for helping him, but then noticed that the sun was going down. He told Petey that he must get home before the sun went down. Petey asked him, "Where is your home?" The small pelican stated, "I live in a wonderful place called Terra Island." Without realizing it, Petey had flown back close to his old home. A smile came across his face and he asked the small pelican, "Do you mind if I go back with you?" The small pelican replied, "I'd like that very much."

Petey returned home to Terra Island to his family and friends. At times, he felt sad about his father's death, but he noticed that his sadness did not seem to last as long as it did when his father first died. He also decided that he wanted to be like his father and teach many other small pelicans how to fly and catch fish. In so doing, Petey was reminded of his father's love for him. The painful memories of Jonathon Christopher gradually became good memories of a father he loved very much. And at the end of each day, Petey would gather the younger and smaller pelicans around him and tell them stories about his pelican ancestors. The young pelicans listened closely to Petey's gentle voice as the diamonds danced on the water.

ACTIVITIES OF DAILY LIVING PROGRAM

GOALS OF THE EXERCISE

1. Function at an appropriate level of independence in the home setting.
2. Increase participation in family responsibilities.
3. Parents and/or caregivers develop an awareness and acceptance of the client's intellectual and cognitive capabilities so that they place appropriate expectations on his/her functioning.
4. Increase parents' praise and positive reinforcement of client for assuming responsibilities and becoming more involved in activities at home.

ADDITIONAL PROBLEMS FOR WHICH THIS EXERCISE MAY BE MOST USEFUL

- Academic Underachievement
- Autism Spectrum Disorder
- Depression
- Oppositional Defiant

SUGGESTIONS FOR PROCESSING THIS EXERCISE WITH THE CLIENT

This intervention utilizes principles of positive reinforcement to reward the child for assuming basic activities of daily living at home. First, it is important to assess the client's overall intelligence, social/emotional maturity, and level of adaptive functioning before implementing the program. Obtain reports of any recent psychoeducational evaluations to gain insight into the child's level of functioning. Conduct or refer the client for a thorough psychoeducational evaluation, if this has not been completed within the past 3 years. Knowledge of the child's level of capabilities will help the parents, child, and you select tasks that are appropriate for this program. After the assessment has been conducted, meet with the parents and client to identify specific activities or tasks of daily living that the client can assume on a regular or daily basis. Next, select the rewards that will be used to reinforce the child for completing the daily tasks. Include the client in the discussions about the specific tasks and rewards so that he/she feels that he/she is a part of the program. This program differs from the homework assignment, "A Sense of Belonging," because it has been designed for children who have been diagnosed with severe and moderate intellectual disability. The program can also be used with clients with a mild intellectual disability who are resistant to performing basic activities of daily living.

ACTIVITIES OF DAILY LIVING PROGRAM
PARENTS' INSTRUCTIONS

This program seeks to increase your child's level of responsibility and independence in the home by allowing the child to assume basic activities of daily living. The program is designed to improve your child's personal hygiene, increase his/her self-help skills, and help him/her become more responsible around the home.

1. First, meet with your therapist and son/daughter to develop a potential list of activities of daily living that your son/daughter can perform on a daily or regular basis. Include your son/daughter in many of the discussions about this program, particularly when it comes to making any final decisions or explaining the program to him/her. However, there may be times when you need to talk privately with your therapist about the nature of the task or responsibility. In choosing the basic activities of daily living, it is important to consider your son's/daughter's intellectual capabilities, social/emotional maturity, and overall level of adaptive functioning. Select tasks that your son/daughter can perform independently. Hopefully your son/daughter can perform the tasks without a lot of supervision or monitoring, although some children may need greater supervision or guidance in the beginning phases of the program. Likewise, some children with severe limitations may need more supervision throughout the entire program. Talk with your therapist about how much supervision you are to provide for your son/daughter.

    Expect your child to perform three to five basic activities of daily living. Here again, the number of these basic activities or tasks can be adjusted to meet the needs of your child. For some children, you may want to begin the program by focusing on one specific task or activity. You can add other tasks or activities later as the child becomes more proficient in performing the initial task.

    Following is a list of tasks or responsibilities that you may want to address in this program. This list is offered as a guide to help you select appropriate tasks. Feel free to select other tasks that you feel are more appropriate for your son/daughter.

    - Comb hair
    - Brush teeth
    - Wash hands or hair
    - Take a bath
    - Dress self in preselected clothes
    - Select own clothes appropriately
    - Dust furniture
    - Vacuum carpet
    - Wash dishes
    - Pick up toys
    - Pick up sticks in the yard
    - Take out trash

- Make bed
- Load the dishwasher
- Get cereal in the morning

- Sweep the floor
- Set the table
- Chew with mouth closed

2. Use a reward system to positively reinforce your son/daughter for assuming the activities of daily living. Rewards can help maintain your son/daughter's interest and motivation in fulfilling the tasks. Following is a list of tangible rewards that you can use to reinforce your son/daughter. Remember, the most powerful reinforcer or reward may be the spoken word, praise, or an affectionate touch or hug. Praise your son/daughter often in addition to using more tangible rewards, such as:
   - Tokens or stickers that can be traded in to purchase larger toys, prizes, or privileges
   - Money
   - Snacks
   - Extended bedtime
   - Rent or go see a movie
   - Read a book together
   - One-on-one time with child in an agreed upon activity
   - Small toys
   - Allow child to invite a friend over to the house to play
   - Extra television time
   - Extra time to play video games or use computer
   - Coloring books
   - Colorful stickers

3. Keep a record of how often your son/daughter successfully completes a task. Use the following Activities of Daily Living Sheet to record when your son/daughter performs the task. The Activities of Daily Living Sheet will help remind you to reward your son/daughter. Post the Activities of Daily Living Sheet in a visible place (such as the refrigerator or a bulletin board in your child's room).

4. Have your son/daughter sign a formal contract if he/she is reading at a third-grade level or above. Use the Activities of Daily Living Contract Form to formalize the agreement. Regardless of whether a formal contract is used, it is important to clearly spell out the terms of this program to your son/daughter in advance. Your son/daughter should be aware of how often he/she needs to perform his/her activities of daily living before he/she receives the reward. Post the contract in a visible place.

ACTIVITIES OF DAILY LIVING CONTRACT

If _____ performs the following task(s): _____ _____
      (Name of child)

_____

_____

_____ per _____ , then _____
   (Frequency)   (Day or week)   (Name of child)

will receive the following reward:

_____

_____

_____

_____

_____   _____

Signature of Child   Signature of Parent

_____   _____

Signature of Parent   Signature of Teacher or Therapist

ACTIVITIES OF DAILY LIVING SHEET

Activity	DAY OF THE WEEK						
	Sun.	Mon.	Tues.	Weds.	Thurs.	Fri.	Sat.
1. _____							
2. _____							
3. _____							
4. _____							
5. _____							
6. _____							
7. _____							
8. _____							

Place a checkmark (√) in the appropriate box when your child performs the task on that specific date.

A SENSE OF BELONGING

GOALS OF THE EXERCISE

1. Promote feelings of acceptance and a sense of belonging in the family system, school setting, or community.
2. Increase participation in family activities or outings.
3. Assist parents in developing greater awareness of client's intellectual capabilities and level of adaptive functioning.
4. Increase parents' praise of client for assuming responsibilities and/or becoming involved in more activities at home, school, or community.

ADDITIONAL PROBLEMS FOR WHICH THIS EXERCISE MAY BE MOST USEFUL

- Academic Underachievement
- Autism Spectrum Disorder
- Depression
- Low Self-Esteem
- Speech/Language Disorders

SUGGESTIONS FOR PROCESSING THIS EXERCISE WITH THE CLIENT

This assignment is aimed at working with clients who have been diagnosed with a mild intellectual disability (IQ scores 55 to 69) or borderline intellectual abilities (IQ scores 70 to 79). Meet with the child and parents to identify tasks or activities that the child can perform that will provide him/her with a sense of belonging. Carefully consider the child's intellectual capabilities, social/emotional maturity, and level of adaptive functioning before assigning a final task. Select tasks that are both challenging and interesting. At the same time, it is important to avoid placing unrealistic expectations on the child by assigning him/her tasks that clearly exceed his/her level of adaptive functioning. Include the child in the discussions, as it is important that he/she be interested in or motivated to perform the task. Select a task that can be performed on a regular, full-time basis or choose a task that can be performed on a temporary or even one-time basis. This exercise provides you with the opportunity to assess whether the parents are being either overprotective of their son/daughter or unrealistic in their expectations of what he/she can accomplish.

A SENSE OF BELONGING
PARENTS' INSTRUCTIONS

We all have a need to feel accepted and experience a sense of belonging to at least one group. Many of us satisfy this need by using our strengths to perform tasks or activities that help us gain acceptance and respect from others. The child who is faced with intellectual limitations or has been labeled a *slow learner* has the same needs as others. Therefore, it is important that such children be provided with opportunities to utilize their own individual strengths and engage in responsible behaviors that allow them to feel accepted. In this exercise, your child will be assigned a task that will allow him/her to feel that he/she is making a contribution to his/her home, school, or community.

1. First, sit down with your therapist and son/daughter to brainstorm a potential list of activities that he/she can perform. Include your son/daughter in many of the discussions, particularly when it comes time to make any final decisions. However, there may be times when you will want to talk privately with your therapist about the nature of the task or responsibility. In selecting a task, it is important to consider your son/daughter's intellectual capabilities, social/emotional maturity, and level of adaptive functioning. After brainstorming, try to select a task that is both interesting and challenging for your son/daughter. Be careful not to pressure or coerce your child into performing any task; this will not promote a sense of belonging. At the same time, it is important that your son/daughter not be assigned a task that exceeds his/her intellectual capability or level of functioning. If he/she selects a task that is unrealistic or exceeds his/her capabilities, then it is important that your therapist and you discuss this issue with him/her. Listen to your son/daughter's desires or requests, but also assert your thoughts and concerns.

    The task can be assigned on a regular, full-time basis or can be performed on a temporary or even one-time basis. For some children, it is best to select a variety of tasks that will help maintain their interest and motivation. You have the option of varying the tasks from day to day or week to week.

    The task or responsibility can be performed at home, at school, or in the community. You may want to consider consulting with the schoolteachers, church officials, or community leaders before you decide on the final activity to be performed. Following is a list of tasks or responsibilities that you may want to review with your son/daughter before making a final decision. This list is offered as a guide to help in the selection of an appropriate task, or it may generate other ideas.

    *   Work alongside parent in preparing a special meal for the family
    *   Work alongside parent in performing a mechanical or construction task

- Assist parents with grocery shopping
- Bake a cake (with parental supervision)
- Wash car
- Go clothes shopping with money earned from allowance
- Learn how to sew or make blankets or clothes (e.g. hats, booties, socks) for young children or infants at a homeless agency
- Plant flowers, bushes, fruits, or vegetables in family garden
- Raise flag at school
- Give a simple announcement on the intercom at school
- Assist with setting up props at a school play
- Sing with choir at a school concert
- Participate in a community hunger walk or walk-a-thon
- Volunteer for assistant trainer or bat boy on school baseball team
- Sign up for sports team
- Sign up for swimming lessons
- Sign up for karate lessons
- Enter Special Olympics events
- Enter local road race or fun run
- Actively participate in church service (sing in choir, sign up as an altar boy/girl, volunteer for community service work)

2. If these tasks do not seem appropriate for your son/daughter, then observe his/her behavior in the next week or in the time before your next therapy session. Record any positive, constructive, or responsible behaviors that he/she exhibits before the next therapy session on the following form. Observe your son's/daughter's reaction to the positive or responsible behavior. Likewise, notice how others respond to his/her positive or responsible behavior.

   Bring the form to your next therapy session. Your therapist can review the form and help you decide on an appropriate task or activity for your son/daughter. This form can also be used throughout therapy to inform the therapist of any positive or responsible behaviors that your son/daughter has performed. The therapist can reinforce him/her for being responsible. This will help to boost his/her self-esteem.

RESPONSIBLE BEHAVIOR FORM

1. Describe the positive or responsible behavior by your son/daughter. _____

   _____

   _____

   _____

   _____

2. What frustrations or obstacles did your son/daughter encounter while engaging in the responsible behavior? _____

   _____

   _____

   _____

3. How did your son/daughter manage these frustrations? _____

   _____

   _____

   _____

4. How did other people respond to the positive or responsible behavior? _____

   _____

   _____

   _____

5. How did your son/daughter feel about his/her actions or behavior? _____

   _____

   _____

   _____

DIXIE OVERCOMES HER FEARS

GOALS OF THE EXERCISE

1. Elevate self-esteem.
2. Identify actions that can be taken to improve self-image.
3. Recognize personal insecurities that prevent or inhibit trying new tasks or engaging in age-appropriate activities.
4. Decrease frequency of statements that reflect fear of failure, rejection, or criticism.

ADDITIONAL PROBLEMS FOR WHICH THIS EXERCISE MAY BE MOST USEFUL

- Anxiety
- Enuresis/Encopresis
- Separation Anxiety
- Social Anxiety
- Specific Phobia

SUGGESTIONS FOR PROCESSING THIS EXERCISE WITH THE CLIENT

This homework assignment involves the reading of the story "Dixie Overcomes Her Fears," which is about a young duck who learns to overcome her fears and insecurities about flying. The parents or caretakers are encouraged to read the story to the child between therapy sessions. After reading the story, the parents or caretakers should review several questions with the child. In responding to the questions, it is hoped that the child will identify his/her own insecurities. Discuss the insecurities with the child to help him/her develop coping strategies (i.e., positive self-talk, cognitive restructuring, relaxation techniques) to overcome his/her insecurities. By developing new coping strategies, it is further hoped that the child will be willing to try new tasks or engage in age-appropriate activities. This story is designed for children approximately 5 to 11 years of age. You may consider using the story with younger children who are more verbal and mature in their development or with older children who are less verbal and mature.

DIXIE OVERCOMES HER FEARS
READER'S INSTRUCTIONS

The story "Dixie Overcomes Her Fears" is about a young duck who learns to master her fears of flying. Dixie lacks self-confidence and self-esteem, but with courage and the help of an unlikely friend, she overcomes her fears and learns to fly.

Storytelling can be a useful way to join with the child to begin to address his/her insecurities or low self-esteem. Before reading "Dixie Overcomes Her Fears" to the child, try to create a relaxed atmosphere. Spend a few minutes talking gently with the child. Feel free to sit on the floor with the child or have the child stretch out on a couch. Familiarize yourself with the story by reading it in advance. This will help you to be more animated or spontaneous in your expressions as you read the story.

The purpose of reading the story is to help the child identify his/her own insecurities or doubts that may prevent him/her from trying new tasks or performing age-appropriate activities. Hopefully, by creating a supportive environment, the child will feel comfortable enough to talk about his/her insecurities. After reading the story, ask the child some questions about his/her own insecurities or fears.

Following is a list of questions that you may find helpful in allowing the child to identify and discuss his/her insecurities or fears. These questions are offered as a guide. Feel free to ask other questions that you may feel are more appropriate for the particular child. Do not feel that you have to ask all the questions. Furthermore, it is very important that you be sensitive to how the child responds to the story or questions. Do not force or pressure the child into responding to any questions that he/she may not be ready to answer. Record any noteworthy remarks that the child may make in the following spaces. This will also help the child to share his/her fears or insecurities with the therapist in the next therapy session. The therapist, with your help, can assist the child in finding ways to reduce his/her fears or insecurities so that he/she can begin to take some healthy risks.

1. What have you been afraid to try in the past? _____

    _____

    _____

    _____

    _____

2. What were you afraid would happen if you tried? _____

_____

_____

_____

_____

3. Think of times when you first felt afraid to try something new, but after trying it anyway, you ended up succeeding or doing well at it. Tell about some of these times. _____

_____

_____

_____

_____

_____

4. How did you feel after you succeeded? _____

_____

_____

_____

5. In the story, Dixie sees herself as being smaller and weaker than the other ducks. What do you see as your weaknesses? _____

_____

_____

_____

_____

6. Dixie felt sad when the other ducks made fun of her. Can you think of times when other kids made fun of you? How did you feel when they made fun of you? Please share your thoughts and feelings about these experiences. _____

_____

_____

_____

_____

7. What is a task or activity that you would like to try at present but, perhaps, have been afraid to try? _____

    _____

    _____

    _____

    _____

8. What can you do to overcome your fears or worries? _____

    _____

    _____

    _____

    _____

9. Who can help you through encouragement and believing in you like Tina did for Dixie? _____

    _____

    _____

    _____

    _____

DIXIE OVERCOMES HER FEARS

The Indian River is a gently flowing river that runs through Northern Michigan, connecting two beautiful lakes, Burt Lake and Mullett Lake. In the winter, the river moves quietly under the frozen cover of ice and snow. Sometimes, it seems that the winters last forever in Northern Michigan, but spring eventually comes. Spring is an exciting time of the year because it brings forth new life. The Canadian geese and wild ducks return from their winter vacation lands and settle in the Indian River area to make their summer homes.

It is here in this quiet river community that the family of a friendly duck, Claire, settled each year. Claire always looked forward to coming back to the Indian River each spring, but this year she was more excited than ever. For this year, she would become a mother. Claire laid eight beautiful eggs. She watched over her eggs with careful love, and when all the eggs were hatched, her neighbors swam over to congratulate her for having eight beautiful ducklings. It was a proud moment for Claire. Claire took good care of her ducklings and made sure that they got the right amount of food. Her ducklings were a lively bunch—full of energy. All of them, with the exception of the youngest and smallest duckling, had an adventuresome spirit, and Claire had to keep a watchful eye over them. But Dixie, the youngest and smallest of her eight ducklings, stayed very close to Claire. She did not venture very far because she was afraid of being harmed by one of the duck's natural enemies, the fox, raccoon, or hawk. Dixie learned to rely on her mother to catch many of her meals.

All of the ducklings continued to grow, and soon it was time for their first flying lesson. Claire taught her ducklings that it was very important that they learn how to fly because they would have to return south for the winter. One by one, Dixie's brothers and sisters took their turns at learning how to fly. They struggled a bit at first, but with their mother's encouragement, the ducklings were all flying and soaring in the air by the end of the day. All of the ducklings, that is, except for Dixie. Dixie told her mother that she was not ready to fly because she was not as big or strong as the others. Claire could see the fear in Dixie's eyes and tried to comfort and calm her. Dixie refused to try that day, but she did agree to go with her mother the following day for her own private flying lesson.

The following day arrived, and although Dixie was still nervous, she knew that she had to follow through with her promise to try to learn how to fly. Dixie tried four times and fell head over tail each time. On the fifth attempt, she found herself soaring in the sky. She flew about 70 yards before she turned around and shouted to her mother, "Look, Mom, I'm flying!" But as she turned her head, she crashed into a huge branch and dropped straight to the ground. She landed on her right wing and screamed out in pain. Claire immediately flew over to Dixie's side and called for one of her other ducklings to go and get the doctor.

The doctor came as soon as he could. He was a serious sort of fellow by the name of Dr. Quack. Dr. Quack carefully looked over Dixie with concern. He paused for a bit and then said, "Well, I think she'll be okay. She has a badly bruised right wing, and she will need some time to rest. But I think she'll be flying before long." Dr. Quack instructed Dixie to rest her wing for the next week, and then he would check her over again.

When the doctor returned a week later, he found that everything was all right. He told Dixie that she could begin to learn how to fly again. Dixie's strength had returned, but unfortunately, her confidence had not. She nervously said to her mother, "I'm afraid I will only get hurt again, and besides, I'm still not as big as the others." Claire told Dixie that she would need to learn how to fly soon because she would need to build up her strength before she could make the long trip south for the winter. Dixie refused to learn how to fly despite her mother's urging.

The neighboring ducks on the Indian River noticed that she was not flying and began to make fun of her. One duck, by the name of Thomas, seemed to take particular pleasure in teasing Dixie. He laughed and said, "Nah nah nah nah nah!! Dixie is a chicken. She's nothing but a landlubber!"

Dixie's feelings were hurt by the teasing and she ran off and hid from the other ducks. She found a lonely riverbank and climbed up on a bumpy rock and began to cry. She sobbed, "I'll never learn how to fly. I'm just too afraid." Suddenly, the rock began to move under her webbed feet. She was surprised to see that she was actually standing on a turtle. The turtle looked up at the tearful Dixie and said, "Hi, my name is Tina, and I couldn't help but overhear you crying."

Dixie apologized, "I'm sorry that I sat on you."

Tina said, "No problem, it's not the first time that it's happened, but I think that before you learn how to fly, you're going to have to start to believe in yourself."

Dixie now became angry at the turtle and shot back, "What do you know about flying; you're just a turtle."

Tina replied, "Well, that's true, I am just a turtle, but I do know that if you don't take any chances, you'll never accomplish what you set out to do. I could hide in my shell and never come out. That way, I'd be safe from any attack from a raccoon or fox, who would love to turn me into turtle soup, but I have to venture out if I want to catch any food. I also enjoy swimming in the Indian River and meeting different friends." She went on to add, "So, you see, I have to take chances just to survive and make friends. You have to take the chance that you might hurt yourself before you learn how to fly."

Dixie was now listening closely to Tina and sadly stated, "But if I even try to learn how to fly, the other ducks will just laugh at me if I don't do it right. I can't take any more of their teasing."

Tina said, "I know a field where hardly any ducks ever go. I can take you there, and I'll watch you as you practice. I promise that I won't make fun of you."

Dixie agreed to meet Tina the next morning before any of her brothers and sisters awoke from their sleep. Dixie tried several times, but still she was not successful. When Dixie began to feel discouraged, Tina quickly challenged her, "Now, now, remember what I told you. You've got to believe in yourself."

Dixie closed her eyes and pictured herself, in her mind, flying in the air. Without realizing it, she began to flap her wings and then run along the ground. She was lifted up by a gust of wind, and before she knew it, she was 30 feet up in the air. Tina cried out, "You can do it, Dixie, just keep flapping your wings." Dixie began flapping her wings and she shouted, "I can't believe it, I'm really flying! I've got to go show my mother. Tina, can you go tell the other ducks that I've learned to fly?"

Tina left the field and ran as fast as her thick, little legs could carry her. She found Thomas and joyfully shared, "You'll never guess what's happened!" Thomas sarcastically replied, "Oh, do tell, you creature of quick feet. Inquiring minds want to know!"

Tina excitedly said, "You may not believe this, but Dixie has learned how to fly." Thomas looked at Tina in disbelief and said, "Not Dixie, she's too much of a chicken. I won't believe it until I see it with my own eyes."

Just then, Dixie flew overhead, and her brothers and sisters looked up to discover that Dixie was flying. They happily flew up to join and congratulate her. Dixie spent the rest of the day flying above the Indian River with her brothers and sisters.

Dixie spent the rest of the summer playing air games with her brothers and sisters and visiting with her special friend, Tina. She grew stronger with each day. The cooler weather came and the fall colors appeared. It was now time for Dixie to make her first trip south. She felt a little nervous about making the long trip, but she realized that she would have her family flying beside her. Before leaving, she went to say good-bye to Tina for the winter. She found her friend busily making her home in the soft mud on the banks of the Indian River. She hugged Tina and said good-bye. Tina gave Dixie the best hug a turtle could give with her short, thick legs. She wished her well, and said, "I certainly hope I see you next summer." Dixie said, "Oh, I'm sure I'll make it back. The Indian River is the best place to spend the summer, especially with friends like you."

And do you know what? Dixie made it to her winter home in the south. She also made it back to the Indian River the following summer. There she spent her summer days catching food, laughing, and playing with her brothers and sisters and her good friend, Tina.

LEARN FROM YOUR MISTAKES

GOALS OF THE EXERCISE

1. Elevate self-esteem.
2. Recognize how failure can become a valuable learning experience.
3. Identify steps that must be taken in order to overcome faults or achieve desired goals.
4. Identify factors that contribute to the failure experience.

ADDITIONAL PROBLEMS FOR WHICH THIS EXERCISE MAY BE MOST USEFUL

- Academic Underachievement
- Anxiety
- Depression
- Social Anxiety

SUGGESTIONS FOR PROCESSING THIS EXERCISE WITH THE CLIENT

In this assignment, the client is asked to write about three experiences in which he/she either lost or failed in some way. The assignment gives the client the opportunity to examine how the experience affected his/her feelings about the self. It provides insight into how the client copes with failure. The exercise is particularly useful for clients who overreact to losing or catastrophize failure. Challenge the client to consider how the failure experience can become a valuable learning experience. It is hoped that the client will also recognize that even though he/she may fail or lose from time to time, he/she is still a person worthy of respect and affirmation. For younger clients or those with a learning disability in the written language area, enlist the help of a parent or other significant adult to help the client respond to the questions.

LEARN FROM YOUR MISTAKES

Losing or failing is not fun. It can create a lot of bad feelings, such as sadness, disappointment, frustration, or anger. Yet, failure is part of life. All people fail from time to time, and it actually can be helpful in the long run. Through failure, you can learn from your mistakes or become more determined to do better next time. Just because you fail sometimes, doesn't make you any less important or special.

In this exercise, you are asked to write about three important times in your life when you experienced failure. Take a few minutes to think about these experiences before you sit down to write. Review the following items or questions before you start to write. If you feel like you need help in responding to these items or questions, feel free to ask a parent, teacher, other adult, or older peer for help.

Please respond to the following items or questions. Fill out a separate form for each failure experience. (*Note*: Your therapist will give you three copies of this form.) Remember to bring the forms to your next therapy session.

1. Describe a sad or painful time when you experienced failure. _____
    _____
    _____
    _____
    _____
    _____

2. How did you respond to the failure experience? _____
    _____
    _____
    _____
    _____

3. At the time, how did the failure experience make you feel about yourself? _____
    _____
    _____
    _____
    _____

4. What factors led up to the failure? _____
    _____
    _____
    _____
    _____
    _____

5. What did you learn from your failure experience, or what would you do differently
    if you had to do it all over again? _____
    _____
    _____
    _____
    _____
    _____

6. How can the experience make you a better person? _____
    _____
    _____
    _____
    _____
    _____

7. What good came out of, or could come out of, the failure experience? _____
    _____
    _____
    _____
    _____
    _____
    _____

SYMBOLS OF SELF-WORTH

GOALS OF THE EXERCISE

1. Elevate self-worth.
2. Identify positive traits and talents about self.
3. Identify actions that can be taken to improve self-image.

ADDITIONAL PROBLEMS FOR WHICH THIS EXERCISE MAY BE MOST USEFUL

*   Anxiety
*   Depression
*   Separation Anxiety
*   Social Anxiety

SUGGESTIONS FOR PROCESSING THIS EXERCISE WITH THE CLIENT

This intervention is designed for the client who is experiencing feelings of low self-esteem and inadequacy. The client is instructed to take an inventory of his/her strengths, interests, or accomplishments. Some clients, particularly younger children, may have difficulty identifying any strengths, interests, or accomplishments because of their developmental level. Parents may need to help him/her identify his/her strengths. After the client identifies his/her strengths, interests, or accomplishments, instruct the client to bring in objects or symbols that represent his/her strengths, interests, or accomplishments. The objects or symbols can give you some insight into what activities provide the client with a sense of joy or happiness. Then you can plan other homework assignments or interventions that will help to elevate his/her self-esteem. This exercise can be modified to work with a number of different emotional or behavioral problems.

SYMBOLS OF SELF-WORTH

Every child is special in some way. We all have been blessed with some talent, strength, or interest that makes each one of us unique. At times, it is difficult to feel good about ourselves when we experience sadness or feel overwhelmed by problems. Yet, it is especially important at these times to step back and think about our own positive qualities. By reflecting on our strengths, interests, or accomplishments, we can start to feel better about ourselves.

1. The first step in this exercise is to step back and spend a few minutes thinking about your strengths, interests, or accomplishments. Ask yourself, "What are my strengths and interests?" and "What accomplishments have made me feel good about myself?" For example, you may feel really good about yourself because you have made good grades in school or have been on a winning basketball team. After identifying your strengths, interests, or accomplishments, write them down in the following spaces. Identify at least five strengths, interests, or accomplishments.

   A. _____
   B. _____
   C. _____
   D. _____
   E. _____
   F. _____
   G. _____

2. Next, think of an object or symbol that represents your strengths, interests, or accomplishments. Bring in these symbols or pictures of such objects to your next therapy session. The symbols or objects will help your therapist learn more about you and discover what your strengths and interests are. Again, think closely about what types of objects or symbols you would like to bring in. Several examples or suggestions follow to help you decide.
   • Girl Scout uniform with pins or badges reflecting past accomplishments
   • Football helmet demonstrating membership on a sports team
   • Instrument representing your musical talent
   • Ski boot reflecting your interest in downhill skiing
   • School report cards reflecting your academic accomplishments
   • Poetry or drawings reflecting your artistic talents

- Medals, awards, or ribbons representing past accomplishments
- Pictures from past vacations reflecting interests and positive memories

Perhaps these examples or suggestions will give you some ideas. Remember to be yourself and select objects or symbols that reflect who you are as a person. Be creative and have fun with this exercise. At the same time, you are encouraged to be practical in selecting your symbols or objects. For example, if you have a strong interest in biking, then it would be very difficult to bring in your bicycle. However, your bike helmet or a picture of you riding your bike would be good symbols of your interest in biking.

3. Bring in three symbols or objects to your next therapy session. Be prepared to discuss these symbols or objects with your therapist. Your therapist will want to know how you developed your strengths and interests or how you achieved your accomplishments. Please respond to the following items or questions to help you prepare for the next therapy session.

Name of first symbol or object: _____

What strength, interest, or accomplishment does this symbol or object represent?

_____

How are you using this strength or interest in your present life? If your symbol or object represents an accomplishment, how did you achieve this accomplishment?

_____

_____

Name of second symbol or object: _____

What strength, interest, or accomplishment does this symbol or object represent?

_____

How are you using this strength or interest in your present life? If your symbol or object represents an accomplishment, how did you achieve this accomplishment?

_____

_____

Name of third symbol or object: _____

What strength, interest, or accomplishment does this symbol or object represent?

_____

How are you using this strength or interest in your present life? If your symbol or object represents an accomplishment, how did you achieve this accomplishment?

_____

_____

_____

THREE WAYS TO CHANGE YOURSELF

GOALS OF THE EXERCISE

1. Elevate self-esteem.
2. Increase awareness of self and ways to change in order to improve self-image.
3. Identify activities that can be taken to improve self-image.
4. Establish rapport with therapist in the beginning stages of therapy.

ADDITIONAL PROBLEMS FOR WHICH THIS EXERCISE MAY BE MOST USEFUL

- Anxiety
- Attention-Deficit/Hyperactivity Disorder (ADHD)
- Conduct Disorder/Delinquency
- Depression
- Gender Identity Disorder
- Overweight/Obesity

SUGGESTIONS FOR PROCESSING THIS EXERCISE WITH THE CLIENT

This activity can often be used as a sequel to the Three Wishes Game exercise. Like the Three Wishes Game, it is recommended that this activity be used in the beginning stages of therapy to help you establish rapport with the client. The Three Ways to Change Yourself activity can be used with children who are exhibiting a variety of behavioral or emotional problems, but it is included in this section because of its potential to increase the client's self-image. In this exercise, the client is asked to draw three separate pictures between therapy sessions that reflect three changes that he/she would like to make with himself/herself. The client is instructed to bring the pictures back to the following therapy session to process with you. In discussing the drawings, assist the client in identifying ways that he/she can bring about positive changes in himself/herself. The information gained from this exercise can also help you and the client establish clearly defined treatment goals.

THREE WAYS TO CHANGE YOURSELF

This activity can be a fun-filled way for your therapist to get to know you better. Here, you are invited to be a creative artist and draw pictures of three changes that you would like to make in yourself. Try to express what is really important to you, but also remember to relax and have fun when you are drawing your pictures.

Before you sit down to begin drawing the pictures, spend a few minutes thinking about the changes that you would most like to see happen in yourself or in your life. You can express your wish to change in a number of different ways. Some people want to develop a talent, skill, or interest in a certain area. For example, they may draw a picture of a ballet dancer, singer, or basketball player. Other people may choose to draw something that has to do with their personality. For instance, some people would like to see themselves control their temper, smile more, or be more cheerful about life. Perhaps you would like to change how you get along with other people. Some people may choose to draw pictures that show that they have more friends, smile or laugh more often, or are friendlier and more caring. Finally, some people may express their wish to change something about their personal appearance.

There are only a couple of rules for this activity. First, think of three different changes that you would like to make in yourself. If you cannot think of at least three changes, then talk with someone you trust in order to develop some ideas. Second, don't use any written words in your drawings. This is because your therapist will attempt to guess what changes you would like to make after you bring your drawings back to the next therapy session. Your therapist will have three chances to guess what your desired changes are. If your therapist cannot guess what changes you would like to make in three tries, then, in baseball terms, your therapist has struck out. At that point, you can tell your therapist how you would like to change.

After you have given thought to the changes that you would like to make in yourself and listed them in the following spaces, please draw them on separate pieces of blank paper. Remember to bring the drawings to your next therapy session, along with your responses to the following items.

1. The first change I would like to make is: _____
    _____
    _____

2. Reasons why I would like to make this change are: _____

_____

_____

3. How will other people know that I have changed? What signs will I show them? How will my behavior be different? _____

_____

_____

_____

4. The second change I would like to make is: _____

_____

_____

5. Reasons why I would like to make this change are: _____

_____

_____

6. How will other people know that I have made this second change? What signs will I show them? How will my behavior be different? _____

_____

_____

_____

7. The third change I would like to make is: _____

_____

_____

8. Reasons why I would like to make this change are: _____

_____

_____

9. How will other people know that I have made this third change? What signs will I show them? How will my behavior be different? _____

_____

_____

Do not show this list to your therapist until he/she has attempted to guess what your desired changes are.

THREE WISHES GAME

GOALS OF THE EXERCISE

1.   Increase ability to identify and verbalize needs.
2.   Identify steps that must be taken to meet needs.
3.   Identify actions that can be taken to improve self-image.
4.   Establish rapport with therapist in the beginning stages of therapy.

ADDITIONAL PROBLEMS FOR WHICH THIS EXERCISE MAY BE MOST USEFUL

•   Anxiety
•   Conduct Disorder/Delinquency
•   Depression
•   Oppositional Defiant

SUGGESTIONS FOR PROCESSING THIS EXERCISE WITH THE CLIENT

The Three Wishes Game is a fun-filled activity that you can use in the early stages of therapy to establish rapport with the client. This activity can be used with children who are experiencing a variety of emotional or behavioral problems, but it has been included in this section on low self-esteem because of its potential to help improve the client's feelings about himself/herself. In this exercise, the client is asked to draw three separate pictures between therapy sessions that reflect his/her own individual wishes. The client is instructed to bring the pictures to the following therapy session for processing.

Assess how realistic or attainable the client's wishes are. If the client has produced a picture that identifies his/her interests or potential talents, then he/she should be encouraged to take steps to develop those interests or talents. For example, if a 10-year-old child expresses a wish to be a basketball star or musician, then he/she should be encouraged to join a basketball team with same-aged peers or to take music lessons. On the other hand, do not be discouraged or consider the assignment a failure if the client draws a picture of a wish that is unattainable or is based solely on fantasy. At the very least, the exercise provides the client with the opportunity to express or identify his/her own individual needs. This game can also be incorporated into a therapy session.

THREE WISHES GAME

The Three Wishes Game is a fun-filled activity that can help your therapist get to know you better. Here, you have the opportunity to be an artist and draw pictures of your three most important wishes.

Just pretend, for the sake of having fun, that you have been granted three wishes, and you can wish for anything in the whole world. Perhaps you would wish for a special toy, object, or thing. You may wish to go someplace special or accomplish some special feat. You can also choose to spend one or more of your wishes on someone else. You may make a wish for someone you really care about, such as a parent, sibling, grandparent, relative, or friend.

1. There are only two rules in this activity. First, you are allowed only three wishes. You cannot use one of your wishes to wish for more wishes. Second, you must draw a picture of something that represents each wish. You cannot use any written words in your drawings to express your wishes. This is because your therapist will attempt to guess what it is that you are actually wishing for after you bring your pictures to the next therapy session. Your therapist will have three chances to guess each one of your wishes. If your therapist cannot guess what each wish is, then you can tell your therapist what it is that you are wishing to come true.

2. In the following space, list your three wishes and your reasons for selecting each one of them. Do not show this list to your therapist until he/she has attempted to guess each one of your wishes. Draw each one of your wishes on a separate piece of paper.

   A. My first wish is for: _____

   Reasons for this wish: _____

   _____

   B. My second wish is for: _____

   Reasons for this wish: _____

   _____

   C. My third wish is for: _____

   _____

   Reasons for this wish: _____

   _____

BAD CHOICE—LYING TO COVER UP ANOTHER LIE

GOALS OF THE EXERCISE

1. Significantly reduce the frequency of lying.
2. Identify negative consequences that can occur as a result of lying.
3. Consistently tell the truth, even when facing possible consequences for wrongful actions or irresponsible behavior.
4. Assist client in establishing and maintaining close, trusting relationships by being honest on a regular basis.

ADDITIONAL PROBLEMS FOR WHICH THIS EXERCISE MAY BE MOST USEFUL

- Attention-Deficit/Hyperactivity Disorder (ADHD)
- Conduct Disorder/Delinquency
- Disruptive/Attention-Seeking
- Oppositional Defiant

SUGGESTIONS FOR PROCESSING THIS EXERCISE WITH THE CLIENT

In this assignment, the client is asked to read a short story about a young boy, Joshua, who has a problem with stealing. The main character in the story actually gets into additional trouble for lying to cover up a previous lie. After reading the story, the client is asked to respond to several questions. Through reading the story and answering the questions, it is hoped that the client will realize the negative consequences that his/her lying can create. The final question requires the client to identify ways to rebuild his/her level of trust with family members and others. The parents are encouraged to read the story and questions to younger children who may have problems with either reading or writing. If the client has problems with writing, then the parents are encouraged to record his/her responses in the appropriate spaces.

BAD CHOICE—LYING TO COVER UP ANOTHER LIE

Please read the following story and answer the questions that follow.

Joshua came home from school on a Friday afternoon and walked into the kitchen. He saw a big plastic bag lying on the counter. He peaked into the bag and saw about 15 large candy bars. They just so happened to be his favorite kind. Joshua quickly glanced around the room and looked to see if anyone was around. He also listened to make sure that he did not hear anyone. When he saw that nobody was around, he reached into the bag and grabbed two of the candy bars. He raced back to his bedroom, then closed and locked the door. A smile crept across his face as he unwrapped a candy bar and took a huge bite. He thought to himself, "What a great start to my weekend!" Joshua finished the first candy bar and decided to also eat the second one. After finishing the candy bars, he tossed the wrappers into his wastepaper basket. He tossed some other papers on top of the wrappers to cover them up.

The next day, Joshua got to sleep in a little later. His younger sister, Erica, had a soccer game. When his mom came home from the soccer game, she was quite angry. She walked into Joshua's bedroom without knocking and asked him in a stern voice, "Did you take some candy bars out of the bag I had lying on the kitchen counter? Somebody took them, because two girls on Erica's soccer team went without their snack after the game." Joshua sat up in his bed and answered his mother in a grumpy tone of voice, "No, I didn't take the candy bars. I don't know anything about them." He did not look at his mother as he answered her. His mother then said, "Are you sure? Because somebody took them." Joshua, sounding more irritated, said, "I already told you no! How come you never believe me?" His mother shot back, "Because you have a history of lying."

A few days later, Joshua's mother was taking out the trash. She went into his room to empty out his wastepaper basket into a large garbage bag. In doing so, some of the trash fell onto the floor, including the two candy bar wrappers. Joshua's mother picked up the wrappers and called out, "Joshua, come here." When Joshua came into his bedroom, his mother said, "I found these wrappers in your trash. Would you mind explaining how they got there?" Joshua nervously stuttered, "Um . . . I . . . um . . . I bought two candy bars with my allowance a couple of weeks ago." His mother replied, "A couple of weeks ago, huh? I took out your trash last week and didn't see them there. Joshua, it looks like you're telling a lie. You first lied about taking the candy bars, and now you're telling a lie to cover up your first lie." His mother was about to lecture him again about lying, but Joshua very angrily commented, "I didn't take them! Why are you always blaming me for things and accusing me of lying? You never believe me!" His mother again said, "That's because you have a history of lying. Listen, I'm going to talk to your father about this and we'll both decide what your punishment will be." Joshua cried, "It's not fair! I always get blamed for things."

Joshua's mother and father talked about the incident. They decided that Joshua would have to do extra chores that weekend to pay for the candy bars. He would also be grounded from being able to play video games or having friends over for the next 3 days because of his lies.

1. In the story, Joshua tells two lies. He first lies about taking the candy bars, and then he tries to cover it up when he is caught by his mother. Please take a few minutes and think about a time when you told a lie to cover up another lie that you told. Write about it in the following space.

   _____

   _____

   _____

   _____

   _____

2. How did your parents react to your lies? _____

   _____

   _____

3. What punishment did you receive? _____

   _____

   _____

4. Joshua could have avoided getting into trouble by making better choices. What are some better choices that Joshua could have made? _____

   _____

   _____

   _____

5. Joshua's mother does not believe his story because he has a history of lying. Joshua complains about his mother not believing him, but the truth is that his lying has caused his mother to doubt him. It will likely take time for Joshua's parents to trust him more. What can you do so that your parents and others can have more trust in you? Please list three to five things below that you can do that will help other people to trust and believe you. Be specific. For example, instead of saying, "Be good," tell exactly how you can be good.

A. _____

B. _____

C. _____

D. _____

E. _____

THE VALUE OF HONESTY

GOALS OF THE EXERCISE

1. Identify the factors contributing to the problem with lying.
2. Teach the value of honesty to help establish and maintain trusting relationships.
3. Significantly reduce the frequency of lying.
4. Consistently tell the truth, even when facing possible consequences for wrongful actions or irresponsible behavior.

ADDITIONAL PROBLEMS FOR WHICH THIS EXERCISE MAY BE MOST USEFUL

- Attention-Deficit/Hyperactivity Disorder (ADHD)
- Conduct Disorder/Delinquency
- Oppositional Defiant
- Peer/Sibling Conflict

SUGGESTIONS FOR PROCESSING THIS EXERCISE WITH THE CLIENT

This assignment has two phases. The first phase involves the parents talking to the child over a two-week period each time he/she is caught telling an obvious or apparent lie. (Note – the duration of phase one can be modified to meet the needs of the client and family.) The parents are instructed to talk to the child in a calm, composed, and assertive manner about the factors that contributed to his/her telling a lie. The parents are further encouraged to "teach" the child about the importance of being honest. In phase two, the parents and client identify how he/she will be rewarded or reinforced for telling the truth. The parents can reinforce the client with a reward if he/she is honest. The parents and client also have the option of reducing the severity of a consequence if he/she admits to engaging in minor behaviors, wrongful actions, or irresponsible acts. The client's admission of fault or responsibility should not protect him/her from the natural or logical consequences of his/her actions, particularly if the offense was serious in nature. Finally, the client, along with the parents' help, is encouraged to complete a questionnaire when he/she tells the truth.

THE VALUE OF HONESTY

Honesty is one of the essential ingredients to building close relationships. If a person has a problem with lying, then this weakens trust and places a great deal of strain on his/her relationships with other people. In this assignment, the parents and child are encouraged to work together to help the child become more honest. There are two phases to this assignment. The first phase of this assignment lasts for approximately two weeks. The length of this phase can be changed to meet your needs. Talk with your therapist about how long you feel the first phase should last. The first phase has two goals: (1) Explore and identify the reasons contributing to the child's need to lie, and (2) Parents teach the child about the importance of honesty. During phase two, the child will either be rewarded for being honest or receive a less severe consequence for being honest about his/her misbehaviors, wrongful actions, or irresponsible acts

PHASE ONE—Explore Factors and Teach Honesty
A. <u>Explore reasons for lying</u>

The first phase of this assignment requires the parents and child to spend time talking about the issue of honesty and the problem with lying. One of the first steps to overcoming a problem is to recognize that a problem exists. Many times, the discussion about a problem leads to positive changes and improvements in behavior. It is hoped that by discussing the problem, the child will be more motivated to tell the truth and resist the urge to lie. Parents are encouraged to talk with their child about the issue of lying in a calm, composed, and matter-of-fact manner. Parents are discouraged from yelling or "lecturing" the child for long periods of time. The child will likely be more willing to explore the reasons for him/her lying if the parents remain calm and composed. Parents may also need to allow the child to calm down before he/she is willing to discuss the reason(s) for lying. The child may need to take a "time-out" (not as a form of punishment) to help him/her calm down and think about the reason(s) why he/she may have lied on this particular occasion.

There are a number of reasons why a child or person may lie. The parents and child are encouraged to sit down and explore and discuss these possible reasons for telling a lie. The following is a list of common reasons why a child may lie. The list is not all-inclusive, so be open to other possible reasons.

Common reasons why a child may lie include:

- Lie to get out of trouble or avoid punishment
- Lie to meet needs or getting something they want (e.g., toy, snack, extra time playing video games)
- Lie to get out of performing chores or homework
- Lie to meet up with a friend or go to a place where he/she is not allowed
- Lie to get sibling in trouble
- Lie because the child was not thinking about possible consequences
- Lie because the child was worried or afraid of disappointing parents or others
- Lie because the child was ashamed or embarrassed about his/her behavior
- Lie to make self look better (e.g., saying you got a hit in a baseball game when you actually struck out)
- Lie to protect self-esteem or not look so bad in the eyes of others
- Lie because the child is tired of "always getting into trouble"
- Lie to protect friend or another important person

After identifying the reason for lying, the parents can teach the child about the importance of being honest in that particular situation. The discussion may also help the child learn to deal with stressful situations.

B. Teach the value of honesty

A key part of this assignment is the opportunity that the parents have to teach the child about the importance of honesty. The parents are encouraged to share with the child the reasons why it is important to be honest. The parents are again encouraged to remain calm and avoid lecturing the child in an overly stern tone of voice. The following is a list of reasons why honesty is important. Here again, the list is not all-inclusive. Your therapist can help you identify other reasons why it is important to be honest.

- Honesty helps to build trust.
- People can depend on your word if you are honest.
- They don't doubt or question you as much.
- Honesty helps a person to make and keep friends.
- A person feels less anxious, afraid, ashamed, or embarrassed in the long run if they are honest because they are not worried about getting caught in a lie.
- A person shows respect and kindness to others by being honest.
- Other people will treat you with greater respect or kindness when you are honest.
- By being honest, you are more willing to accept responsibility for yourself, instead of blaming others.

- Other people will be more willing to believe you when you are suspected of doing something wrong because you have a history of telling the truth. On the flip side, other people will tend not to believe you when you are actually telling the truth because you have a history of lying.
- You will feel better about yourself if you are an honest person.
- Your punishment, many times, will be less severe if you are honest about your misbehavior or irresponsible behaviors.

PHASE TWO—Reward and Reinforce Honesty

It is important to praise, reward, and/or reinforce positive changes in behavior when they occur. In this phase, the parents are encouraged to reward or reinforce the times when the child is honest. The parents and child are encouraged to discuss ways to reward or reinforce the child's honesty. Your therapist can also help you identify ways to reward or reinforce honesty.

The following is a list of rewards that can be given to the child if he/she is honest:

- Words of praise
- Physical display of affection (e.g., hug, pat on the back, high-five)
- Small toy
- Extra time playing video games or watching TV
- Snacks
- Extended bed time
- Money
- Spending one-on-one time with parent in game or other recreational activity
- Tokens that can be "cashed in" for a larger reward or privilege at a later time

The goal of this program is also to reinforce the child when he/she is telling the truth about his misbehavior, wrongful actions, or irresponsible acts. In this case, it may be appropriate to assign a natural or logical consequence for the misbehavior or irresponsible actions. Yet, it is recommended that the consequence or punishment not be so severe or long-lasting. The following is a list of ways for how the child's punishment can be reduced when he/she is honest:

- Less time spent in time-out
- A privilege (e.g., watching TV or playing video games) is removed for less time
- Spend less time performing chore as restitution for wrongful actions
- Loss of points or tokens in reward system or token economy
- Perform act of kindness to person who was the victim of wrongful or irresponsible action
- Compliment or help sibling or peer who was the victim of wrongful or irresponsible action
- Write apology letter to person who was hurt by wrongful or irresponsible action

Finally, the problem of lying will not likely magically disappear for good. The parents and child are encouraged to consult with the therapist about how to deal with the child's lying when it does occur.

The parents and child are encouraged to complete The Value of Honesty Questionnaire on the following page. This will help to inform your therapist of times when the child has been honest. The parents are encouraged to help the child complete the questionnaire. Please remember to bring the questionnaires back to the following therapy session.

THE VALUE OF HONESTY QUESTIONNAIRE

1. Describe an incident where you told the truth. _____
   _____
   _____
   _____

2. How did you feel while you were telling the truth?

   ____ Happy   ____ Anxious/worried   ____ Mad
   ____ Proud   ____ Embarrassed   ____ Sad
   ____ Relieved   ____ Ashamed   ____ Other _____

3. What reward did you receive for being honest? _____
   _____
   _____

4. On the other hand, if you told the truth about your misbehavior or irresponsible act, how was your punishment reduced? _____
   _____
   _____

5. How did your parents respond to your honesty? _____
   _____
   _____

6. How would you have liked your parents to respond differently, if at all? _____
   _____
   _____

7. How did you feel about yourself after talking with your parents? _____
   _____
   _____

TRUTHFUL/LYING INCIDENT REPORTS

GOALS OF THE EXERCISE

1. Explore factors contributing to the client's decision to either be truthful or dishonest.
2. Significantly reduce the frequency of lying.
3. Identify negative consequences that can occur to self and others as a result of lying.
4. Consistently tell the truth, even when facing possible negative consequences for wrongful actions or irresponsible behavior.
5. Assist client in establishing and maintaining close, trusting relationships by being honest on a regular basis.

ADDITIONAL PROBLEMS FOR WHICH THIS EXERCISE MAY BE MOST USEFUL

- Attention-Deficit/Hyperactivity Disorder (ADHD)
- Conduct Disorder/Delinquency
- Disruptive/Attention-Seeking
- Oppositional Defiant

SUGGESTIONS FOR PROCESSING THIS EXERCISE WITH THE CLIENT

In this assignment, the client is asked to complete either a Truthful or a Lying Incident Report. Parents and teachers should be given copies of both of these Incident Reports so that they can use the appropriate form when the situation arises. The Lying Incident Report should obviously be used when the client has been caught in a lie. It is hoped that the Incident Report will help the client identify the factors contributing to his/her decision to lie or be deceitful. The Truthful Incident Report should be given to the client on those occasions when he/she told the truth even when he/she could have received a possible negative consequence for some wrongful action or irresponsible behavior on his/her part. In processing the client's responses in follow-up therapy sessions, the therapist can challenge the client to assume greater responsibility for his actions by being truthful. Reinforce the client for being honest when he/she could have received possible negative consequences for doing so. The therapist should also teach and/or reinforce any effective coping strategies that the client can use to be honest on a regular basis in the future. It is further hoped that the assignment will help the client realize the importance of being honest in building/maintaining close interpersonal relationships.

TRUTHFUL/LYING INCIDENT REPORTS
TRUTHFUL INCIDENT REPORT

Date: _____

1. Please describe a recent situation when you felt the urge to lie, but instead told the truth. _____
    _____
    _____

2. What made you decide to tell the truth instead of lie? _____
    _____
    _____

3. What good things happened as a result of you telling the truth? _____
    _____
    _____

4. On the other hand, what bad things happened as a result of you telling the truth? (For example, you still may have received a punishment for doing something wrong or failing to do something that you should have done.) _____
    _____
    _____

5. How did your parents (or teachers) react to you telling the truth? What did they say or do? _____
    _____
    _____

6. What would you have liked your parents (or teachers) to say or do that they did not?
    _____
    _____

7. How do you feel about yourself now for having told the truth? _____
    _____
    _____

TRUTHFUL/LYING INCIDENT REPORTS
LYING INCIDENT REPORT

Date: _____

1.   What lie did you tell? Who did you lie to? Where were you? _____
_____
_____

2.   What were your reasons for lying? (For example, did you lie to try to get something you wanted or get out of trouble? Did you lie to make yourself look good around others?) _____
_____
_____

3.   How did your lie affect others? _____
_____
_____

4.   How did your parents (or teachers) react to your lie? _____
_____
_____

5.   What was your punishment for lying? _____
_____
_____

6.   If you were in the same situation again in the future, what would you do differently?
_____
_____

7.   What can you do or tell yourself in the future to help you be more honest with others? _____
_____
_____

DEALING WITH CHILDHOOD ASTHMA

GOALS OF THE EXERCISE

1. Share feelings triggered by the knowledge of the medical condition and its consequences.
2. Explore and identify reasons for the client's resistance in following through with recommended treatment interventions for asthmatic condition.
3. Accept the illness and adapt life to necessary changes.
4. Follow through consistently and comply with all recommendations regarding treatment interventions.

ADDITIONAL PROBLEMS FOR WHICH THIS EXERCISE MAY BE MOST USEFUL

- Academic Underachievement
- Speech/Language Disorders

SUGGESTIONS FOR PROCESSING THIS EXERCISE WITH THE CLIENT

In this assignment, the client and parents are both asked to fill out their respective questionnaires pertaining to the client's asthmatic condition. The responses to the questionnaires will not only provide insight into the client's and parents' thoughts, feelings, and attitudes about the asthma, but will also indicate whether the client has gained an acceptance of his/her health condition. The client is given the opportunity to share how the asthma has impacted his/her life. The assignment allows the therapist to assess how compliant or resistant the client has been in following through with the recommended treatment interventions. It is not uncommon for children who have been diagnosed with asthma to experience conflict with their parents over treatment issues. The client's and parents' responses to the questionnaires will provide insight into the nature and degree of any frustration or conflict between them. The client's reasons for failing to follow through with his/her recommended treatment plan should be processed in the therapy sessions. The therapist can help the client and parents identify ways to reduce the degree of conflict and tension. It is ultimately hoped that the client will come to an acceptance of his/her asthma and cooperate in following through with the recommended treatment interventions. The assignment can be used with a variety of other health problems. The therapist can simply change the name of the medical condition (e.g., change asthma to diabetes) and modify or delete some of the questions.

DEALING WITH CHILDHOOD ASTHMA
PARENT FORM

Please answer the following questions to help your therapist gain a greater understanding of your child's thoughts, feelings, and attitude about his/her asthma.

1. At what age was your child first diagnosed with asthma? _____ years old

2. How severe is your child's asthma?

Borderline	Mild	Moderate	Severe	Very severe

3. What factors or conditions cause your child's asthma to flare up or become worse?

_____

_____

4. What type(s) of medication or treatment is your child receiving for his/her asthma?

_____

_____

5. Has your child ever had to be hospitalized because of the asthma? If so, how often, and when was the last hospitalization? _____

_____

_____

6. How has your child reacted emotionally to having asthma? _____

_____

_____

7. How has the asthma affected your child's life and/or what is your child unable to do because of the asthma? _____

_____

_____

8. How have you reacted emotionally to your child's asthma? What effect has it had on your life? _____

_____

_____

9. How does your child's asthma affect your relationship with him/her? _____

_____

_____

_____

10. How compliant or cooperative is your child in following through with his/her treatment?

Very cooperative	Cooperative	So-so	Uncooperative	Very uncooperative

11. What is your child's biggest complaint about the treatment procedures? _____

_____

_____

_____

12. If your child is not consistent in following through with the treatment, what are the biggest factors that contribute to his/her lack of consistency in following through with the treatment plan?

_____

_____

_____

13. What have you found to be effective in getting your child to cooperate with the treatment plan?

_____

_____

_____

14. On the other hand, what approach does not work and causes your child to become even more frustrated or uncooperative? _____

_____

_____

_____

DEALING WITH CHILDHOOD ASTHMA
CLIENT FORM

Please answer the following questions to help your therapist better understand your thoughts and feelings about what it is like to have asthma.

1. How do you feel about having asthma? _____
   _____
   _____
   _____

2. How has the asthma affected your life? _____
   _____
   _____
   _____

3. What is the worst thing about having asthma? _____
   _____
   _____
   _____

4. What activities or things are you unable to do because of your asthma? _____
   _____
   _____
   _____

5. How good are you at following through with your treatment? For example, do you regularly use your inhaler or breathing machine?
   _____
   _____

6. How do you feel about the way your parents have handled your asthma? _____
   _____
   _____
   _____

7. If you were free to say anything to your doctor or parents about your treatment for the asthma, what would you tell them? _____

_____

_____

_____

8. What changes would you like to see your parents make in the way that they deal with your asthma? _____

_____

_____

_____

9. What things do you do or fail to do that make your asthma worse? _____

_____

_____

_____

_____

10. What changes or things could you do differently to help yourself deal better with having asthma? _____

_____

_____

_____

_____

GAINING ACCEPTANCE OF PHYSICAL HANDICAP OR ILLNESS

GOALS OF THE EXERCISE

1. Explore the client's thoughts and feelings about how his/her life has been affected by physical handicap or serious illness.
2. Assess how the physical handicap or serious illness impacts family and peer relationships.
3. Develop greater acceptance of physical handicap or serious illness.
4. Engage in social, productive, and recreational activities that are possible despite the medical condition.

ADDITIONAL PROBLEMS FOR WHICH THIS EXERCISE MAY BE MOST USEFUL

- Attention-Deficit/Hyperactivity Disorder (ADHD)
- Autism Spectrum Disorder
- Social Anxiety
- Speech/Language Disorders

SUGGESTIONS FOR PROCESSING THIS EXERCISE WITH THE CLIENT

In this assignment, the client is asked to read a story about an injured beagle, Sam, and then respond to several follow-up questions. It is hoped that in processing this assignment, the client will feel comfortable in sharing his/her thoughts and feelings about the effect that his/her physical handicap or serious illness has had on his/her life. The client will also be given the opportunity to discuss how his/her handicap or health problem has impacted his/her interpersonal relationships. Furthermore, the client is asked to identify his/her personal strengths and interests that can help him/her develop a positive self-image. The therapist should also encourage the client to become involved in social or extracurricular activities that will provide him/her with the opportunity to establish meaningful friendships. The therapist should be alert to any resistance or feelings of insecurity on the client's part that may keep him/her from reaching out to others. The parents or caregivers are encouraged to read the story to the client. With younger clients, the parents or caregivers may very well need to record their responses.

GAINING ACCEPTANCE OF PHYSICAL HANDICAP OR ILLNESS

Please read the following story and then answer the questions that follow it.

Sam, a young beagle, stood eagerly in the garage, wagging his tail as he watched his master, Mr. Thompson, and his three sons pack all the supplies they would need to go on their first big hunting trip of the fall. Sam loved to go hunting, and so did his five brothers and sisters. He could tell that they were all excited to go hunting, as well. His brothers and sisters were wagging their tails and jumping all around the garage. After loading up the supplies in his truck, Mr. Thompson let Sam's brothers and sisters jump up into the back of the truck. Sam limped over to the truck as fast as he could go. Mr. Thompson saw Sam limping over to the truck and sadly walked over to him. Kneeling down, Mr. Thompson softly said, "I'm sorry, Sam, I can't take you hunting with us this year. You couldn't keep up with us, not with your bad leg and all." Mr. Thompson patted Sam on the head and led him back into the house. Before leaving on the trip, Mr. Thompson turned to Sam and said, "You'll have to take care of Missy this weekend." Sam's heart sank as the door closed. He cried and whimpered, hoping Mr. Thompson would change his mind and allow him to go. But he didn't, and Sam felt left out for the first time in his life.

Sam limped into the living room and lay down next to the couch. His thoughts turned back to last winter when he injured his right leg on a hunting trip. He remembered chasing a raccoon when all of a sudden he collapsed in pain. His leg was caught in a trap. Mr. Thompson came running over right away and was able to free him from the trap, but his leg was badly hurt. Sam would now always walk with a limp. He would never be able to run as fast as he used to. Sam looked back on the accident with sadness because he knew, deep down, that he would probably never go hunting again.

Sam continued lying on the floor, feeling sorry for himself, until Missy came bursting through the front door after school. She cried out to her mother, "Mom, I have a big favor to ask you." Mrs. Thompson said, "What is that?" Missy exclaimed, "Jenny is having everybody over to her house. They're first going to an afternoon movie and then they're having pizza later on. Oh mom, could you please do my paper route for me? I really want to go!" She begged, "Please . . . please!" Mrs. Thompson said in reply, "I'm sorry, Missy, but I can't help you. I've got a meeting with the ladies at church in an hour. I'd be willing to take you over there later on this evening when they're having pizza." Missy protested, "But I'll miss the movie . . . it's not fair! Why do I have to do this stupid paper route?" Mrs. Thompson said, "Well, Missy, it is your job and you can't just quit." With that, Missy cried, "I hate this stupid job! I'm quitting at the end of the month." Missy grabbed her heavy paper route bag and started to leave to deliver her papers. She was met at the door by Sam, who stood there wagging his tail. Irritated, Missy said, "You can come with me, Sam. I might as well have some company since I can't be with my friends. This stinks." Sam followed Missy to the street corner where she folded the papers and placed them in plastic bags. After she folded all the papers, Missy said, "Come on, Sam. Let's get this over with as fast as we can."

Sam limped alongside Missy as she delivered the first few papers. Sam could tell that Missy was still in a bad mood. Trying to make her feel better, Sam jumped up on his hind legs and grabbed a paper out of her bag with his mouth. He trotted over to the next house with the paper in his mouth and dropped it at the feet of an elderly man, Mr. Crowley. The elderly man looked up at Missy and growled, "Why would I want a paper that a dog has drooled all over? I'll take one from out of your bag and not from that dog's mouth." Missy quietly said, "Yes, sir" and handed him another paper. She said, "Come on, Sam." She then added, "Don't let it bother you, Sam. He's always grumpy." When they came to the next house, they were met by a friendlier face. It was Mr. Jenson, who always smiled when she delivered his paper. Mr. Jenson said, "Well, Missy, I see you brought a special friend along with you today. I'd be honored if your friend would bring me the paper." Missy hesitantly gave the paper to Sam, who grabbed it with his mouth and brought it over to Mr. Jenson. Mr. Jenson patted him on the head and said, "My friend, I hope you brought me good news and not bad news. Hopefully my Yankees beat those Red Sox last night." The kind, elderly man took the paper out of Sam's mouth and said, "Wait here a minute." He went into the house and came out with a small treat. He gave it to Sam who quickly scarfed it down. Missy said, "Thanks, Mr. Jenson." Mr. Jenson replied, "Have a good day, Missy, and I hope you bring your friend along with you tomorrow."

Missy and Sam walked down the street delivering the rest of the papers. Sam delivered about half of the papers. Many of Missy's customers smiled or laughed when they saw her dog helping her with the paper route. When they got home, Missy gave Sam another doggie treat and said, "Thanks, Sam. You were a big help. I'll let you help me tomorrow, too." Sam gobbled down the treat and felt happy that he could help Missy. Missy was able to join her friends later that evening and enjoy pizza with them.

From that day on, Sam often went with Missy to help her with the paper route. Many of her customers would greet her each day to say hello to Sam. Even Mr. Crowley began taking his papers from Sam after a while. Although Sam missed hunting, he felt very good about being able to help Missy.

1. Sam, the beagle, is not able to go hunting because of his injury. How has your physical handicap or health problem affected your life? _____

_____

_____

_____

_____

2. What things are you unable to do because of your physical handicap or health problem that you would really like to do? _____

_____

_____

_____

3. In the story, Sam feels sad and left out when Mr. Thompson and his sons leave to go hunting. Have you ever felt sad about being left out? If so, please tell about a time when you felt this way. _____

_____

_____

_____

4. How do your family members and many of the other kids at school treat you because of your physical handicap or illness? _____

_____

_____

_____

5. Would you like to be treated differently by other kids? _____ yes _____ no
If YES, please tell how you would like to be treated differently. _____

_____

_____

_____

6. In the story, Sam feels happy about being able to help Missy deliver the newspapers. What activities or things do you do that help you feel good about yourself? _____

_____

_____

_____

7. What activities would you like to become involved in the future that would help you to feel liked and accepted by the other kids? _____

_____

_____

_____

CONCERNS, FEELINGS, AND HOPES ABOUT OCD

GOALS OF THE EXERCISE

1. Describe the nature, history, and severity of obsessive thoughts and/or compulsive behavior.
2. Obtain from the parents a working knowledge of the disorder and its effects on their child.
3. Instill a sense of realistic hope for parents and child.
4. Develop and implement specific strategies for minimizing OCD symptoms.

ADDITIONAL PROBLEMS FOR WHICH THIS EXERCISE MAY BE MOST USEFUL

- Anxiety
- Specific Phobia

SUGGESTIONS FOR PROCESSING THIS EXERCISE WITH THE CLIENT

This exercise will be most effectively processed with the parents from an open, encouraging perspective, as the possibility or likelihood of their child having this disorder will be quite upsetting. For most parents, this disorder will evoke images of Howard Hughes from books they have read about him or from the film *The Aviator*. These behaviors will need to be put in perspective as being the extreme of the disorder and where it could go if it is not treated. Realistic hope needs to be at the center of the processing alongside giving key information, addressing concerns, and starting to develop strategies for minimizing the symptoms.

CONCERNS, FEELINGS, AND HOPES ABOUT OCD

This exercise will help you begin to express your feelings and concerns about OCD and to look optimistically at how you can begin to assist your child in handling and minimizing the symptoms.

1. Describe briefly your responses to when the possibility that your child may have this disorder was first presented to you. _____
    _____
    _____

2. What was the most disturbing thing about the disorder that you heard? _____
    _____
    _____

    What was the most encouraging thing you remember hearing? _____
    _____
    _____

3. Identify the feelings you have experienced around hearing the diagnosis of OCD (circle all that apply). _____

Angry	Upset	Afraid	Helpless
Worried	Anxious	Hopeless	Sad
Numb	Overwhelmed	Encouraged	Other _____

4. Do either you or your partner have any relatives who have or may have had this disorder?
    _____ yes _____ no

    If yes, who was it and how did the disorder affect them? _____
    _____
    _____

5. From the following list of OCD symptoms, check all the ones that your child exhibits:

___ Fear of dreadful illness

___ Obsession about one's body

___ Inability to discard anything

___ Repeating questions over and over

___ Accumulating useless objects

___ Asking over and over for reassurance

___ Needing to do it over and over until it is "just right"

___ Repeatedly checking things (e.g., is the door locked, appliance turned off)

___ Excessive concerns about diet and germs

___ Overwhelming need to align objects

___ Saving useless trash or other things

___ Repeating routine activities for no reason

___ Blinking or staring rituals

___ Counting compulsions

6. Of the symptoms checked, rate their overall severity: (circle one)
   Minimal   Mild   Moderate   Severe   Very severe

7. Which of the checked symptoms causes you the greatest concern? _____
   _____

8. How could you best be helped and supported in coping with and addressing this disorder, in particular the symptoms you previously identified? (Check all that would be helpful.)

   _____ Seek out a support group

   _____ Meet on a regular basis with a therapist to develop strategies/ways to address symptoms

   _____ Obtain books and articles on the disorder

   _____ Attend a conference on treating the disorder

   _____ Go to a child psychologist who has a specialty in this area

REFOCUSING

GOALS OF THE EXERCISE

1. Train the client in the use of refocusing.
2. Learn to refocus attention away from obsessions and compulsions by engaging in other positive or useful activities.
3. Significantly reduce the time involved with or interference from obsessions.
4. Significantly reduce frequency of compulsive or ritualistic behavior.

ADDITIONAL PROBLEMS FOR WHICH THIS EXERCISE MAY BE MOST USEFUL

- Anxiety
- Separation Anxiety
- Specific Phobia

SUGGESTIONS FOR PROCESSING THIS EXERCISE WITH THE CLIENT

The purpose of this exercise is to train the client (and parents) in the use of the therapeutic technique, refocusing, to help him/her reduce the frequency and severity of his/her obsessive thoughts and compulsive behaviors. The therapist should first educate the client and parents about the refocusing technique. To learn more about this technique, the therapist and parents are encouraged to read *Brain Lock: Free Yourself from Obsessive-Compulsive Behavior* (Schwartz). The exercise has two parts. The first part requires the client and parents to identify and list three to five alternative behaviors that will help the client refocus his/her attention away from the obsessions or compulsions by engaging in other positive or useful activities. After identifying the alternative behaviors, the client is required to practice the refocusing technique on at least three occasions before the next therapy session. The client, with assistance from the parents, is encouraged to write about his/her experiences and how successful he/she felt the refocusing technique was in managing the obsessions and/or compulsions. The parents are encouraged to help the client, particularly younger ones, record his/her responses on the Refocusing Incident Report.

REFOCUSING

Refocusing is a therapeutic technique that has proven to be helpful in decreasing how often a child experiences obsessions or compulsions. Refocusing simply calls for the person to turn his/her thoughts or attention away from the obsession or compulsion by doing something else that is positive or more useful. Sit down with your parents and take a few minutes together to think about what positive or useful activities you can do to take your attention away from your obsessions or compulsions. Please list three to five alternative behaviors in the following spaces.

1. _____
   _____

2. _____
   _____

3. _____
   _____

4. _____
   _____

5. _____
   _____

Studies have shown that it is helpful to have a support person or "coach" who can help turn your attention away from the troubling thoughts, ideas, or urges. Name at least three people who can help turn your attention away from your obsessions or compulsions.

1. _____
2. _____
3. _____

After identifying the three to five alternative behaviors and your coaches, you will now be asked to practice the refocusing technique at least three times before the next therapy session. You are certainly encouraged to practice the refocusing technique more than three times if you choose to. Use the Refocusing Incident Report on the next page. Your parents are allowed to help you answer the questions and record your responses.

REFOCUSING INCIDENT REPORT

Please answer the following questions to describe your experience with using the refocusing technique.

1. What alternative behavior did you try to take your attention away from the obsessive thoughts or compulsive behaviors? _____

    _____

    _____

    _____

2. How successful was the alternative behavior in taking your thoughts or attention away from the obsession or compulsion?

    |_____|_____|_____|_____|

    Very   Successful   So-so   Unsuccessful   Very
    successful   unsuccessful

3. Did you receive help from a coach or support person? _____ yes _____ no
    If yes, please tell how the coach was helpful in taking your mind away from the obsession or compulsion. _____

    _____

    _____

4. Would you continue to use the same alternative behavior in the future to resist the obsession or compulsion? _____ yes _____ no
    If no, please state why you would not continue to use this same alternative behavior. _____

    _____

    _____

    _____

5. What other alternative behaviors would you be willing to try to help turn your attention away from your obsessions or compulsions? _____

    _____

    _____

    _____

RITUAL EXPOSURE AND RESPONSE PREVENTION

GOALS OF THE EXERCISE

1. Increase motivation to resist urge to engage in compulsive behavior or talk about obsessive thoughts.
2. Identify support persons who can help the client manage obsessions/compulsions.
3. Significantly reduce time involved with or interference from obsessions.
4. Significantly reduce frequency of compulsive or ritualistic behaviors.

ADDITIONAL PROBLEMS FOR WHICH THIS EXERCISE MAY BE MOST USEFUL

- Anxiety
- Separation Anxiety
- Specific Phobia

SUGGESTIONS FOR PROCESSING THIS EXERCISE WITH THE CLIENT

The primary goal of this assignment is to decrease the frequency of the ritualistic behavior and/or the amount of time the client spends engaging in the compulsive behavior or talking about his/her obsessive thoughts. There are several steps to this assignment. The therapist should educate the client and his/her parents about the various steps. The client and parents are first asked to identify the specific compulsive behavior or obsessive talk that they hope to eliminate or manage more effectively. The client and parents may need to first gather a baseline (generally lasting 1–2 weeks) to determine how often the client engages in the ritualistic behavior each day. The unit of measurement can be either frequency or time. After gathering the baseline, the therapist should help the client and parents set a realistic goal to gradually reduce the frequency or time spent performing the ritualistic behavior. The goal (either the frequency or amount of time spent performing the ritual) should be lowered when the client demonstrates mastery and is able to manage his/her anxiety effectively. A reward system should be utilized to reinforce the client for achieving his/her goal. The therapist should train the client in the use of various therapeutic techniques (i.e., exposure/response delay, deep breathing, muscle relaxation, thought-stopping, distraction) to help the client resist the urge to engage in the compulsive behavior or obsessive talk. Assist the client and parents in identifying three support persons or "coaches" whom the client can turn to for help in resisting the urge to engage in the ritualistic behavior.

RITUAL EXPOSURE AND RESPONSE PREVENTION
PARENT AND CLIENT INSTRUCTIONS

The goal of this exercise is to reduce the frequency or amount of time the child spends performing his/her ritual each day. A ritual is defined as either obsessive talk about a particular topic or compulsive behavior. Examples of obsessions include excessive talk about germs, dirt, or possible illnesses; troubling thoughts about religion and/or bad behavior; excessive worrying about catastrophes (e.g., storms, earthquakes, accidents); and frequent worrying about school performance or grades. Examples of compulsions include excessive hand-washing, frequent checking to make sure that a door is locked or homework is done correctly, and a strong need to arrange objects or toys in a certain order.

1. Identification of the Ritual

The first step in this exercise is to identify the specific obsession or compulsion that you would like to reduce or manage more effectively. What is the specific obsession/compulsion that you would like to reduce or manage better? (Note, if the child is exhibiting more than one obsession or compulsion, then discuss the specific ritual you would like to address first.) _____

_____

_____

2. Gather Baseline

After identifying the specific obsession/compulsion, the next step involves taking a baseline to help measure the strength of the obsession or compulsion. The baseline period usually lasts 1–2 weeks. The unit of measurement can be either frequency (i.e., how often the child actually does the behavior) or time (i.e., how much time the child spends each day performing the ritual or obsessing about a particular topic). Your therapist can help you determine whether the unit of measurement should be frequency or time. As a general rule, it may be helpful to measure the strength of an obsession by identifying how much time the child spends talking about the particular topic each day. For compulsions, it may be better to count how often the child performs the ritual (for example, count the number of times the child washes his/her hands per day, rechecks to make sure that the door is locked, or the number of times he/she arranges objects in a certain order). Use the baseline sheet at the end of this assignment to record either the frequency or the time spent performing the ritual.

3. Gradual Reduction of the Ritual

Typically, the child experiences anxiety around the time that he/she is troubled by the obsessive thoughts or is engaging in the compulsive behavior. For many children, it is difficult to "just stop" a compulsion or stop talking about the obsession. Therefore, it is recommended that the client seek to gradually reduce the frequency or the time spent performing the ritual by setting realistic goals for each day or week. For example, if you find after gathering the baseline that the child spent 45 minutes each day talking about a particular topic, the goal may be to initially reduce the amount of time the child spends talking about this topic to 30–35 minutes per day. Over time, the duration can gradually be reduced to 20 minutes, then 15, then 10, and so on. As for compulsions, if you found after gathering the baseline information that the child washed his/her hands 20 times each day, then you may set a goal for the client to wash his/her hands only 14 times per day. As the child achieves success and manages his/her anxiety, the frequency can be lowered to 10, then 7, then 5 or 3 times. The goal should not be lowered until the child feels comfortable resisting the urge to engage in the compulsion or obsession. Your therapist can help you set new goals.

4. Reward Success

It is strongly recommended that the child be rewarded for achieving his/her daily or weekly goal. You can use a variety of rewards. The following is a list of rewards that you might find helpful to reward your child for successfully achieving his/her goal:

- Snacks
- Small toys
- Extended bed time
- Extra time to play video games or use computer
- Child spends one-on-one time with parent in agreed-upon activity
- Tokens or stickers that can be exchanged for larger toys, prizes, or privileges

It is recommended that the child be rewarded each day for achieving his/her goals. Keep a record of how often the child is successful in achieving his/her goal. The Daily Reward Contract has a box for each day of the week to record the day's results in minutes or response frequency. Have the child sign the Daily Reward Contract identifying the specific reward he/she will receive if he/she is successful in achieving the daily goal.

5. Use of Therapeutic Techniques

By now, your therapist has trained your child and you in the use of different techniques or strategies to help your child resist the urge to perform the ritual. You have been trained in the use of strategies such as response delay, deep breathing, muscle relaxation, thought-stopping, and distraction. Research has shown that these techniques are helpful in reducing the frequency and duration of the obsession/compulsion. Remember, the more time your child spends practicing these techniques, the more likely it is that he/she will achieve success in resisting the urge to engage in the ritual.

Oftentimes, a support person or coach can help the child resist the urge to engage in the ritual. Help the child identify a list of three to five support persons or coaches whom the child can talk with to resist the urge to engage in the ritual. Following is a list of support persons or coaches (parents qualify, too):

1. _____
2. _____
3. _____
4. _____
5. _____

What intervention(s) does your child plan to use to resist the urge to engage in the obsession/compulsion? Please a checkmark next to the interventions the child plans to use.

_____ Deep breathing/Muscle relaxation   _____ Response delay

_____ Thought-stopping   _____ Talk to coach or support person

_____ Distraction   _____ Other: _____

BASELINE MEASUREMENT
First Week

Unit of Measurement	MO	TU	WE	TH	FR	SA	SU
Frequency (number of times child performs ritual each day)							
Time (approximate time spent each day performing ritual)							

Second Week

Unit of Measurement	MO	TU	WE	TH	FR	SA	SU
Frequency (number of times child performs ritual each day)							
Time (approximate time spent each day performing ritual)							

DAILY REWARD Contract

If (name) _____ either: (a) engages in obsessive talk for _____ minutes or less each day; or (b) limits the number of times he/she performs the compulsive behavior each day to _____ or less; then he/she will receive the following reward:

_____

Record of Results

Week #	MO	TU	WE	TH	FR	SA	SU	Total #

Observations: _____

_____

_____

_____   _____
Signature of Child   Signature of Parent

_____   _____
Signature of Parent   Signature of Therapist

_____
Signature of Teacher

FILING A COMPLAINT

GOALS OF THE EXERCISE

1. Decrease the number of complaints about life and other people.
2. Increase the focus and specificity of identified complaints.
3. Identify the difference between a complaint and a request.
4. Develop the ability to request things from others in a manner of mutual respect.
5. Reach a level of reduced tension, increased satisfaction, and improved communication with family and/or other authority figures.

ADDITIONAL PROBLEMS FOR WHICH THIS EXERCISE MAY BE MOST USEFUL

- Attention-Deficit/Hyperactivity Disorder (ADHD)
- Conduct Disorder/Delinquency
- Peer/Sibling Conflict

SUGGESTIONS FOR PROCESSING THIS EXERCISE WITH THE CLIENT

Those who are oppositional defiant or who have that tendency often have a long litany of gripes and complaints. Nearly always, the complaints are wide open and nonspecific, making them difficult to pin down and quite impossible to resolve. In order to interrupt this pattern, it is essential to focus the client on one complaint and work with him/her to make that complaint as specific and clear as possible; with this comes the possibility of some type of solution or resolution. The client should be deterred from voicing another issue until he/she has reasonably settled the first. Once the client has done this, he/she can present the complaint to parents in a family session or be encouraged to try it again with another complaint. After the client has worked through two or more complaints, he/she should then be encouraged or challenged to try changing one of the complaints into a request. When the client completes the request form, he/she needs to present the request to the person who could fulfill it. Afterward, the experience can be processed and the results compared to that of complaining.

FILING A COMPLAINT

It's natural to sometimes become irritated when you're part of a social group or family. In order to resolve such conflicts, it is important to focus on one complaint at a time. Use these forms to help you specify what you do not like and then how you want things to change.

1. Using your experience in your family, with a group, or with a friend, complete the following form to specifically describe what irritates you about a situation or person.

COMPLAINT FORM

Name of person making the complaint: _____

Date: _____ Location at time of incident: _____

Nature of complaint (include names and be clear, specific, and detailed in describing the event or situation involved in the complaint):

_____

_____

_____

_____

_____

_____

How often has something like this occurred?
___ All the time ___ Most of the time ___ Sometimes ___ Once in a while ___ Rarely

How would you like to see this situation improved? (Be specific.)

_____

_____

_____

_____

_____

Signature: _____

---

2. Having completed the Complaint Form, try to put the complaint in the form of a request for change. This may be difficult, but give it a try.

SPECIAL REQUEST FORM

Date of request: _____ Person making request: _____

To: _____

Nature of request (be positive, specific, and as detailed as possible in order to assure the request will be accurately filled):

_____

_____

_____

_____

_____

_____

Additional Comments:

_____

_____

_____

Signature: _____

---

3. Now that you have completed each of the two forms, which form do you prefer?

_____

_____

_____

4. Why do you prefer that one over the other?

_____

_____

_____

5. Which of the two forms do you think would be more likely to get you what you want?

_____

_____

_____

6. File your Complaint and Request Forms with your therapist.

IF I COULD RUN MY FAMILY

GOALS OF THE EXERCISE

1. Identify the changes desired in the family system in terms of rules.
2. Develop an awareness of what it is like to be in charge and be responsible.
3. Reduce opposition by understanding what it is like to be in charge.
4. Display a marked reduction in the intensity and frequency of hostile and defiant behaviors toward adults.

ADDITIONAL PROBLEMS FOR WHICH THIS EXERCISE MAY BE MOST USEFUL

- Peer/Sibling Conflict
- School Refusal
- Sexual Abuse Victim

SUGGESTIONS FOR PROCESSING THIS EXERCISE WITH THE CLIENT

Being in charge or calling the shots can seem like a wonderful thing and even a dream come true. But one of the things you lose by taking charge is your power to resist, oppose, and defy. Being in charge greatly restricts these options, especially if you want to be effective. Children who have strong oppositional defiant tendencies are good at making others, especially parents, feel inadequate and ineffective. This exercise turns the tables by putting the oppositional person in charge. You have the opportunity to introject the reality of what it is like for the client to have responsibility and try to get others to cooperate with him/her. A good follow-up assignment is to have the client organize and lead a family activity of his/her choice.

IF I COULD RUN MY FAMILY

We all dream that we could call the shots and be the boss in our homes. It can be fun to sit back and imagine how things would be if this were the way it was. Here is your chance to be just that: the boss.

Answer the following questions.

1. If I could run my family, the first thing I would change would be: _____
   _____
   _____
   _____

2. Why would you change what you described in question 1? _____
   _____
   _____
   _____

3. What are the things you would keep the same? _____
   _____
   _____
   _____

4. List several of the rules you would have for the family. _____
   _____
   _____
   _____
   _____

5. Would there be consequences for breaking the rules? What would those consequences be?
   _____
   _____
   _____
   _____

6. List all the things that you would like about being in charge. _____

_____

_____

_____

7. What are the things you would not like about being in charge? _____

_____

_____

_____

8. How would you like parents and siblings to treat you? How could they disagree with you?

_____

_____

_____

_____

9. Is there any one thing that you would not allow? Why? _____

_____

_____

_____

_____

10. What are the things you would do to keep peace within the family and to encourage each member to treat each other respectfully? _____

_____

_____

_____

11. If your brothers or sisters said, "I hate you," "You're so mean," "You're stupid," "Other kids do it," or "I'm not going to do it because I'm not your slave," how would you handle these situations?

_____

_____

_____

_____

12. Being in charge would be (check one):

_____ A breeze, no problem   _____ Quite problematic

_____ Somewhat problematic   _____ A nightmare

_____ Sometimes good, sometimes bad

13. Would there be a way for you to quit the job if you got tired or did not like how things were going? How would that happen and who would you like to see take charge? _____

_____

_____

_____

_____

14. In the end, do you think your family members will love you or be more annoyed with you for the way you did the job? Give two reasons for your choice. _____

_____

_____

_____

_____

15. How do you think your parents do at being in charge, making decisions, and keeping the peace?

_____

_____

_____

SHARE A FAMILY MEAL

GOALS OF THE EXERCISE

1. Assist in meeting needs for closeness by sharing regular meals with family.
2. Increase the frequency of positive interactions with parents and other family members.
3. Decrease the frequency and intensity of temper outbursts and arguments.
4. Reach a level of reduced tension, increased satisfaction, and improved communication with family and/or other authority figures.

ADDITIONAL PROBLEMS FOR WHICH THIS EXERCISE MAY BE MOST USEFUL

- Attention-Deficit/Hyperactivity Disorder (ADHD)
- Blended Family
- Conduct Disorder/Delinquency
- Peer/Sibling Conflict

SUGGESTIONS FOR PROCESSING THIS EXERCISE WITH THE CLIENT

In this assignment, the client and his/her family members formally agree to eat meal(s) together a specified number of times per week. Hold a session with all the family members present and discuss how often the family can realistically or reasonably eat together. Require the family members to sign a contract that reinforces their commitment to following through with the assignment. Consider using an optional clause where family members receive a minor consequence if they miss the family meal without a legitimate reason. Instruct all the family members to complete a rating form to assess the quality of the time spent together during the meal. The feedback from the rating form can provide insight into family dynamics and facilitate discussions of how to improve the quality of time spent together as a family. The family also has the option of completing a questionnaire that describes the mealtime experience.

This assignment is ideal for families who rarely find time to eat a meal together. The assignment can be given to clients who are experiencing a variety of emotional or behavioral problems. The assignment has been included in this section on oppositional and defiant children because it is not uncommon for children to demonstrate an increase in temper outbursts and negativistic behaviors when their needs for affection and acceptance are not being met.

SHARE A FAMILY MEAL
PARENTS' INSTRUCTIONS

Many families live such fast-paced lives that they seldom share a meal together, either because their schedules do not allow it or they choose to eat separately for other reasons. There can be a number of legitimate reasons why the entire family cannot eat a meal together. Some adults are required to work the second shift. Teenage children may have to work after school hours. Some activities may also require a family member to miss a meal; for example, soccer practice or music lessons may be scheduled at dinnertime. Other families choose not to eat together for other reasons. Perhaps, they prefer to watch television or play video games while eating, instead of sitting down as a whole family. Other families may find that it is too hectic or stressful when everyone tries to sit down at one time. What is supposed to be a time of family togetherness may turn out to be more a time of family chaos. Siblings may quarrel, make faces at one another across the table, or kick each other under the table. Parents may feel too drained or exhausted after coming home from work to want to prepare a meal for the entire family. It may be difficult for the parent to carry on a stimulating conversation with the child when his/her mind is preoccupied with work or by a number of other things. Or, sometimes parents will ask the children how their days went at school, and the children will matter-of-factly state, "Fine," without elaborating any further.

Despite all the obstacles or problems that prevent your family from eating a meal together, it is strongly recommended that your family finds time to eat together as a unit. Sharing a meal is not the only way to spend quality time together, but it can be a very valuable time when family members check in with one another. It can help provide a sense of stability and consistency. Two of the basic ingredients for healthy self-esteem are stability and consistency. Some children respond to instability or too many changes in their environment by becoming sad, depressed, or withdrawn. It is not uncommon for other children to become more angry, irritable, and demanding when they feel insecure or feel that their basic needs for love and affection have not been met. Sharing a meal together can be one way to meet these important needs.

1. Encourage your family to sit down together and discuss this issue. This meeting can be held in the therapy session or at home. Discuss how often your family can realistically or reasonably eat a meal together each week. Allow all the family members to share their thoughts and feelings on this topic. Remember, sharing a meal together does not pertain only to supper or dinner. If your family cannot eat together at supper or dinner, then consider sharing your family meal at breakfast or lunch (brunch or late-night snacks can also be included).

Ideally, all the family members will agree on how often the family can eat together. However, if an agreement cannot be reached, then the final decision should be made by the parent(s). Parents are encouraged to consider the needs of all the children when making any final decisions. After a final decision has been reached, it is recommended that you formalize the agreement by signing the following Family Meal Contract. Signing the contract reflects the seriousness of the issue and will also reinforce your family's motivation for and commitment to following through with the agreement. Post the contract in a prominent place, such as on the refrigerator.

2. Consider having an optional clause where family members receive a minor consequence if they fail to appear for the scheduled meal without a legitimate reason. For example, a child may experience a consequence, such as having to wash the dishes, because he/she was spending time with friends. Likewise, a parent may receive a consequence, such as having to perform a chore for his/her spouse or child(ren), if he/she ends up spending more time on the golf course than originally planned. If your family agrees to include this clause in your agreement, then please fill in the appropriate blank on the contract.

3. During the initial stages of this assignment, all the family members are asked to complete a rating form at the end of each meal. Please complete the following Family Meal Rating Form to rate the quality of the time spent together. A separate scale has been provided for all of the family members. The family members do not all have to agree in their ratings. Please bring the rating forms to the next therapy session. The rating forms can provide feedback to your therapist and facilitate a discussion on the quality of the time spent together.

You may also complete the following questionnaire, which goes into greater depth. The responses to the questions can provide insight for your therapist on the quality of your family's relationships.

FAMILY MEAL RATING FORM

Each family member is asked to rate, from his/her own perspective, the quality of the time spent together during the meal. Please use the following scale to rate your level of satisfaction with the mealtime experience.

RATING SCALE POINT DEFINITION

No satisfaction	Low satisfaction	Moderate satisfaction	High satisfaction	Very high satisfaction
1	2	3	4	5

Family Member's Rating
Mother

1	2	3	4	5

Father

1	2	3	4	5

Oldest Child

1	2	3	4	5

Second Child

1	2	3	4	5

Third Child

1	2	3	4	5

Fourth Child or Significant Other

1	2	3	4	5

FAMILY MEAL CONTRACT

We, the _____ family, agree to share a family meal together _____ times per
(Last name of family)   (Frequency)
week.

_____   _____
Signature of Mother   Signature of Father

_____   _____
Signature of Oldest Child   Signature of Second Child

_____   _____
Signature of Third Child   Signature of Fourth Child or Significant Other

_____   _____
Signature of Significant Other   Signature of Therapist

Provisional Clause:
If a family member does not attend the scheduled family meal, without a good reason,
then he/she will receive the following consequence(s):

_____

_____

_____

_____

_____

_____

_____

FAMILY MEAL QUESTIONNAIRE

Date: _____

Type of Meal (check one): ____ Breakfast ___ Lunch ____ Supper ___ Other

Family members present for meal:

_____

_____

What did you talk about during the meal?

_____

_____

_____

How did the family members communicate with one another?

_____

_____

_____

What did you like about the meal experience?

_____

_____

_____

What did you dislike about the meal experience?

_____

_____

_____

What can be done to improve future family meals?

_____

_____

_____

SWITCHING FROM DEFENSE TO OFFENSE

GOALS OF THE EXERCISE

1. Identify the child's behaviors that are most problematic for parents.
2. Increase parents' focus on interventions for a child's specific, targeted problem behaviors.
3. Develop parental consistency in intervening with and giving consequences for undesirable behaviors when they occur.
4. Develop specific positive reinforcements that parents can give for cooperative behavior or negative consequences they can give for oppositional defiant behaviors.
5. Parents learn and implement good child behavioral management skills.

ADDITIONAL PROBLEMS FOR WHICH THIS EXERCISE MAY BE MOST USEFUL

- Attention-Deficit/Hyperactivity Disorder (ADHD)
- Conduct Disorder/Delinquency
- Peer/Sibling Conflict

SUGGESTIONS FOR PROCESSING THIS EXERCISE WITH THE CLIENT

Oppositional defiant children are masters at manipulation, making parents feel inadequate and constantly on the defensive. To change this, parents must be focused on modifying their child's specific, targeted, problematic behaviors in a consistent, nonreactive manner. They will need focus, guidance, and encouragement to stick to this goal. Review parents' interventions and assist them by using modeling and role-playing of more effective interventions. Remember to emphasize consistency and positive reinforcement for desired behaviors.

SWITCHING FROM DEFENSE TO OFFENSE
PARENTS' INSTRUCTIONS

As you have been working with an oppositional defiant child, you know how quickly you are put on the defensive. Once there, you seem to never get the ball back and subsequently feel like you always lose. To start to change this pattern, you must move to the offense where you can gain control of the game and be an effective parent. Like any offense, you need a game plan, which is specific, focused, and consistent, and then success comes through effectively implementing that plan.

Identify Problematic Behaviors

1. List *as specifically as possible* several of the problematic behaviors of your child.

_____

_____

_____

_____

_____

_____

_____

_____

_____

_____

_____

_____

2. Now go back over the list and select three of the behaviors that are the most problematic. (It is necessary to limit your focus in order to maximize your effectiveness.)

    A. _____

    B. _____

    C. _____

Describe Desired Positive Behaviors

For each of the behaviors you selected, describe the desired or expected behavior you would like to see from your child. Make the expectation as specific and as realistic as possible.

Example:
Problem: Always argues and then refuses to do any reasonable request or task.
Expected / Desired Behavior: Comply with request in a reasonable amount of time with minimal resistance.

Problem	**Expected/Desired Behavior**
1. _____	_____
2. _____	_____
3. _____	_____

Identify Rewards for Positive Behaviors

It is necessary to reward or reinforce the positive behavior when it is done by your child in a reasonable way. This is crucial if you want to see more of that behavior. Remember, the rewards do not have to be big things (see example). List two rewards for the desired behaviors you described in the preceding section.

Reward examples:
1. Thank you for doing that.
2. You sure did a nice job of cleaning up.

Desired behavior: _____

Reward 1: _____

Reward 2: _____

Desired behavior: _____

Reward 1: _____

Reward 2: _____

Desired behavior: _____

Reward 1: _____

Reward 2: _____

Identify Consequences for Problem Behaviors

Now, develop two or three negative consequences for each of the problem behaviors. Keep in mind that consequences are most effective when they are logical and tied as closely as possible to the behavior/offense. Also, it is best if consequences are brief in nature.

Example: Not allowed to go anywhere or have anyone over until the request/task is done.

Problem behavior: _____

Consequence 1: _____

Consequence 2: _____

Consequence 3: _____

Problem behavior: _____

Consequence 1: _____

Consequence 2: _____

Consequence 3: _____

Problem behavior: _____

Consequence 1: _____

Consequence 2: _____

Consequence 3: _____

Rewards or consequences should be given in a prompt manner as near as possible to the achievement or misbehavior. It will take attention and focus to do this consistently.

Plan Ahead to Avoid Problems

To increase your effectiveness, it is helpful to anticipate and plan for possible misbehavior. This will better prepare you to intervene in a timely manner, on your terms, and make you less likely to overreact. For each of the three problem behaviors, develop a strategy for trying to make the positive behavior occur and avoid the problem behavior.

Example: Let the child know ahead of time that you plan to ask him/her to do something in the afternoon.

1. _____

_____

2. _____

_____

3. _____

_____

DEVELOPING AND IMPLEMENTING
A HEALTHIER DIET

GOALS OF THE EXERCISE

1. Terminate overeating and implement lifestyle changes (e.g., get more exercise, eat more vegetables and fruits, eat healthy snacks) that lead to weight loss and improved health.
2. Gain knowledge of healthy nutrition and eating patterns.
3. Develop and implement new healthy eating habits.
4. Decrease portion size and opportunities for spontaneous eating.

ADDITIONAL PROBLEMS FOR WHICH THIS EXERCISE MAY BE MOST USEFUL

- Depression
- Low Self-Esteem
- Posttraumatic Stress Disorder (PTSD)

SUGGESTIONS FOR PROCESSING THIS EXERCISE WITH THE CLIENT

All parties (i.e., therapist, parent, and client) will need to be actively involved in the development and processing of this exercise. The exercise is designed to be done over multiple sessions in order to build confidence and to direct focus toward small, effective steps. The therapist needs to help the family assess and make any adjustments to their plan that may be appropriate. Also, this makes for a structured routine that allows opportunities for the therapist to give appropriate praise and encouragement to the family. A further part of processing this exercise will be to work with the parent(s) to get them to buy into giving incentives (or rewards) over praise as often parents think that the child should just do what is right or best out of their own inner drive.

Two final points for the therapist: (1) directing the family not to take on the challenge of changing dinner, as this is the most complicated, until they have effectively implemented changes in the other five areas; and (2) Observing that the client is actively involved in the process and in decision-making process.

(Answers to Nutrition Knowledge T/F: 1. True; 2. False; 3. True; 4. True, 5. True, 6. True; 7. True; 8. False)

DEVELOPING AND IMPLEMENTING A HEALTHIER DIET

A. Nutrition Knowledge

As a way of starting to look for things to change in our diets, it is important to learn more about nutrition. Below are some true/false statements regarding nutrition for you and your child to answer. When completed, process your answers with your therapist.

1.	T F	Eating a healthy breakfast improves cognitive functioning (especially memory) and improves mood.
2.	T F	Most American youth eat the recommended 2½ to 6½ cups of fruits and vegetables daily.
3.	T F	Overconsumption of sweetened drinks and soda has been linked to increased rates of obesity in American children.
4.	T F	A child can detect hunger or fullness better when encouraged to eat slowly.
5.	T F	The eating habits children pick up when they are young help them maintain a healthy lifestyle when they become adults.
6.	T F	A diet around low-fat or non-dairy products, skinless poultry, lean meats, and whole grain breads and cereals are the four key factors in promoting healthy weight.
7.	T F	The most important aspects of healthy eating for children are portion control and limiting how much fat a child eats.
8.	T F	Planned low-calorie snacks are not an important part of healthy nutrition.

B. Developing, Implementing, and Evaluating Healthy Changes in Our Diet

Listed below are the six key areas that will need to change in order for you as a family to develop and maintain a healthy diet and eating routine. Please rate the six below in terms of change, with 1 being the easiest for you to change and 6 being the most difficult.

_____ breakfast   _____ lunch (school)   _____ lunch (home)

_____ snacks   _____ dinner   _____ portions

As change can be overwhelming, it is best to break it down into parts and start with the one thing that would be the easiest for you to change. This starts as a small test and a confidence builder as you move forward to changing more difficult areas. List your #1 from above and complete and implement the plan below.

#1 Easiest Change: _____
Research: Google search "Children's Nutrition" or find a book on children and nutrition togather some key facts on this area. The facts we found connected to this area are: _____

_____

_____

Changes we would like to make: _____

_____

_____

Steps: 1. _____

2. _____

3. _____

Evaluation and changes (1 week after implementing) to discuss with therapist.
Adjustments: _____

_____

How we plan to sustain these healthy changes: _____

_____

_____

#2 Easiest Change: _____
Research: Google search "Children's Nutrition" or find a book on children and nutrition to gather some key facts on this area. The facts we found connected to this area are: _____

_____

_____

Changes we would like to make: _____

_____

_____

Steps: 1. _____

2. _____

3. _____

Evaluation and changes (1 week after implementing) to discuss with therapist.
Adjustments: _____

_____

How we plan to sustain these healthy changes: _____

_____

_____

#3 Easiest Change: _____
Research: Google search "Children's Nutrition" or find a book on children and
nutrition to gather some key facts on this area. The facts we found connected to
this area are: _____

_____

_____

_____

Changes we would like to make: _____

_____

_____

Steps: 1. _____

      2. _____

      3. _____

Evaluation and changes (1 week after implementing) to discuss with therapist.
Adjustments: _____

_____

How we plan to sustain these healthy changes: _____

_____

_____

For changes 4, 5, and 6 please copy a new form.

C. Praise and Incentives

Both praise and incentives (or rewards) are helpful to us as we tackle big changes. This
is especially true for children, as gains that are in the future seem far off and not easy
for them to see. So to aid this process, develop several incentives for your child and one
incentive that the whole family would enjoy for actively and cooperatively working on
these changes. Daily and/or weekly incentives would be best as reinforcers are big
motivators. Examples are incentives for trying new foods, taking part in picking
healthy snacks, and/or sticking to reasonable portions.

1. Incentives
   for the Child   A. For doing this specific thing: _____
                         Incentive: _____
                      B. For doing this specific thing: _____
                         Incentive: _____

   Incentives
   for the Family   A. For doing: _____
                         Incentive: _____
                      B. For doing: _____
                         Incentive: _____

2. Praise—Now develop specific praise statements that you can use to recognize and affirm the efforts you see your child making in terms of planning, implementing, and following through on establishing a healthy nutrition pattern.

   A. _____

   B. _____

INCREASING MY PHYSICAL ACTIVITY

GOALS OF THE EXERCISE

1. Identify changes in daily lifestyle activity conducive to improved health and good weight management.
2. Increase amount of daily exercise and physical activity.
3. Sustain regular exercise and physical activity leading to weight loss and improved health.

ADDITIONAL PROBLEMS FOR WHICH THIS EXERCISE MAY BE MOST USEFUL

- Anxiety
- Depression
- Low Self-Esteem
- Medical Condition

SUGGESTIONS FOR PROCESSING THIS EXERCISE WITH THE CLIENT

This assignment seeks to increase the client's overall level of daily physical activity that will hopefully lead to sustained lifestyle changes and improved health. The assignment has two parts. The client and his/her parents are first asked to identify various forms of exercise or physical activity under the following categories: Play/Daily Activities, Family Activities, Regular Exercise, and Participation in Organized Sports or Physical Activities. After identifying the various forms of exercise/physical activity, the client is encouraged to incrementally increase his/her daily amount of exercise/physical activity. The client, along with help from his/her parents, is asked to record the type and amount of exercise or activity on the Weekly Exercise Journal. The client should be discouraged from engaging in overly strenuous exercise at the beginning stages so that he/she does not become exhausted or frustrated to the point where he/she wants to quit the program. It is hoped that the client will understand that the assignment seeks to help him/her make sustained lifestyle changes over time.

INCREASING MY PHYSICAL ACTIVITY
PARENT AND CLIENT INSTRUCTIONS

Your agreement to participate in this assignment shows that you are taking your health seriously. The goal of the assignment is to increase your amount of daily exercise or physical activity to improve your overall health. Before actually beginning the program, you and your parents are first asked to identify various types of exercise or physical activity. Please take the time to list different types of exercise/physical activity under each of four categories. If you think of a different category, then by all means create a different category. Feel free to ask your therapist for help in identifying different types of exercise or activity for each category. You may also find that some types of exercise or physical activity may fall under more than one category. For example, you may decide to walk one mile (falling under the category of Regular Exercise) to the store with your parents to buy something (falling under the category of Play/Daily Activities). Don't worry about what category your exercise or activity may fall under; the point is that you want to increase your overall amount of activity. Examples of different types of exercise or activity are given in each category. Feel free to include this example on your list. Please identify at least five different types of activity in each category.

Part 1—Identify Different Types of Exercise/Physical Activity

CATEGORY A—Play/Daily Activities
Examples: playing tag at recess, exploring the woods close to your home, riding your bike to a friend's house instead of having your parents drive you to their home, taking the stairs at a mall instead of using the elevator or escalator, vacuuming the play room or sweeping the garage (your mom and dad will love this one!). Be creative with this category and remember to have fun!

1. _____   5. _____
2. _____   6. _____
3. _____   7. _____
4. _____   8. _____

CATEGORY B—Family Activities
Examples: play Wii Fit games with parents or siblings, play catch with your mom or dad, shoot hoops with brother or sister in driveway, hike in county or state park with family, go for a bike ride with family. Exercise and physical activity can be a great way to spend time with your family and bring you closer together!

1. _____   5. _____
2. _____   6. _____
3. _____   7. _____
4. _____   8. _____

CATEGORY C—Regular Exercise

Examples: walking or jogging a certain distance, calisthenics (e.g., push-ups, sit-ups, jumping jacks), lifting weights, riding stationary bike. Getting into a regular routine of daily exercise is a great way to improve your health.

1. _____   5. _____
2. _____   6. _____
3. _____   7. _____
4. _____   8. _____

CATEGORY D—Participation in Organized Sports or Physical Activities

Examples: sign up for soccer or baseball team (or some other sport), enter local 1-mile fun run, sign up for yoga or exercise class at local fitness club. Participation in organized sports can be a lot of fun and help you make new friends.

1. _____   5. _____
2. _____   6. _____
3. _____   7. _____
4. _____   8. _____

Part 2—Commit to Increasing Physical Activity

After identifying the different types of exercise or physical activity, you are asked to commit to doing a certain amount of exercise or physical activity each day. Please use the Weekly Exercise Journal to record the types and amount of exercise or physical activity that you did each day. You can use different types of measures (time spent, distance, frequency or number of repetitions) to record the amount of exercise or physical activity. For example, you can write down the amount of time you spent doing the activity (e.g., 30 minutes playing catch with your family or rode a stationary bike for 20 minutes). You can use distance as a measure and record that you walked one mile or rode your bike for approximately three miles. As for frequency or number of repetitions, you can write that you did 15 push-ups or 20 sit-ups. Space is provided for you to express any thoughts or feelings you have about the type or amount of activity under the Comments column. For example, you can record whether you liked or disliked the activity. You can also note whether you felt the exercise was too easy or too difficult. Your parents can help you to record the information at the end of each day. Talk with your physician or therapist about what is a realistic amount of exercise to do, especially in the beginning stages. It is important that you set realistic goals for yourself. Try not to overdo it in the early stages of the program because you might become so exhausted or frustrated that you want to give up. Gradually increase your amount of exercise or physical activity over time. Remember that you are making changes in your everyday life that will last and lead to better health. Bring the Weekly Exercise Journal(s) to your therapy sessions so that you can discuss your progress with your therapist.

WEEKLY EXERCISE JOURNAL		
Day of Week	**Type and Amount of Exercise**	**Comments**
MONDAY Date: _____		
TUESDAY Date: _____		
WEDNESDAY Date: _____		
THURSDAY Date: _____		
FRIDAY Date: _____		
SATURDAY Date: _____		
SUNDAY Date: _____		

MY EATING AND EXERCISE JOURNAL

GOALS OF THE EXERCISE

1. Establish a baseline for 7 days, documenting the client's food consumption and amount of time spent in exercise/physical activity.
2. Terminate overeating and implement lifestyle changes (e.g., get more exercise, eat more vegetable and fruits, eat healthy snacks) that lead to weight loss and improved health.
3. Increase daily exercise and/or amount of physical activity to achieve weight loss and improve overall health.

ADDITIONAL PROBLEMS FOR WHICH THIS EXERCISE MAY BE MOST USEFUL

- Anxiety
- Depression
- Medical Condition

SUGGESTIONS FOR PROCESSING THIS EXERCISE WITH THE CLIENT

The purpose of this assignment is to help the client begin to make healthy lifestyle changes regarding his/her diet and amount of time spent in exercise/physical activity. The client and parents are instructed to gather baseline data for 7 days focusing on the client's eating habits and amount of time spent in exercise. Using the Daily Eating and Exercise Journal, the client and parents are asked to record the type of foods that he/she consumed that day along with portion sizes. The client is further instructed to record the amount of time he/she spent engaging in exercise or physical activity during the morning, afternoon, and evening hours. Space is provided for the client and parents to share their thoughts, feelings, and observations about the daily meals or type of activity. After processing the data, the therapist, client, and parents can discuss what lifestyle changes the client can make regarding his/her diet and exercise regimen. The client can continue to use the Daily Eating and Exercise Journal after the baseline has been completed to monitor his/her eating and exercise habits. The assignment will require active parental involvement and supervision.

MY EATING AND EXERCISE JOURNAL
PARENT AND CLIENT INSTRUCTIONS

Your agreement to participate in this exercise means that you, along with help from your parents, have decided to begin to make healthy changes regarding your daily eating and exercise habits. You will be asked to gather baseline data over the course of 7 days using the Daily Eating and Exercise Journal and to write down the types and amount of food you ate each day for breakfast, lunch, and dinner. In addition, you should write down any snacks that you ate during the day. As for the amount of food, please record either portion sizes or the approximate calories. You will also be asked to write down how much time you spent in exercise/physical activity during the morning, afternoon, and evening hours. Space is provided for you to write down any thoughts, feelings, or comments you would like to make regarding your daily eating or exercise habits. It is recommended that you record the information after each meal or at the end of the day. Parents are encouraged to help their child record this information. Make a copy of the form for as many days needed before recording data.

After gathering the baseline data of your daily eating and exercise habits, please take time to answer the following questions.

1. After reviewing your list, what foods do you think were the most healthy and unhealthy? Please list five to seven foods you thought were the most healthy and unhealthy:

    Healthy Foods   Unhealthy Foods

    _____   _____
    _____   _____
    _____   _____
    _____   _____
    _____   _____
    _____   _____

2. What new healthy foods would you like to add to your diet? (Please list three to six.)

    _____   _____
    _____   _____
    _____   _____

3. What particular foods do you think you should reduce or restrict in your daily diet? (Please list three to six.)

    _____   _____
    _____   _____
    _____   _____

4. What types of exercise or physical activity did you like the best? (Please list three to six.)

    _____   _____
    _____   _____
    _____   _____

5. What, if any, of the type of exercise or physical activities did you find the most difficult? _____

    _____
    _____
    _____

6. What new exercise or physical activity would you like to do in the future? (Please list three.)

    1. _____
    2. _____
    3. _____

Please bring your Daily Eating and Exercise Journal entries for the entire baseline period to your next therapy session. Your therapist will process your daily Journal entries along with reviewing your answers to the questions listed above. Your therapist, along with help from your parents, can help you make decisions about what kinds of changes you can make regarding your eating and exercise habits. You are encouraged to continue to use the Daily Eating and Exercise Journal after the baseline period has ended.

DAILY EATING AND EXERCISE JOURNAL		
Date:	**Foods Consumed and Portion Size or Approximate Calories**	**Thoughts, Feelings, and Attitudes About the Food**
BREAKFAST Time:		
LUNCH Time:		
DINNER Time:		
SNACK(S) Time(s):		
Period of Exercise	**Exercise/Physical Activity and Amount of Time Spent**	**Thoughts, Feelings, and Attitudes About Exercise/Physical Activity**
Morning Exercise or Activity		
Afternoon Exercise or Activity		
Evening Exercise or Activity		

BEING A CONSISTENT PARENT

GOALS OF THE EXERCISE

1. Reduce or eliminate barriers to being consistent in parenting.
2. Establish a daily pattern of being consistent in parenting.
3. Develop and maintain the focus and confidence to be consistent in parenting.
4. Achieve a level of competent, effective parenting.

ADDITIONAL PROBLEMS FOR WHICH THIS EXERCISE MAY BE MOST USEFUL

- Attention-Deficit/Hyperactivity Disorder (ADHD)
- Conduct Disorder/Delinquency
- Oppositional Defiant

SUGGESTIONS FOR PROCESSING THIS EXERCISE WITH THE CLIENT

The processing of this exercise needs to be done in a manner that does not increase anxiety, but instead works to establish focus and to develop the parent's confidence. It is important to normalize the parenting struggle as an issue that all parents deal with to varying degrees. Also, as part of the processing, it is strongly suggested that the parents be directed to consult with older, experienced parents to gain ideas on how they handled the consistency issue. Lastly, the weekly follow-up evaluation is seen as essential to reinforcing progress, providing encouragement, and making any adjustments in a timely way.

BEING A CONSISTENT PARENT

No one is consistent 100% of the time. To expect this is to set yourself up for failure. You need to use self-discipline to try to make consistency your norm of parenting day after day. This takes into account that on occasion you will not be consistent. This exercise is designed to help you evaluate your consistency and to strengthen areas in which you are weak.

1. Rate the percentage of time that you are consistent with your children. (Circle one.)

Percentage

0–20	61–80
21–40	81–100
41–60	

2. How many times do you find yourself reminding your child to stop a behavior or to do some request? _____

Area I

3. What do you see as the main factors that keep you from being consistent? (Check one or all that apply.)

_____ Avoid conflicts   _____ Feel bad or sympathetic for child

_____ Avoid meltdowns   _____ Do not want to be the mean or bad parent

_____ Give up easily

_____ Want to be more of a friend   _____ Want peace at almost any cost

Take one of the factors that you identified and develop one way you can now begin to strengthen this weakness.

Factor: _____

How I can strengthen myself: _____

_____

Area II

4. Being manipulated is another important factor that can affect your consistency. Rate yourself on how easy it is for your children to manipulate you. (Circle one.)

Very easy   Easy   So-so   Difficult   Very difficult

Identify specifically how you are most easily manipulated by your children.

_____

_____

Now develop a plan to strengthen yourself against this manipulation.

_____

_____

Area III

5. The following three things can impact your consistency:

Too busy   Preoccupied   Easily distracted

Which of these do you see as having the biggest impact on your being consistent? (Circle one.)

Now identify one thing you can do to decrease this factor's impact.

_____

_____

_____

Area IV

6. Three key components of consistency are:

1. Clear expectations   2. Minimal talk   3. Regular follow-up

Of the three, which do you identify as being your strongest, and which is your weakest component?

Strength: _____ Weakness: _____

Identify one thing you can do to begin to strengthen your identified area of weakness.

_____

_____

_____

7. Over the next 4 weeks, rate yourself in carrying out the plans you identified to strengthen your consistency in the four areas.

Rating scale: Plan Implementation: 1. A little of the time   2. Some   3. A lot

Results: 1. A little   2. Some   3. A lot

	Week 1 Plan/Results	Week 2 Plan/Results	Week 3 Plan/Results	Week 4 Plan/Results
Area I				
Area II				
Area III				
Area IV				

On a weekly basis, process your ability to implement your plans and the results you see with your children. Make any adjustments that may increase your effectiveness.

PICKING YOUR BATTLES

GOALS OF THE EXERCISE

1. Develop parents' skills to focus on the important issues of conflict with the children.
2. Decrease parental feelings of frustration and ineffectiveness.
3. Increase parents' skills in effectively fighting key battles with their children.
4. Terminate ineffective and/or abusive parenting and implement positive, effective techniques.

ADDITIONAL PROBLEMS FOR WHICH THIS EXERCISE MAY BE MOST USEFUL

-   Attention-Deficit/Hyperactivity Disorder (ADHD)
-   Oppositional Defiant

SUGGESTIONS FOR PROCESSING THIS EXERCISE WITH THE CLIENT

This exercise can be completed by just one parent, by both parents separately, or by parents conjointly. The processing should be focused on identifying which battles with the children are important enough to gain attention. The selection of the battles is a major factor in determining a successful outcome and in training parents how to discern between what to battle over and what to let go. The other key area of focus needs to be on teaching the parents how to avoid or let go of unimportant battles. For many parents, this will be difficult as they will see all issues as equally important. They need to see how their children can manipulate them into conflicts, especially when they are busy, preoccupied, tired, or overwhelmed. Weekly review of progress is important to adjust the plan, reinforce success, and to give encouragement.

PICKING YOUR BATTLES

One of the unfortunate parts of parenting is the unavoidable "battling" with children. All children can be oppositional and this characteristic is more present at certain stages/ages (e.g., 6 to 11) than at others. Also, there are children with personality types who battle on what seems like a constant basis regardless of their age. Being engaged in constant battles with children can make parents feel tired, frustrated, and inadequate. In order to avoid feeling overly tired, frustrated, and inadequate, it is therefore important that we learn to pick which battles we will fight and which ones we will let go. This exercise will help you begin that process.

1. List all the "battle issues" you find yourself fighting over with your child.

   A. _____
   B. _____
   C. _____
   D. _____
   E. _____
   F. _____
   G. _____
   H. _____
   I. _____

2. Now choose from the list the two battles that you see as being the most important for you to focus on with your children. Then identify what makes the battle important, what results you desire in winning that battle, and what you see as the benefit for your child.

   A. Battle #1:_____
      Reason it is important: _____
      Results that are desired: _____
      Benefit for child: _____
   B. Battle #2:_____
      Reason it is important: _____
      Results that are desired: _____
      Benefit for child: _____

3. Develop a two- or three-step "battle plan" for each issue to help you reach your desired result.

A. Battle plan #1

Step 1 _____

Step 2 _____

Step 3 _____

B. Battle plan #2

Step 1 _____

Step 2 _____

Step 3 _____

4. To make your plan successful, all other battles must be avoided or let go. Rate yourself on what you think it will be like for you to let go. (Circle one.)

Very difficult   Difficult   A struggle   Quite easy   Easy

5. How are you planning to avoid/let go of all the other battles that your child would like to engage you in?

_____

_____

_____

6. What do you see as one thing that could draw you into any of the battles you are wanting to avoid? How might you avoid this?

_____

_____

_____

7. Track and rate yourself on your implementation of your plan and on avoidance of the other battles. Use a scale of 1 to 5, with 1 being "poor" and 5 being "good."

Battle #1:	Week 1	Week 2	Week 3	Week 4
Implementing plan	_____	_____	_____	_____
Avoiding battles	_____	_____	_____	_____
Battle #2:	Week 1	Week 2	Week 3	Week 4
Implementing plan	_____	_____	_____	_____
Avoiding battles	_____	_____	_____	_____

JOSEPH, HIS "AMAZING TECHNICOLOR COAT," AND MORE

GOALS OF THE EXERCISE

1. Accept the reality of parental favorites and sibling conflict.
2. Increase awareness of own part in contributing to the conflict.
3. Identify specific things that could be done to help reduce the conflict.
4. Accept the possibility of resolution of the conflict.
5. Form respectful, trusting peer and/or sibling relationships.

ADDITIONAL PROBLEMS FOR WHICH THIS EXERCISE MAY BE MOST USEFUL

- Low Self-Esteem
- Oppositional Defiant
- Physical/Emotional Abuse Victim

SUGGESTIONS FOR PROCESSING THIS EXERCISE WITH THE CLIENT

Two things that are very difficult for us to accept are that most parents have favorites and there is sibling conflict in all families. To know and to accept these things as a normal occurrence, if they are not too extreme, normalizes them and can make them easier to deal with. The Old Testament has three stories (Cain and Abel, Jacob and Esau, and Joseph) that are great examples of this conflict and how it can have bad results or be resolved to good ends. Stories stay with us and help us look at our own situation and perhaps see different possibilities. It could be beneficial to have the client review his/her responses with both the parents and the therapist.

JOSEPH, HIS "AMAZING TECHNICOLOR COAT," AND MORE

Surprising to most of us, sibling and peer conflicts are almost as old as time. Even in Jesus's time, his disciples argued over who would sit at his right hand in heaven but that's far from where these conflicts started. Cain and Abel, Jacob and Esau, and Joseph and his brothers are older examples of siblings who had big conflicts. Listen to the story of Joseph for an example of sibling conflicts and their resolution. The story can be found in the Bible in Genesis, Chapters 37 through 50, or in a shorter version, in most books of Bible stories for children.

Carefully read the story and think about it, then answer the following questions.

1. What were the conflicts between Joseph and his brothers? _____
   _____
   _____
   _____
   _____
   _____
   _____

2. Can you identify the causes of these conflicts? _____
   _____
   _____
   _____
   _____
   _____
   _____

3. In this story, do you identify more with Joseph or his brothers? Give a brief explanation for your choice. _____
   _____
   _____
   _____
   _____

4. What are your thoughts about parents like Joseph's dad, Jacob, who have favorite children?

_____

_____

_____

_____

5. What do you think is the number of parents who have favorites among their children? (Circle one.)

All   **Most**   **Some**   **A few**   **None**

6. Your dad's favorite child is _____

Your mother's favorite child is _____

What do you think makes each of them your parent's favorite? _____

_____

_____

_____

7. From the following list, can you identify feelings that Joseph's brothers had about him being the favorite? (Circle as many as you think may fit.)

Angry	Happy	Unloved
Sad	Hurt	Second best
Relief	Lonely	It was no big deal
Envious	Left out	Unwanted
Ignored	Lucky	Nice for him

8. If you are not a parent's favorite (in your opinion), which of the preceding feelings have you felt? (List at least three.)

A. _____ B. _____ C. _____

9. How do you think you would feel if your brother or sister shared his/her dream where you and the rest of the family were bowing down to him/her? _____

_____

_____

_____

_____

10. Joseph's brothers made a plan to get rid of Joseph. What do you think of their plan and its results? Have you ever made plans in your head to harm or get rid of a brother or sister? What was your plan? _____

    _____

    _____

    _____

    _____

11. After the plan worked, what feelings do you think Joseph's brothers might have had? (Circle the feelings.)

Angry	Upset	Guilty
Worried	Overjoyed	Sad
Glad	Nervous	Lonely

12. It was a long time before Joseph saw his brothers again. In the following list, check what you think might have gone through his mind in those many years.

    _____ Maybe I shouldn't have bragged so much.

    _____ Why did they do that to me?

    _____ Just wait till I can get my hands on them. I'll . . .

    _____ Boy, they were sure ticked off with me!

    _____ Acting so special really upset them.

13. What did you think of how they became friends again? Could you have done that if you were Joseph? _____

    _____

    _____

    _____

    _____

14. Since it was possible for Joseph to make peace with his brothers, how might you possibly resolve things with your brothers or sisters? _____

    _____

    _____

    _____

    _____

    _____

    _____

NEGOTIATING A PEACE TREATY

GOALS OF THE EXERCISE

1. Increase a general understanding of issues that cause conflict and what it might take to resolve them.
2. Identify specific personal issues that cause conflict and possible resolutions.
3. Identify barriers to reaching a state of peace.
4. Develop an understanding of the need to give and take in relationships in order to make them work.
5. Obtain the skills required to build positive peer relationships.

ADDITIONAL PROBLEMS FOR WHICH THIS EXERCISE MAY BE MOST USEFUL

- Attention-Deficit/Hyperactivity Disorder (ADHD)
- Conduct Disorder/Delinquency
- Oppositional Defiant

SUGGESTIONS FOR PROCESSING THIS EXERCISE WITH THE CLIENT

As in most serious emotional conflicts, we as human beings get locked into a position from which we either knowingly or unknowingly have difficulty shifting. This exercise is designed to look for cracks, little openings, and possibilities for further dialogue. When processing, suggest possible alternatives, different views, and possibilities. Hold out the ultimate hope of the client feeling better by reaching a settlement of the interpersonal conflict.

NEGOTIATING A PEACE TREATY

Most disagreements or wars between countries are worked out and settled by a peace treaty. The process of reaching that point is the result of hours of talking to work things out, with perhaps both sides getting a little and giving a little. The process starts by exploring the possibilities of both parties getting together. To understand what they are thinking and wanting, papers similar to this questionnaire are filled out and exchanged between the people who will attempt to work out the peace treaty.

As a beginning for you, answer the following questions.

1. Clearly state reasons for the disagreement or war you have with your brother or sister or peer.

   _____

   _____

   _____

2. What are the specific things he/she has done to you that caused the disagreement/war?

   A. _____

   B. _____

   C. _____

   D. _____

3. What is one thing he/she could start doing now to show you that he/she is serious about trying to get along?

   _____

   _____

4. Is there one thing you could begin to do now to show that you are serious about making things better between you?

   _____

   _____

5. Name one specific thing that would have to change in order for you to make peace.

   _____

   _____

6. List other things that would need to change or stop for you to make peace with your sibling(s) or peers.

_____

_____

_____

7. To get what we want, we often have to give, at least a little. What do you think you need to do or give up to make peace a possibility? (Write down only those things you are really prepared to do or give up.)

_____

_____

_____

8. Others can often be helpful in making a peace treaty truly work. Are there some specific things your parents could do to help make your peace agreement successful?

_____

_____

_____

9. What should your parents not do, in your opinion, because these things would only make the conflict between you and your sibling(s) worse?

_____

_____

_____

10. If one or both of you in the conflict fail to live up to what is agreed upon for making peace, what do you feel needs to be done?

_____

_____

_____

11. As you have started to think about the possibility of making peace, how hopeful are you of this working out?

| No chance | Doubtful | Maybe | Likely | Very sure |

Now that you have completed this questionnaire, share it with your therapist and explore the possibilities, based on your answers here, of you and the other party meeting with a third party to try to negotiate a peace treaty.

LETTER OF EMPOWERMENT

GOALS OF THE EXERCISE

1. Tell the story of the physical abuse by writing a letter.
2. Identify and express the feelings connected to the abuse.
3. Recognize and verbalize how physical abuse has impacted life.
4. Decrease feelings of shame and guilt by affirming the perpetrator as being responsible for the abuse.

ADDITIONAL PROBLEMS FOR WHICH THIS EXERCISE MAY BE MOST USEFUL

- Depression
- Oppositional Defiant
- Posttraumatic Stress Disorder (PTSD)
- Sexual Abuse Victim

SUGGESTIONS FOR PROCESSING THIS EXERCISE WITH THE CLIENT

In this assignment, the client is instructed to write a letter to the perpetrator in order to allow the client to express his/her feelings connected to the physical abuse. It is also hoped that the client will gain a sense of empowerment through writing the letter. First, the client is asked to respond to a series of questions before actually writing the letter to help him/her organize his/her thoughts. The questions listed on the following pages are offered as guides to help write the letter. Some of the questions may not be relevant to your particular client. Encourage the client to express other thoughts and feelings that may be unique to his/her traumatic experience. After the client responds to the questions, he/she can then begin to write the letter. Instruct the client to bring the letter to the following therapy session to process with you. This assignment is also appropriate for children who may not have been actual victims of physical abuse, but may have witnessed the victimization of other family members. Be sensitive and do not assign this task to clients who dislike writing or have a learning disability in written expression.

LETTER OF EMPOWERMENT

Physical abuse produces a lot of pain and hurt, both physically and emotionally. It is very important for the person who has suffered the pain and hurt of physical abuse to be able to express his/her thoughts and feelings. In this assignment, you are asked to write a letter to the perpetrator or person who hurt you. Writing the letter not only gives you the opportunity to share your thoughts and feelings, but also the chance to tell how the physical abuse has affected your life. Bring the letter to your next therapy session so your therapist can discuss the letter with you and better understand your thoughts, feelings, and experiences. Your therapist will also talk with you about what you want to do with the letter.

First, find a quiet or relaxing place where you can write the letter. After finding a quiet or relaxing place, please respond to the following questions. These questions will help you organize your thoughts and feelings before you actually begin to write the letter to the perpetrator. These questions are offered as a guide to help you write your letter. Feel free to write down whatever thoughts or feelings come into your mind at this stage of the assignment. You can decide later whether you want to include these thoughts in your final letter.

1. What events occurred shortly before the physical abuse? _____
   _____
   _____

2. When did the physical abuse occur and with whom? At what times and/or in what places? _____
   _____
   _____

3. What thoughts and feelings did you experience toward _____
   (Name of perpetrator)

   during the abuse? _____
   _____
   _____

4. What thoughts and feelings did you experience toward _____
   (Name of perpetrator)
   after the abuse?

   _____

   _____

   _____

5. How did the physical abuse make you feel about yourself? _____

   _____

   _____

   _____

6. How has the physical abuse affected your life? _____

   _____

   _____

   _____

7. Have you experienced any shame or guilt about the physical abuse? If so, please
   explain. _____

   _____

   _____

   _____

8. If you were free to say anything to _____, what would you say to
   (Name of perpetrator)
   him/her?

   _____

   _____

   _____

9. How do you feel toward _____ today? _____
   (Name of perpetrator)

   _____

   _____

10. What is your relationship like with _____ today?
    (Name of perpetrator)

   _____

Please express any other thoughts or feelings that you would like to include in the
letter on the back of this page or on a separate piece of paper.

11. Next, review your responses and begin to write your letter on a separate piece of paper. Remember, this is your letter, so share the thoughts and feelings that are important to you. Bring the completed letter to your next therapy session to go over with your therapist. After discussing the letter, please consider what you would like to do with the letter—do you want to destroy it or throw the letter away? Would you like to share the letter? Your therapist can help you answer these questions.

MY THOUGHTS AND FEELINGS

GOALS OF THE EXERCISE

1. Increase ability to identify and verbalize thoughts, feelings, and needs.
2. Help establish rapport with therapist in the beginning stages of therapy.
3. Gain insight into family dynamics or the quality of relationships with family members and/or significant others.
4. Identify and express the feelings connected to the abuse.
5. Express feelings about family members or individual(s) associated with the physical abuse.

ADDITIONAL PROBLEMS FOR WHICH THIS EXERCISE MAY BE MOST USEFUL

- Low Self-Esteem
- Oppositional Defiant
- Posttraumatic Stress Disorder (PTSD)
- Sexual Abuse Victim

SUGGESTIONS FOR PROCESSING THIS EXERCISE WITH THE CLIENT

In this exercise, the client is instructed to fill out a form that is similar in format to an incomplete-sentences blank. It is recommended that this exercise be used in the beginning stages of therapy to help you establish rapport with the client and to allow the client to begin to express his/her thoughts, feelings, or needs. The fill-in-the-blanks form can be used with children who are experiencing a variety of emotional or behavioral problems. It has been included in this section for physical abuse victims because of its potential to help the client express his/her feelings about the individual(s) associated with the physical abuse. Use the exercise as a homework assignment or as an intervention in a therapy session. The significance of the responses on the form will vary. Some clients may produce responses of little therapeutic value, while other clients will produce very meaningful responses.

MY THOUGHTS AND FEELINGS

In this exercise, you are asked to complete several statements to express your true thoughts and feelings. There are no right or wrong answers, only your answers. Please complete the following statements. Please try to do all of them.

1. The best day of my life was when _____

   _____

2. The worst day of my life was when _____

   _____

3. I felt very proud of myself when _____

   _____

4. I felt very embarrassed when _____

   _____

5. The one thing I wish I could do all over again is _____

   _____

6. If I were stranded on a deserted island, the person(s) I would most like to have
   with me is/are _____

   _____

7. If I were stranded on a deserted island, the person(s) I would least like with me
   is/are _____

   _____

8. The place I would most like to go to in the world is _____ because
                                                                   (Name of place)

   _____

   _____

9. If I could send my mother/_____ anywhere in the world, I would
                                       (Name of adult female)

   send her to _____ because _____
               (Name of place)

10. If I could send my father/_____ anywhere in the world, I would
                                      (Name of adult male)

    send him to _____ because_____
                (Name of place)

    _____

11. If I could send _____ anywhere in the world, I would send
(Name of sibling or peer)
him/her to _____ because _____

_____

12. I think I am most like the following animal: _____ because

_____

13. I think my mother/_____ is most like the following animal: _____
(Name of adult female)
because _____

14. I think my father/_____ is most like the following animal:_____
(Name of adult male)
_____ because _____

15. I think _____ is most like the following animal: _____
(Name of sibling or peer)
because _____

16. If I were free to say anything to my mother/_____, I would tell
(Name of adult female)
her: _____

_____

17. If I were free to say anything to my father/_____, I would tell
(Name of adult male)
him: _____

_____

18. If I were free to say anything to _____, I would tell him/her:
(Name of sibling or peer)

_____

19. I would like to add or change the following rule at home: _____

_____

_____

20. During times that I was being abused, my feelings toward the abuser were _____

_____

21. During times of the abuse, my feelings about myself were _____

_____

22. My father _____

23. My mother _____

24. I wish _____

_____

FINDING MY TRIGGERS

GOALS OF THE EXERCISE

1. Identify specific triggers for the client.
2. Describe the traumatic event in as much detail as possible.
3. Begin to make a connection between triggers and past traumatic events.
4. Expand awareness of how past traumas still impact the client and his/her life.
5. Develop and implement strategies to effectively handle triggers.

ADDITIONAL PROBLEMS FOR WHICH THIS EXERCISE MAY BE MOST USEFUL

- Physical/Emotional Abuse Victim
- Separation Anxiety
- Sexual Abuse Victim
- Sleep Disturbance

SUGGESTIONS FOR PROCESSING THIS EXERCISE WITH THE CLIENT

This assignment will likely need to be done in session with the therapist's assistance. Given the nature of the subject matter, it may require more than one session to be completed. The therapist will need to be supportive and encouraging as the assignment's questions will more than likely stir up a traumatic response that may include some varying degrees of dissociation. Subsequently, time should be allowed at the end of the session to shift away from this emotional material with a "controlled breathing" exercise or other de-escalating activities. The information gathered from the exercise needs to be shared and processed with parents to help develop helpful strategies to advance emotional regulation and decrease meltdowns. Parents could also complete the exercise to increase their skills in detecting triggers so they can then intervene in a more timely and effective manner.

FINDING MY TRIGGERS

Many times there are sounds, smells, things, and so on that can trigger feelings in us. Often we don't know this and it leads to behavior that can cause us problems and make us feel bad about ourselves. The purpose of this exercise is to help you begin to see the things that cause the feelings that may set you off. Your therapist will help you complete this exercise and help you find better ways to handle these feelings.

1. Which of the following sounds might make you feel upset, mad, anxious, or afraid? (Place a checkmark next to all that apply.)

    _____ Door(s) slamming   _____ Yelling   _____ Crying

    _____ People whispering   _____ Loud footsteps   _____ Loud music

    _____ Arguing   _____ Can being opened   _____ Other _____

    _____ Knocking on door   _____ Loud voices   _____

    _____ Tires squeaking   _____ Sirens

    When I hear one of the sounds I checked, I feel (circle one):

    Mad   Anxious   Afraid   Worried

    On a scale of 1 to 10 (1 is very little; 10 is a lot), I feel this: _____

    I feel this most in which part of my body? (Circle one.)

    Head   Arms/hands   Face   Stomach   Other _____

        Other _____

    Then I do_____

    _____

2. Which of the following sights might make you feel upset, mad, anxious, or afraid? (Place a checkmark next to all that apply.)

    _____ Blood   _____ People high or drunk   _____ Someone crashed on sofa

    _____ A messy room   _____ Parent with a stranger

    _____ Alcohol   _____ Note on door or counter   _____ A sad face

    _____ An angry look   _____ Someone touching someone   _____ Dark rooms

    _____ Knives   _____ Closed bedroom doors

    _____ Something broken   _____ Many empty cans or bottles

    _____ Small plastic bags   _____ Other _____

    _____ Police cars   _____ People laughing   _____

When I see one of the sights I checked, I feel (circle one):

Mad   Anxious   Afraid   Worried

On a scale of 1 to 10 (1 is very little; 10 is a lot), I feel this: _____

I feel this most in which part of my body? (Circle one.)

Head   Arms/hands   Face   Stomach   Other _____

    Other _____

Then I do_____

_____

3.   Which of the following smells might make you feel upset, mad, anxious, or afraid? (Place a checkmark next to all that apply.)

_____ Perfume/cologne   _____ Lighter   _____ Sweat

_____ Alcohol   _____ Mints   _____ Cigarette or other smoke

_____ Scented candle or incense   _____ Food cooking or burning   _____ Other _____

_____

When I smell one of the smells I checked, I feel (circle one):

Mad   Anxious   Afraid   Worried

On a scale of 1 to 10 (1 is very little; 10 is a lot), I feel this: _____

I feel this most in which part of my body? (Circle one.)

Head   Arms/hands   Face   Stomach   Other _____

    Other _____

Then I do_____

_____

4.   When you hear the following statements or remarks, which might make you feel upset, mad, anxious, or afraid? (Place a checkmark next to all that apply.)

_____ "No"   _____ "I'll be back in a minute"   _____ "Be quiet"

_____ Swearing/cursing   _____ "That's not important"

_____ "I don't have time"   _____ "I love you"

_____ "That's nothing"   _____ "Do it now"   _____ Other _____

_____ Promises   _____ "Wait a minute"   _____

When I hear one of the statements I checked, I feel (circle one):

Mad   Anxious   Afraid   Worried

On a scale of 1 to 10 (1 is very little; 10 is a lot), I feel this: _____

I feel this most in which part of my body? (Circle one.)

Head   Arms/hands   Face   Stomach   Other _____

                                                                               Other _____

Then I do _____

_____

5.   Which of the following events might make you feel upset, mad, anxious, or afraid? (Place a checkmark next to all that apply.)

_____ Bedtime   ___ Mealtime   _____ Change in plans

_____ Vacations/trips   ___ Birthdays   _____ Holidays

_____ No one home   ___ Adults being late   _____ Other _____

                                                                            _____

When I experience one of the events I checked, I feel (circle one):

Mad   Anxious   Afraid   Worried

On a scale of 1 to 10 (1 is very little; 10 is a lot), I feel this: _____

I feel this most in which part of my body? (Circle one.)

Head   Arms/hands   Face   Stomach   Other _____

                                                                               Other _____

Then I do_____

_____

PTSD INCIDENT REPORT

GOALS OF THE EXERCISE

1. Help the client to identify or recognize trigger events that precipitate flashbacks, painful memories, or nightmares.
2. Parents verbalize an accurate understanding of PTSD and how it develops.
3. Facilitate expression of emotions connected to traumatic event and emergence of PTSD symptoms.
4. Develop effective coping strategies to reduce the frequency and severity of PTSD symptoms associated with the past trauma.

ADDITIONAL PROBLEMS FOR WHICH THIS EXERCISE MAY BE MOST USEFUL

- Divorce Reaction
- Grief/Loss Unresolved
- Physical/Emotional Abuse Victim
- Sexual Abuse Victim

SUGGESTIONS FOR PROCESSING THIS EXERCISE WITH THE CLIENT

In this exercise, the client and parents are given a PTSD Incident Report that is to be completed soon after the client has experienced any of the following PTSD symptoms: flashback, painful memory, or nightmare. (For nightmares, the child should complete the Incident Report the following morning or day.) Many children, especially younger clients, may need assistance in completing the Incident Report. Parents are given instructions that will allow them to help the child complete the report. It is acceptable for the parents to record the client's verbal statements for them. The completion of the Incident Report can help the therapist assess the frequency of the PTSD symptoms. It is further hoped that the parents and client will be able to recognize the specific trigger events that lead to the emergence of the PTSD symptoms. Ultimately, the client should be helped to develop effective coping strategies that will reduce his/her emotional distress and return him/her to a regular or stable mood state. It is not necessary for the parents and child to complete the Incident Report each time he/she experiences the PTSD symptoms. The child also should not be forced or required to complete the Incident Report if he/she does not feel emotionally ready. The Incident Report can easily be used with preadolescent and adolescent clients, as well.

PTSD INCIDENT REPORT
PARENTS' INSTRUCTIONS

Children who suffer from a posttraumatic stress disorder (PTSD) exhibit various signs or symptoms of emotional distress. It is not uncommon for children who have endured some type of trauma to experience nightmares, flashbacks, and/or painful memories. Oftentimes, these PTSD symptoms are accompanied by intense emotions. The client may feel very depressed, anxious, frightened, or angry while experiencing the flashback, painful memory, or nightmare. It is not uncommon for children to experience these symptoms after they have been exposed to a trigger event that reminds them of the past trauma or stressful event. For example, some children may have a flashback or nightmare after they have watched a TV show dealing with abuse. Likewise, the child may experience PTSD symptoms if they come in contact with a person who in some way is connected to the traumatic event.

Your therapist has given you and your child a PTSD Incident Report that is to be completed soon after your child experiences a nightmare, flashback, or painful memory. For nightmares, the Incident Report should be completed the following morning or day. (*Note:* Some children may not recall the specific details of their nightmare, especially if they appear confused or disoriented after waking up from the nightmare. In these cases, you may not be able to complete the entire Incident Report.)

The Incident Report serves several purposes. First of all, it can inform your therapist as to approximately how often your child experiences these PTSD symptoms. In completing the report, your child will be asked to describe the specific nature of the flashback, painful memory, or nightmare. It is further hoped that the Incident Report will help you to identify some of the trigger events that cause your child to re-experience the traumatic event. By completing the Incident Report, your therapist can also help your child develop positive coping strategies to decrease the intensity of his/her emotional distress.

You are encouraged to exercise good judgment when filling out the Incident Report. First of all, your child should not be forced or required to complete the report. For some children, filling out the form may cause them to become upset again. It is not necessary that the Incident Report be completed each time your child experiences a flashback, painful memory, or nightmare. Younger children may also need your help in filling out the report. Feel free to verbally ask the questions to your child and record his/her answers for him/her. Older children may feel more comfortable filling out the Incident Report by themselves. Please bring the Incident Reports to the following sessions.

PTSD INCIDENT REPORT

1. Date: _____

2. What PTSD sign or symptom did you experience? (Please check the appropriate space.)
    _____ Nightmare _____ Flashback _____ Painful memory

3. Describe the flashback, painful memory, or nightmare (use extra paper or write on the back of this form if needed). _____
    _____
    _____
    _____
    _____

4. What things or events happened shortly before you had the flashback or painful memory? Or, what upsetting things happened on the day before you had the nightmare? _____
    _____
    _____
    _____
    _____

5. How did you feel while experiencing the flashback or bad memory? Or, how did you feel after you woke up from the nightmare? _____
    _____
    _____
    _____

6. Who or what helped you to calm down after having the flashback, painful memory, or nightmare? _____
    _____
    _____
    _____
    _____

A PLEASANT JOURNEY

GOALS OF THE EXERCISE

1. Disengaged or distant parent to help the child attend school regularly.
2. Increase the time spent between the client and the disengaged parent in play, school, or work activities.
3. Attend school on a consistent, full-time basis.
4. Reduce anxiety and expression of fears prior to leaving home and after arriving at school.
5. Cease temper outbursts, regressive behaviors, complaints, and pleading associated with attending school.

ADDITIONAL PROBLEMS FOR WHICH THIS EXERCISE MAY BE MOST USEFUL

- Academic Underachievement
- Anxiety
- Separation Anxiety
- Social Anxiety
- Specific Phobia

SUGGESTIONS FOR PROCESSING THIS EXERCISE WITH THE CLIENT

In working with the school-phobic child, it is not unusual to find an overly involved or enmeshed parent and also a disengaged or distant parent. The purpose of this assignment is to enlist the aid of the disengaged or distant parent in helping his/her child to attend school regularly. (The disengaged parent is generally the father, but this is not always the case.) By enlisting the help of the distant parent, this will help to decrease the degree of enmeshment between the client and the overly involved parent. The distant parent in this assignment is instructed to transport the child to school each day. You may need to call or write the parent's employer to obtain permission for that parent to transport the child to school each day. You should also work with the distant parent to help him/her manage his/her child's temper outbursts, regressive behaviors, clinging, or pleading. The distant parent is further encouraged to reduce the child's anxiety by engaging the child in conversation or some activity on the way to school. It is important that you obtain the verbal commitment from both parents in following through with this plan of action.

A PLEASANT JOURNEY
PARENTS' INSTRUCTIONS

This assignment is designed to help your child attend school on a regular, consistent basis by enlisting your involvement and cooperation. Your involvement as a parent will help your child learn to manage his/her fears and anxiety about attending school. You are asked to transport your child to school each day. Your therapist is willing to call or write a letter to your employer to obtain permission for you to drive your son/daughter to school each day. Don't be surprised if your child cries in protest on the way to school, but stand firm in your expectation that your son/daughter must attend school. You are encouraged to use the strategies discussed in the therapy sessions to manage your child's temper outbursts, regressive behaviors, clinging, or pleading.

Your child may exhibit signs of anxiety or fearfulness in the car as you travel to school. Try to reduce your child's fears or anxiety by engaging him/her in conversation or some activity. The car trip provides you with the opportunity to spend some quality time with your child in the morning. It is hoped that this time will reinforce and/or strengthen your relationship with your son/daughter. Following is a list of topics that you can discuss or activities that you can perform as you transport your child to school:

- Play a game with your child to see who can count the most cars of one color.
- Allow child to play hand-held video game.
- Count the number of out-of-state license plates you see on the way to school.
- Play the "sign game" (that is, find all of the letters of the alphabet on street signs).
- Find the oldest or tallest tree.
- Find the oldest car.
- Tell a story.
- Allow the child to draw in the car on the way to school.
- Tell your child a story about your childhood experiences.
- Tell your child a story about when you were dating your spouse.
- Share some of your past, positive school experiences.
- Check out a book from the library on jokes and riddles and have your child share the jokes or riddles in the car on the way to school.

Your child is instructed to keep a journal of his/her daily school experiences. Please sit down with your son/daughter at the end of the school day or in the evening to discuss his/her experiences for the day. Your child may use his/her own notebook or the daily journal notes on the following page. This exercise gives you the opportunity to reinforce your child's positive school experiences. On the other hand, if your child has had negative experiences, it gives you the opportunity to discuss his/her fears and anxieties and help the child learn more effective ways to manage the stress.

A PLEASANT JOURNEY

DAILY JOURNAL NOTES

Date: _____

What were your positive school experiences?

_____
_____
_____

What new or interesting things did you learn today? _____
_____
_____
_____

Describe any humorous events (if any) that happened today. _____
_____
_____
_____

What negative school experiences did you have? _____
_____
_____
_____

How did you handle this problem? _____
_____
_____
_____

What would you do differently (if anything)? _____
_____
_____
_____

What did you do to reduce your fears or anxieties? _____
_____
_____
_____

LETTER OF ENCOURAGEMENT

GOALS OF THE EXERCISE

1. Attend school on a consistent, full-time basis.
2. Reduce anxiety and expression of fears.
3. Cease temper outbursts, regressive behaviors, complaints, and pleading associated with attending school.
4. Parents cease sending inconsistent messages about school attendance and begin to set firm, consistent limits on excessive clinging, pleading, crying, and temper tantrums.

ADDITIONAL PROBLEMS FOR WHICH THIS EXERCISE MAY BE MOST USEFUL

- Academic Underachievement
- Separation Anxiety
- Social Anxiety
- Specific Phobia

SUGGESTIONS FOR PROCESSING THIS EXERCISE WITH THE CLIENT

It is not uncommon for the parents of school-phobic children to act in ways that either reinforce or maintain the child's symptoms. The parents may send mixed messages to the child about the importance of attending school. For example, the parents may verbally tell the child to go to school, but then allow the child to cling excessively to them when it is time for him/her to leave for school. In this case, the parents' inability to set limits with the excessive clinging or pleading reinforces the child's symptoms.

In this assignment, you enlist the cooperation of the parents by having them send a clear, consistent message about the importance of the child attending school. The parents are instructed to write a letter to the child that seeks to calm his/her fears or anxieties. The letter is placed in the child's notebook. Instruct the child to read the letter at school during appropriate times when he/she begins to feel anxious or fearful. Help the parents set limits with the child's temper outbursts, regressive behaviors, or pleading before the child leaves for school. Likewise, work with the client to help him/her develop coping strategies to reduce his/her fears and anxieties.

LETTER OF ENCOURAGEMENT
PARENTS' INSTRUCTIONS

The purpose of this task is to help your child attend school on a regular, consistent basis by enlisting your cooperation. Your role as parents can be very important in helping your child learn how to manage fears and anxieties about attending school. Through your participation in this task, you will send a message to your child that you care about him/her and believe in his/her ability to master fears and anxieties. Your expression of confidence in your child's ability to overcome fears will go a long way toward helping the child develop more self-confidence.

1. In this task, you are asked to write a letter to your child that he/she can read at appropriate times during the school day to help reduce his/her anxiety or fears. The letter should be relatively brief (i.e., two to four paragraphs) so that your child can read it quickly. Place the letter inside your child's notebook so he/she can have easy access to it. Use words that are appropriate for your child's reading level. If your child has just started reading or has low reading abilities, then you may want to consider using a voice recorder to send a message of encouragement to your child. Consult with your child's teacher about this option, as it is important that the child not disrupt the classroom by listening to the recorded message at inappropriate times.

    The letter should be positive. Offer encouragement and express your belief that your child can overcome his/her fears and anxieties. An example of a letter follows to help you write your own letter to your child. This letter is offered only as a guide to help you organize and record your own thoughts and feelings.

Dear Jennifer,
We hope that as you read this letter you are having a good day at school. We are so glad that you are at school and have the chance to learn many new things and meet other kids your own age. School can help you achieve your goals and live out your dreams.

Yet, we know that there may be times when you feel nervous or afraid. Remember, everyone feels nervous from time to time, and your nervousness or fears will not last forever. Practice the things we've talked about in counseling and at home. Replace your bad thoughts with good thoughts. Pray for God's support. Smile and talk to your teacher and the other kids when you get to school or are at recess. Pay attention to the teacher and try your best to do your schoolwork. If you do these things, we are sure that your worries will go away.

We know that you can do it. We remember when you were 5 years old and you wanted to ride your bike without any training wheels. Even though you were afraid of falling down and hurting yourself, you did not let your fears stop you from learning how to ride your bike. It did not take you very long at all to learn how to ride your bike. Now, look at you! You're able to go on long bike trips with your family.

Hang in there—you'll get through this day and we'll see you when you get home. We love you!

Love,
Mom and Dad

2. After reviewing this letter, spend a few minutes thinking about what it is you would like to say in your letter. Write a draft of your letter in the following space. Bring the draft letter to your next therapy session to review with your child's therapist. The therapist can discuss the letter with you to see if any changes or additions should be made. After the final draft has been written, read the letter to your child so he/she clearly understands what you are trying to communicate. Place the letter in his/her notebook and encourage the child to read it at appropriate times during the day.

_____

_____

_____

_____

_____

_____

_____

_____

_____

_____

_____

_____

_____

_____

SCHOOL FEAR REDUCTION

GOALS OF THE EXERCISE

1. Comply with a systematic desensitization program and attend school for increasingly longer periods of time.
2. Reduce anxiety and expression of fears prior to leaving home and after arriving at school.
3. Cease temper outbursts, regressive behaviors, complaints, and pleading associated with attending school.

ADDITIONAL PROBLEMS FOR WHICH THIS EXERCISE MAY BE MOST USEFUL

- Separation Anxiety
- Social Anxiety
- Specific Phobia

SUGGESTIONS FOR PROCESSING THIS EXERCISE WITH THE CLIENT

This exercise is designed for the school-phobic child who is exhibiting very high levels of anxiety and has already missed a substantial amount of time from school. Meet with the client, parents, and school officials to develop a systematic desensitization plan that gradually allows the client to attend school for longer periods of time. The client incrementally works his/her way back to attending school on a full-time basis. The highly anxious and resistant client may begin attending school for 2 hours each day in the beginning phase of this program. (*Note:* This time can be adjusted depending on the client's level of anxiety and degree of pathology.) Once the client shows that he/she can attend school without exhibiting a significant amount of emotional distress, then the length of the school day is increased either in time (i.e., 45 minutes to 1 hour) or by the number of classes attended. Use a reward system to reinforce the client for attending school for increasingly longer periods of time. Expect more anxiety or resistance around the periods when the length of the school day increases. Teach the client coping strategies (e.g., positive self-talk, thought substitution, relaxation techniques) during the therapy sessions to help the client manage his/her anxiety and stress.

SCHOOL FEAR REDUCTION
PARENTS'/TEACHERS' INSTRUCTIONS

This systematic desensitization program is designed for the student who is experiencing a high level of anxiety and has already missed a substantial amount of time from school because of anxiety and fearfulness. In this program, the student is gradually expected to return to school on a full-time basis. Before beginning the program, it is imperative that the student, parent(s), teacher(s), and therapist all sit down together as a team to work out the specific details of this plan. The team will develop a schedule that gradually increases the time the student is expected to be in school each day or week. The student will spend increasingly longer periods of time at school as he/she becomes more confident and self-assured. Use a reward system to reinforce the student for attending school without exhibiting a lot of emotional distress.

1. The first order of business is for the team to come together to work out the specific details of this plan. The child should be informed that the goal of this program is for him/her to eventually attend school on a full-time basis. However, in recognition of the child's high level of anxiety and fearfulness, the team will structure the plan so that he/she begins attending school on a part-time basis. It is suggested that the child begin attending school under this plan for a minimum of 2 hours. This time can be adjusted, depending on his/her level of anxiety and fearfulness. For example, a severely anxious child may start this program by attending school for 1 1/2 hours per day; whereas a less anxious child may start the program by attending school for 3 hours a day. The child is strongly encouraged to use the coping strategies (e.g., positive self-talk, thought substitution, relaxation techniques) that he/she has practiced in therapy sessions.

2. The length of the school day is increased in increments when the child shows that he/she can attend school without exhibiting a significant amount of emotional distress. A significant amount of emotional distress can be demonstrated in any of the following ways:

   - Crying
   - Excessive pleading and whining
   - Excessive clinging to parents before leaving home/after arriving at school
   - Numerous somatic complaints
   - Frequent verbalizations of unrealistic fears
   - Temper outbursts (yelling, screaming, swearing)
   - Refusal to enter school building or classroom
   - Leaving classroom or school grounds
   - Trembling and shaking
   - Refusal to talk when appropriate

3. It is recommended that the child attend school 80% of the time (i.e., 4 out of 5 days, 8 out of 10 days) without showing a significant amount of emotional distress before increasing the length of the school day. If the child successfully meets this criterion, then it is suggested that the expected time spent at school be increased by 45 minutes to an hour. The steps of the program are then repeated before moving on to the next level, where the child attends school for an even longer period of time.

4. Use a reward system. The child should be reinforced for attending school for the expected period of time without displaying significant distress. The child and other team members should identify the specific reward(s) to reinforce him/her for attending school. Use the following contract form as a means of formalizing the agreement with the child. Establish a new contract for each phase of the program. Place the contract in the child's notebook or post it in his/her room as a reminder of the agreement. The team should consult with the child about appropriate rewards that can be used to reinforce school attendance. A list of potential rewards follows.
    *   Extra time for watching television or playing video games
    *   One-on-one time with child (e.g., attend a movie, exercise together, play a board game)
    *   Extended bedtime
    *   Extra time on telephone or computer
    *   Allow child to invite a friend over or go over to friend's house after school or invite friend to sleep over at house
    *   Outing to favorite fast-food restaurant
    *   Money
    *   Snacks
    *   Stickers or tokens that can be cashed in for a larger reward or privilege at a later date

SCHOOL ATTENDANCE CONTRACT

I, _____, agree to attend school for _____ per day, in a calm,
(Name of student)   (Time)

cooperative manner, and without showing a significant amount of emotional distress. A
significant amount of emotional distress is defined as:

_____

_____

_____

If _____ attends school for the agreed upon period of time and
(Name of student)

without resistance, then he/she will receive the following reward:

_____

_____

In witness of this contract, we have signed our names on this date _____.

_____   _____
Signature of Student   Signature of Parent

_____   _____
Signature of Parent   Signature of Teacher or School Official

_____   _____
Signature of School Principal   Signature of Therapist

EXPLORE YOUR WORLD

GOALS OF THE EXERCISE

1. Tolerate separations from parents or attachment figures without exhibiting heightened emotional distress, regressive behavior, temper outbursts, or pleading.
2. Increase the frequency and duration of time spent in independent play away from major attachment figures.
3. Foster greater interests and curiosity about the surrounding world.
4. Decrease the intensity of fears about the surrounding environment being a foreboding or ominous place.

ADDITIONAL PROBLEMS FOR WHICH THIS EXERCISE MAY BE MOST USEFUL

- Anxiety
- Depression
- School Refusal
- Social Anxiety
- Specific Phobia

SUGGESTIONS FOR PROCESSING THIS EXERCISE WITH THE CLIENT

Children who suffer from separation anxiety are often afraid to venture far from home. It is not uncommon for them to perceive the world as a frightening or foreboding place. They worry that some harm or catastrophe will befall them or their major attachment figures. This homework assignment is designed to encourage the child to spend greater time in independent play or activities. In the process, it is hoped that the child will enjoy the activity, become less anxious, and see the world as a less frightening place. The child, parents (or attachment figures), and therapist are encouraged to develop a list of activities or outings that are both safe and enjoyable. The frequency and duration of the child's explorations outside of the home can be modified to meet the individual needs of the client. Process the child's feelings about each activity, focusing on the positive, enjoyable aspect of the experience.

EXPLORE YOUR WORLD

This exercise is designed to help you to get out of your house, explore your world, and enjoy the sights and sounds of your neighborhood. You are asked to go on an outing or perform an activity outside of your home every day of the week. This exercise will help you to gradually feel more comfortable being on your own for longer periods of time. Talk with your parents and therapist about what outings or activities are permissible. Following are some suggestions of outings or activities that you can do as you explore your surrounding world. Feel free to use your imagination and come up with a list of other ideas about things to do.

1. Select an activity to do each day from the following list:
    *   Ride your bike around the neighborhood and find other same-aged children.
    *   Walk to a local park or schoolyard and climb on the jungle gym.
    *   Go rollerblading or skating.
    *   Go sledding with a friend.
    *   Collect five different bugs in jars or containers.
    *   Look for frogs and turtles at a local pond.
    *   Go fishing in a safe place.
    *   Put on a puppet play for neighborhood kids.
    *   Set up a lemonade stand.
    *   Draw a picture outside using sidewalk chalk. (Parents cannot see your artwork until it is finished.)
    *   Find the tallest tree in the neighborhood.
    *   Find the oldest or coolest car in the neighborhood.
    *   Walk to neighborhood convenience store with a friend.
    *   Play basketball at local park or schoolyard.
    *   Pick wildflowers in nearby woods.
    *   Play jumprope with other neighborhood kids.
    *   Play hopscotch.
    *   Go swimming at community pool with neighborhood kids.

2. At the end of each outing or activity, write down three things in the following spaces that you discovered or enjoyed as you explored your world:

    Day 1

    A. _____

    B. _____

    C. _____

Day 2

A. _____

B. _____

C. _____

Day 3

A. _____

B. _____

C. _____

Day 4

A. _____

B. _____

C. _____

Day 5

A. _____

B. _____

C. _____

Day 6

A. _____

B. _____

C. _____

Day 7

A. _____

B. _____

C. _____

3. Draw a picture of your favorite outing or activity on a separate piece of paper, and bring it to your next therapy session.

PARENTS' TIME AWAY

GOALS OF THE EXERCISE

1. Tolerate separation from attachment figures without exhibiting heightened emotional distress, aggressive behaviors, temper outbursts, or pleading.
2. Parents or attachment figures take active steps toward helping the child to function more independently.
3. Parents establish and maintain appropriate parent-child boundaries, and set firm limits when the child exhibits temper outbursts or manipulative behaviors.

ADDITIONAL PROBLEMS FOR WHICH THIS EXERCISE MAY BE MOST USEFUL

*   School Refusal
*   Social Anxiety

SUGGESTIONS FOR PROCESSING THIS EXERCISE WITH THE CLIENT

The parents of a child who struggles with separation anxiety often act in ways, either consciously or unconsciously, that reinforce or maintain the child's excessive clinging or distress around separation points. The parents may be reluctant or unwilling to separate from their child for fear that the anticipated separation will produce excessive crying, clinging, or heightened emotional distress. The child's distress or temper outburst can be a powerful tool in ensuring that the parents remain in close proximity. In this homework assignment, the parents are encouraged to take active steps toward establishing greater independence from their child. The parent(s) are asked to go on a variety of outings that will gradually increase in duration and/or frequency. The outings or breaks will provide the child with the opportunity to learn to master his/her fears or anxieties. It is recommended that the parents give advanced notice of when they will be going on the outings. This will allow the parent(s) an opportunity to talk with their child about what coping strategies (e.g., positive self-talk, relaxation techniques, calling a friend, playing with sibling) that the child can utilize to decrease fears or anxieties. The frequency and duration of the planned separations can be negotiable. It is suggested that the parent(s) initially plan to take three to four breaks per week that last approximately 15 to 30 minutes. The frequency and/or duration of the breaks can be increased as the child tolerates and feels more comfortable with the separations.

PARENTS' TIME AWAY
PARENTS' INSTRUCTIONS

Your child has been having difficulty managing separations from you. He/she may experience fear or anxiety, believing that some potential catastrophe or calamity will occur to him/her or you upon separation. These fears or worries are usually unrealistic. In order to help your child learn to overcome unrealistic fears or worries, you will be asked to go on regularly scheduled outings or breaks without your child. The outings or breaks will gradually increase in frequency and/or duration. For example, during the first week you will be asked to go on three outings without the child for approximately 15 to 30 minutes. The length of these outings will gradually increase as your child becomes more comfortable with managing the separations. You are encouraged to talk with your child about the coping strategies (e.g., positive self-talk, relaxation techniques, talking with a friend on the phone, playing with a sibling) that he/she can use to decrease his/her anxiety or fears during the actual separation.

1. Plan these outings in advance. For younger children, you may need to obtain the services of a babysitter or other relatives to care for the children while you are on your outing. Remember, the purpose of the homework assignment is to give you a break and provide the child with an opportunity to become more independent. Following is a list of suggested ideas for outings, but feel free to be creative and add to the list:
    *   Go on a walk with your spouse or friend.
    *   Go to a grocery or convenience store to pick up groceries.
    *   Run an errand (e.g., go to the dry cleaners).
    *   Go rollerblading.
    *   Go out for coffee or dessert.
    *   Visit with a neighbor.

2. After you have completed the outing, process your experience(s) with your child. Review the following questions or points of discussion with your child.
    A. Share or write down event(s) that you witnessed or experienced on your outing.

        1. _____

        2. _____

        3. _____

B. What event(s) did your child witness or experience while you were on your outing?

    1. _____

    2. _____

    3. _____

C. What coping strategies did your child use to help eliminate or reduce his/her fears or anxiety? _____

    1. _____

    2. _____

    3. _____

D. In the event that your child experienced distress, what can he/she do to eliminate or reduce anxiety or fear during the next outing?

    1. _____

    2. _____

    3. _____

Additional comments: _____

_____

_____

_____

_____

_____

_____

_____

Remember to bring the completed worksheet to your child's next appointment.

MY STORY

GOALS OF THE EXERCISE

1. Tell the entire story of the abuse.
2. Identify and express feelings connected to the abuse.
3. Verbalize how sexual abuse has impacted life.
4. Begin the healing process by working through thoughts and feelings associated with the sexual abuse.
5. Decrease feelings of shame and guilt, and affirm self as not being responsible for the abuse.

ADDITIONAL PROBLEMS FOR WHICH THIS EXERCISE MAY BE MOST USEFUL

- Grief/Loss Unresolved
- Low Self-Esteem
- Physical/Emotional Abuse Victim

SUGGESTIONS FOR PROCESSING THIS EXERCISE WITH THE CLIENT

The child is instructed to keep a journal at home to help him/her express his/her feelings about the past sexual abuse. The journal can be utilized throughout therapy, but can be particularly helpful during the initial stages of therapy when you are attempting to join with the child and fully understand his/her experiences. The child is given a list of questions that he/she can respond to in order to help express his/her thoughts and feelings. Encourage the child to use the journal to express his/her story in his/her own words. Inform the child that he/she may find the journal particularly helpful around the time that he/she is experiencing strong or distressing emotions. Instruct the child to bring the journal notes to the therapy sessions for processing. The journal notes may help prepare the child to perform other therapeutic tasks such as verbally confronting the perpetrator or sharing his/her thoughts and feelings about the sexual abuse with other key family members. The journal notes can also help the child prepare for a formal apology from the perpetrator. Be sensitive to any signs that the child blames himself/herself for the sexual abuse. Seek to empower the child and affirm him/her as not being responsible for the abuse.

MY STORY

Sexual abuse can produce many confusing and strong emotions. Keeping a journal can help you identify, express, and work through your many thoughts and feelings about the sexual abuse. The journal gives you the opportunity to share your own story and tell how the abuse has affected your life. Bring the journal notes to your therapy session each week to help your therapist better understand your thoughts and feelings.

How people choose to write in a journal varies. Some people find it useful to set aside a certain time each day to write in a journal, such as when they wake up in the morning or after supper. This option allows them to spend some personal time alone each day to record their thoughts and feelings. Other people prefer to write down their thoughts and feelings as they occur throughout the day.

1. Find a quiet or relaxing place to write down your thoughts and feelings. This will help you to concentrate and block out any distractions. Many people find it best to record their thoughts in a quiet room in the home, such as in the privacy of their own bedroom. Other people find it helpful to go to a favorite place such as a park, farm, or beach, to write their thoughts and feelings.

    Remember, this is your journal, and you have the option of writing in it in the time and place in which you feel most comfortable. Feel free to express your thoughts and feelings without worrying about being judged or criticized. Don't worry about spelling or grammar errors; just get your thoughts and feelings down on paper.

2. Following is a list of questions or items that you may choose to respond to in your journal. Respond to those that you feel are appropriate to your experience.
    *   Describe some of the events leading up to the sexual abuse. Where did the sexual abuse occur and with whom? At what times or at what places?
    *   Where were other people in the family when the abuse occurred?
    *   What thoughts and feelings did you experience toward the perpetrator before the abuse?
    *   What thoughts and feelings did you experience toward the perpetrator during the actual sexual abuse?
    *   What thoughts and feelings did you experience toward the perpetrator after the sexual abuse occurred?
    *   How has the sexual abuse made you feel about yourself?
    *   What effect has the sexual abuse had on your life?
    *   How has the discovery of the sexual abuse affected your family members' lives?
    *   How have the other family members acted toward you since the sexual abuse came out in the open?

- Do you think someone besides you and the perpetrator was aware that the sexual abuse was occurring and did nothing about it? If so, who was it and why did he/she do nothing?
- How did other people find out about the sexual abuse?
- What was the reaction of others when they found out that you were abused?
- How did you feel about the reaction of others when they found out you were abused?
- What has been the most painful or difficult part about your sexual abuse experience?
- If you were free to say anything to the perpetrator, what would you say to him/her?
- Whom do you hold responsible for the sexual abuse?
- Have you ever experienced any guilt about the sexual abuse? If so, please explain further.

YOU ARE NOT ALONE

GOALS OF THE HOMEWORK

1. Identify and express feelings connected to the sexual abuse in the context of a supportive, therapeutic environment.
2. Verbalize the way sexual abuse has impacted life and feelings about self.
3. Begin the healing process by working through thoughts and feelings associated with the sexual abuse.
4. Decrease feelings of shame and guilt, and affirm perpetrator as being responsible for sexual abuse.

ADDITIONAL PROBLEMS FOR WHICH THIS EXERCISE MAY BE MOST USEFUL

- Depression
- Grief/Loss Unresolved
- Physical/Emotional Abuse Victim
- Sleep Disturbance

SUGGESTIONS FOR PROCESSING THIS EXERCISE WITH THE CLIENT

The sexual abuse experience often produces a myriad of confusing and ambivalent emotions for the victim. This exercise seeks to help the client identify and express his/her feelings associated with the sexual abuse. The client is instructed to read a short story about a girl, Jenny, who has experienced the pain of both sexual abuse and subsequent removal from her home. After reading the story, the client is asked to respond to a series of process questions. The process questions allow the client to compare and contrast his/her experience with that of the main character. Instruct the client to bring his/her answers back to the next therapy session for processing. Be alert to any signs that the client blames himself/herself for the sexual abuse. In this event, the therapist should identify the perpetrator as being responsible for the sexual abuse and not the client.

YOU ARE NOT ALONE

Read the following story of a young girl, Jenny, who has experienced the hurt of sexual abuse, as well as the pain and loneliness of being removed from her home. As you read the story, you may find that some of your experiences are similar to Jenny's in some ways, but different in others. You may have experienced some similar life changes as Jenny, but perhaps your experiences have been much different. In either case, your therapist has assigned this exercise to give you the opportunity to express your own thoughts and feelings about your experiences.

Jenny sat quietly, staring out the window of her bedroom in her foster home. Her mind was taking her away again to a familiar and comfortable place. Jenny was daydreaming about visiting with her best friend, Alisha. She was remembering a time when she and Alisha got into a huge water fight with some of the neighborhood boys. A smile came across her face. Alisha was her very best friend. She could always count on Alisha to be there to listen and understand.

Jenny missed Alisha now. She was saddened by not being able to visit her friend nearly every day like she used to before she was placed in the foster home. Jenny was removed from her home 3 months ago and was placed in the Jacksons' foster home. The Jacksons seemed like friendly people. They tried to be supportive and make her feel welcome and at home, but no matter how hard they tried, Jenny still did not feel like it was her home.

Jenny longed to be with her mother and two brothers, yet that thought also made her feel frightened. She was afraid of her stepfather, Joe, who had sexually abused her over a 2-year time period. The sexual abuse usually occurred in her bedroom late at night or when her mother was out running errands. Jenny recalled feeling confused when the "bad touches" first began. Part of her liked the attention and affection she received from Joe, but at the same time, it also made her feel ashamed and dirty. As time went on, the bad touches just made her feel more helpless and trapped. When the sexual contact occurred, Jenny would try to escape the pain by allowing her mind to drift away to a more peaceful place—Alisha's house.

Jenny was warned by her stepfather not to tell anyone. She held on to the secret until the guilt and shame increased so much that she just had to share the hurt with someone else. She thought about telling her mother, but was afraid that her mother would become angry and not believe her. Alisha realized that something was wrong with Jenny, so Jenny eventually told her. Alisha said she had to tell someone who could help and went with Jenny to tell the school counselor about the sexual abuse. Jenny felt some relief in telling Alisha and the school counselor, but her worries increased when she found out that Children's Protective Services would have to be informed.

Children's Protective Services removed Jenny from her home. Her stepfather, Joe, strongly denied the charges that he had sexually abused Jenny. Jenny's older brother, Joshua, became very angry and called Jenny a liar. Her youngest brother, Brian, chose not to say anything. Perhaps, what hurt the most was that her mother did not know whom to believe. Her mother felt caught in the middle, and in choosing not to choose sides, Jenny felt like her mother chose to side with Joe.

It seemed so strange to go into a new home. Jenny felt like she was being punished because she was the one who had to leave. She missed her mother and two brothers. She missed visiting with Alisha every day after school. Jenny was able to visit with Alisha five or six times after she was placed in the foster home. However, she often wished that she could see her more, especially since Jenny was attending a new school and had to make new friends. Jenny was meeting with her counselor, Mrs. Wohlford, every week for counseling. Mrs. Wohlford helped her sort through her feelings and told Jenny that the sexual abuse was not her fault. She found the counseling sessions helpful. Still, Jenny needed a friend like Alisha to talk to on a regular basis.

A tear rolled down Jenny's face as she stared out the window and thought about Alisha. She was awakened out of her daydream by a knock on her bedroom door. Jenny called out, "Come on in." Mrs. Jackson peeked her head in and said, "You've got a phone call from Alisha." Jenny ran downstairs to get the phone. She picked up the phone and smiled when she heard the friendly and familiar voice say, "Hi, Jenny, this is Alisha."

Please respond to the following questions that relate to you. Bring your responses back to your next therapy session.

1. How were your experiences similar to Jenny's? _____

    _____

    _____

    _____

2. How were your experiences different than Jenny's? _____

    _____

    _____

    _____

3. What are your strongest feelings about the sexual abuse? _____

    _____

    _____

    _____

4. In the story, Jenny was hurt by the response of her mother and two brothers. How did your family members respond when they first learned about the sexual abuse?

_____

_____

_____

_____

5. How did the person who sexually abused you respond when he/she learned that the abuse had been reported? _____

_____

_____

_____

_____

6. What is your relationship like with your family members today? _____

_____

_____

_____

_____

7. What is your relationship like with the sexual abuser today? _____

_____

_____

_____

_____

8. If you were removed from your home, describe how you felt when you were first placed in another home or setting. _____

_____

_____

_____

9. If another family member was removed from your home, describe how you felt when he/she had to leave the home. _____

_____

_____

_____

10. Alisha was a special friend to Jenny because she provided a lot of understanding and support. Who are the special people in your life whom you have been able to count on for understanding, support, and to be there when you needed them? _____

_____

_____

_____

_____

11. Jenny used daydreaming as a way to escape the pain of the actual sexual abuse and to deal with the sadness of being removed from her home. How have you dealt with the pain and hurt of your sexual abuse experience? _____

_____

_____

_____

_____

List three things that you have found helpful in dealing with your hurt or pain:

A. _____

B. _____

C. _____

CHILDHOOD SLEEP PROBLEMS

GOALS OF THE EXERCISE

1. Assess the severity and nature of sleep problems.
2. Describe stressful experiences and emotional trauma that continue to disturb sleep.
3. Identify effective strategies that help to induce calm and allow the client to experience restful sleep.

ADDITIONAL PROBLEMS FOR WHICH THIS EXERCISE MAY BE MOST USEFUL

- Depression
- Enuresis/Encopresis
- Medical Condition
- Posttraumatic Stress Disorder (PTSD)
- Separation Anxiety

SUGGESTIONS FOR PROCESSING THIS EXERCISE WITH THE CLIENT

In this exercise, the parents are instructed to complete a questionnaire regarding the client's sleep problems. The parents' responses will provide the therapist with a clearer picture of the specific nature of the client's sleep problems. The exercise may be useful in identifying possible stressors or emotionally upsetting events that contribute to the client's sleep problems. The parents are further asked to identify what strategies or approaches they have attempted to try to help the client sleep better at night. The parents are asked to identify strategies that have proven to be either helpful or not helpful.

CHILDHOOD SLEEP PROBLEMS
PARENTS' FORM

In order for your child's therapist to help your child sleep better at night, it is important to first recognize the specific nature of his/her sleep problems. In addition, it helps to know what strategies or approaches you have already tried—what strategies have been found to be effective, as well as what approaches have not proven to be helpful. Please respond to the following questions.

1. What types of problems does your child experience that are associated with his/her sleep? Review the following list and check all that apply.

____ Trouble falling asleep—often takes 45 minutes or longer to fall to sleep

____ Frequent early morning awakenings—repeatedly wakes up at night and/or wakes up and can't fall back to sleep

____ Rises very early in the morning (e.g., 5:30 a.m.)

____ Frequent nightmares

____ Sleep talking

____ Sleep walking

____ Sleepless nights

____ Refusal to sleep alone at night—enters parents' or sibling's room

____ Tiredness or fatigue because of poor sleep

____ Sleep apnea

____ Excessive sleep

____ Trouble waking up in the morning

____ Fearfulness at night before going to bed or while trying to sleep

____ Difficulty settling down to go to sleep

____ Manipulative or attention-seeking behavior at bedtime

____ Repeatedly coming out of room at night after bedtime rituals have been performed

____ Talking with siblings or playing with toys in room

____ Other (please list)

_____

_____

2. How long has your child had sleep problems?

_____ less than 1 month   _____ 1 to 2 years

_____ 1 to 6 months   _____ 2 to 3 years

_____ 6 months to 1 year   _____ over 3 years

3. It is not uncommon for children to develop sleep problems after they have experienced a stressful or emotionally upsetting event. Has your child experienced any stressful or upsetting events that may contribute to his/her sleep problems? If so, please describe the stressful event and tell when it occurred. _____

_____

_____

_____

4. What activities before bedtime cause your child to become more aroused, stimulated, or upset and thus have more trouble sleeping? _____

_____

_____

_____

5. Parents often try different strategies or approaches to help their child sleep at night. What strategies have you tried to help your child sleep at night? Please check all that apply.

_____ Restrict physical activities about 1 hour before bedtime

_____ Limit television or video game usage before bedtime

_____ Instruct child to perform quiet, calming, or relaxing activity before bedtime

_____ Allow child to read in room at bedtime

_____ Allow child to listen to calming or relaxing music

_____ Encourage child to replace negative or fearful thoughts with positive ones

_____ Medication

_____ Read or tell bedtime story

_____ Snuggle with child in bed to help him/her fall asleep

_____ Allow protein snack before bedtime

_____ Surround child with stuffed animals

_____ Use nightlight

_____ Pray or ask for guardian angel to watch over child at night

_____ Use "dream catcher"

_____ Allow pet to sleep in room

_____ Allow child to sleep in same room as sibling

_____ Other (please list) _____

_____

_____

6. Which of these strategies has proven to be helpful in allowing your child to sleep better? _____

_____

_____

_____

_____

7. Which of these strategies has not been helpful in allowing your child to fall or stay asleep? _____

_____

_____

_____

_____

8. What questions do you have for your child's therapist about your child's sleep problems? _____

_____

_____

_____

_____

REDUCE NIGHTTIME FEARS

GOALS OF THE EXERCISE

1. Eliminate or significantly reduce nighttime fears as evidenced by remaining calm, sleeping in own bed, and not attempting to go into parents' or sibling's room at night.
2. Develop and utilize coping strategies to manage nighttime fears.
3. Parents establish and maintain appropriate parent-child boundaries by encouraging child to sleep in his/her own bed at night.
4. Parents consistently adhere to a bedtime routine as developed in a family therapy session.

ADDITIONAL PROBLEMS FOR WHICH THIS EXERCISE MAY BE MOST USEFUL

- Physical/Emotional Abuse Victim
- School Refusal
- Separation Anxiety
- Sexual Abuse Victim

SUGGESTIONS FOR PROCESSING THIS EXERCISE WITH THE CLIENT

Children who experience symptoms of separation anxiety or have endured physical or sexual abuse frequently display their fearfulness at night when it is time to get ready for bed. The child may exhibit his/her distress by protesting about having to go to bed or needing too much supervision to get ready for bed. The child may continue to make requests after his/her needs have been satisfied or may cry about having to sleep alone without parents close by. Likewise, the child may attempt to enter the parents' or sibling's room at night. In this exercise, the child is required to utilize security objects and/or perform a ritual to help alleviate his/her fears. The use of the security objects or performance of the ritual can be combined with the other coping strategies (e.g., positive self-talk, thought substitution, relaxation techniques) to help the child fall asleep. The parents are encouraged to be present while the child performs the ritual.

REDUCE NIGHTTIME FEARS

It is important for a growing child to get a good night's rest, but this can be difficult when you are afraid or anxious. This assignment is designed to help you learn new ways to manage your nighttime fears. You will be asked to use security object(s) or to perform a bedtime ritual to help you feel safer at night. A *ritual* is a routine pattern of behaviors that is repeated every night in the same sequence before you go to bed. The bedtime ritual or the use of the security object(s) will remind you of your parents' love and protection after they say goodnight and leave your room. (Parents are encouraged to be present during the performance of the bedtime ritual.)

1. The following ideas are to help you to feel relaxed and get ready for bed. Talk with your therapist and parent(s) to select the security object(s) or ritual(s) that you will use to feel safer at night. You are encouraged to think of other ideas that may be used to help you feel safe, cozy, and comfortable while you are in bed and falling asleep.
   - Ask your parents to read a favorite bedtime story to you.
   - Ask your parents to sing bedtime songs or lullabies to calm you.
   - Place a fortress of stuffed animals around the bed to protect you from monsters.
   - Place a dreamcatcher above your bed to help eliminate nightmares.
   - Have Mother spray small amount of perfume on your wrist to remind you of your parents' love and presence in the home.
   - Have Father spray small amount of cologne on you to remind you of your parents' love and presence in the home.
   - Ask your parents to allow family pet to sleep in your room.
   - Develop a bedtime routine (e.g., put on pajamas, get a snack, brush teeth, take a drink, read a short story, say a prayer, kiss and hug goodnight, turn on nightlight) that is followed every night.

2. Use the following Contract form as a means of formalizing the promise that you will sleep in your own bed. Post the contract prominently in your room as a reminder of the promise.

   Following is a list of suggested rewards that you may receive for sleeping in your room at night:
   - Purchase book(s) by your favorite author
   - Rent or go see a movie
   - Extra time to play video games
   - Extended bedtime

- One-on-one time with your mother or father in an agreed-upon activity
- Invite friend over to spend the night at your house
- Your favorite meal
- Snacks
- Small toys
- Tokens or stickers that can be traded in to purchase toys, prizes, or privileges

CONTRACT

If _____sleeps in his/her own bed for the entire night without crying,
(Name of child)

whining, or complaining, then the following reward will be given in the morning:

_____
_____
_____
_____
_____
_____
_____
_____
_____
_____

_____   _____

Signature of Child   Signature of Parent

_____   _____

Signature of Parent   Signature of Therapist

GREETING PEERS

GOALS OF THE EXERCISE

1. Interact socially with peers on a consistent basis without excessive fear or anxiety.
2. Increase frequency of social interactions with same-aged peers or acquaintances.
3. Learn and implement social skills to reduce anxiety and build confidence in social interactions.
4. Begin to take steps toward building peer friendships.

ADDITIONAL PROBLEMS FOR WHICH THIS EXERCISE MAY BE MOST USEFUL

- Anxiety
- Depression
- Low Self-Esteem

SUGGESTIONS FOR PROCESSING THIS EXERCISE WITH THE CLIENT

This homework assignment is designed for the extremely shy or reserved child in the beginning stages of therapy. The anxious and shy child often withdraws or shrinks away from social contacts for fear that he/she will be met with criticism, disapproval, or rejection. The shy child avoids eye contact as well as the act of greeting others. In this assignment, the child is asked to initiate three social contacts per day. (The frequency of the social contacts per day or per week can be modified to meet the child's needs.) The child should be encouraged to maintain good eye contact and avoid looking away from others when greeting them. The child may also need to be coached in the therapy sessions as to how to greet others. Role-play a positive greeting (i.e., strong voice, good eye contact, smile) in advance. The child is further requested to rate his/her anxiety level during the social contacts. The rating scale can help you determine when the child feels comfortable enough to take on more challenging or complex social interactions. The child is asked to record his experiences on a greeting log. The log will help keep the child accountable to the treatment goals.

GREETING PEERS

The purpose of this exercise is to help you feel more comfortable around your peers at school and in your neighborhood. You are to initiate three social contacts per day with peers or acquaintances (close or regular friends are excluded from this assignment). Remember to maintain good eye contact and avoid looking away when greeting others. Good eye contact lets others know that you are interested in talking to them. Greet the other person with some of the expressions (such as "good morning," "how are you today?") that were practiced in the therapy session. Don't forget to smile!

In this exercise, you are asked to record the names of three individuals with whom you initiated contact during the day. It is important that you record their names because this will help you to stay focused on performing the task. Put the assignment sheet in your notebook or place it in your desk so that you can easily record the names of the individuals you greeted. Hopefully, some of these simple greetings will lead to longer conversations, but that is not the main goal of this assignment. The main goal is for you to feel comfortable and less anxious as you give a simple greeting.

Use the following rating scale to identify your anxiety level during each social contact, and then write the number on the following pages in the blank space under the column marked Anxiety Level:

Anxiety Level

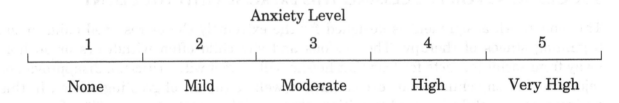

1	2	3	4	5
None	Mild	Moderate	High	Very High

Use the following sheet to record the names of the three peers with whom you initiated contact each day. Remember to rate your anxiety level for each contact. Please feel free to make any additional comments about your experiences or contacts, which can be discussed in therapy.

Please remember to bring the assignment sheets to your next appointment.

GREETING LOG

First Greeting

Person's Name: _____ Place: _____

Date and time: _____ Anxiety level: _____

How did the other person respond? _____

Comments: _____

_____

_____

_____

Second Greeting

Person's Name: _____ Place: _____

Date and time: _____ Anxiety level: _____

How did the other person respond? _____

Comments: _____

_____

_____

_____

Third Greeting

Person's Name: _____ Place: _____

Date and time: _____ Anxiety level: _____

How did the other person respond? _____

Comments: _____

_____

_____

_____

LEARN TO BE ASSERTIVE

GOALS OF THE EXERCISE

1. Interact consistently with adults and peers in mutually respectful manner.
2. Demonstrate improved self-esteem by asserting thoughts and feelings in a calm manner, accepting compliments from others, and handling hurtful teasing effectively.
3. Develop the essential social skills that enhance the quality of interpersonal relationships.

ADDITIONAL PROBLEMS FOR WHICH THIS EXERCISE MAY BE MOST USEFUL

- Anger Control Problems
- Anxiety
- Low Self-Esteem

SUGGESTIONS FOR PROCESSING THIS EXERCISE WITH THE CLIENT

The goal of this exercise is to help the client become more assertive. The exercise has three parts. The client is first taught to differentiate among aggressive, assertive, and passive behavior. The client is asked to identify whether he/she primarily views himself/herself as being aggressive, assertive, or passive. Secondly, the client is taught how to use "I" statements and deep breathing to help himself/herself express his/her thoughts and feelings in a calm, assertive manner. Finally, the assignment focuses on helping the client to become more assertive in three different areas: expressing one's opinion, receiving positive compliments, and handling hurtful teasing. This assignment can be processed over the course of two to three sessions and need not be completed in one session. The therapist may also choose to help the client become assertive in other areas, such as saying "no" to other people.

LEARN TO BE ASSERTIVE

It is important for each of us to learn to stand up for ourselves by expressing our thoughts and feelings in a calm, firm, and respectful manner. Expressing ourselves in a firm, respectful way helps us to feel good about ourselves. Being able to express our thoughts and feelings in a calm and respectful manner is called *being assertive*.

I. Learning About Assertiveness

A. The Difference Among Aggressive, Assertive, and Passive Behavior
Before learning to become assertive, it is first important to know the difference among being aggressive, assertive, and passive. Below are examples of such behavior.

Aggressive	• Push my way onto others • Demand that I get my way most of the time • Tell others what to do • Call others names or hurt them physically • Seek to get from others and rarely give to others • Blame others for problems
Assertive	• Let others know my thoughts and feelings in a respectful way • Stand up for myself • Respect others' ideas, feelings, and wishes • Give as well as receive • Use "I" statements to express myself
Passive	• Almost always do what others want me to do • Keep my thoughts and feelings to myself • Almost never say what I like or do not like • Let others have their way or make decisions for me • Feel "pushed around"/not important • Give to others and only once in a while seek to get

B. All of us behave in these three ways from time to time. Which one of the three listed above best fits you most of the time? _____

_____

C. Draw a circle on a separate piece of paper. Pretend the circle stands for you as a person. Divide the circle (like a graph) into three portions to show how often you are aggressive, assertive, and passive. In each of the sections, write down some ways you have shown this side of yourself. Please bring this filled-in circle back to the next session.

D. Here, you have the choice of being either an artist or an actor. Please choose one of the following options:

1. Draw pictures of yourself showing times when you acted in an aggressive, assertive, or passive way. Please bring the drawings back to your next session.

2. Talk with your parents about times when you acted in an aggressive, assertive, or passive way. Create a play that shows how you acted at those times. Be ready to recreate your play for your therapist in the next session.

E. Talk with your therapist and parents about how becoming more assertive may change your life and the way you feel about yourself. What would be good about becoming more assertive?

_____

_____

_____

On the other hand, what negative changes or bad things might happen if you become more assertive?

_____

_____

_____

_____

II. Helpful Starting Skills

Now is the time to start learning and practicing some ways to become more assertive.

A. Deep Breathing—It is important to remain calm when expressing your thoughts and feelings in an assertive manner. Deep breathing is very helpful in calming our bodies down when we confront a situation that makes us feel anxious, worried, or fearful. One way of learning to do this is to use your hand (palm down) and imagine it as a slice of pizza; then use your nose to smell it. You want to smell it completely, so take as deep a breath as you can and hold it. Slowly let your breath out by blowing it on the slice of pizza to cool it off. Repeat this three times, trying to take a deeper breath each time. Practice this daily for a week at home. (Use a pinwheel to test how well you are doing.) Also ask your therapist about other ways of doing deep breathing (e.g., bubbles, balloons, etc.).

B. Good Eye Contact and "I" Statements—It is important to make good eye contact and make "I" statements when communicating your thoughts and feelings to other people in a calm, assertive way. Practice these skills by completing these statements while looking directly at an object.

I like _____   I wish _____

I believe _____   I want _____

I love _____   I hate _____

III. Areas of Assertiveness

There are many ways you can become assertive in your life. Here are three different ways that you can practice being more assertive:

A. Giving Your Opinion—One way to become assertive is to express your opinions while also listening to other people's thoughts and feelings. Use an "I" statement to answer the following:

Which restaurant would you like to go to tonight? _____

What did you think of that movie? _____

How do you like the class you are in? _____

What do you think of our President? _____

Your therapist can also help you become more assertive by asking you other questions that you can answer with "I" statements. (Remember to make eye contact with your therapist as you answer.)

Take a few minutes to think of a situation that is coming up in the near future that will give you the opportunity to state your opinion. What situation is coming up that will allow you to express your opinion? _____

_____

How can you express your opinion in an assertive way? _____

_____

_____

B. Accepting Compliments or Positive Feedback—We all need positive feedback or compliments and it is polite to receive these in a respectful, assertive manner. Talk with your therapist and parents about polite ways to respond to compliments or positive feedback about yourself. After talking with your therapist or parents, please write how you would respond to the following compliments:

"You look great today." _____

_____

"You did a nice job on your paper." _____

_____

"That was a good idea."

_____

"I appreciated your help today."_____

_____

You can practice more by having your parents or therapist give you two to three new compliments (remember to make good eye contact as you respond to the compliment). During the next week, record three positive remarks or compliments you received from other people and how you responded to each incident. Write your responses to the three compliments below:

1. _____

_____

2. _____

_____

3. _____

_____

C. Handling Hurtful Teasing—Most of us have teased and received teasing in return from others. There are two types of teasing: playful and hurtful. Playful teasing happens with friends and family members who say or do things out of fun. Playful teasing helps us to laugh at ourselves. It does not cause hurt or pain. Hurtful teasing (or bullying) involves saying or doing things that cause hurt or pain. Hurtful teasing is done out of meanness.

1. We have all received both playful and hurtful teasing. Think of a time when you were playfully teased by others. How did you feel? How did you respond?

_____

_____

2. Now think of a time when you were teased in a hurtful or mean way. How did you feel? How did you respond?_____

_____

_____

Below are some ways to deal with hurtful teasing. Talk with your therapist and parents about other ways to deal with hurtful teasing.
• Stick with friends. You are less likely to be teased if you are around other friends or people.
• Avoid teasers or bullies. As much as possible, try to stay away from bullies.

- Ignore teasing and act as if it doesn't bother you. It is important that you not show that the teasing is bothering you on the outside. The bully or teaser is more likely to stop if they do not feel that they are getting a response out of you. If you show that you are hurt, then they may very well continue to tease you in a hurtful way.
- Laugh. Sometimes it helps to laugh. Here again, this shows that you are not bothered by the teasing and they will likely stop if they are trying to get a response out of you.
- Calmly say to the bully in an assertive and confident manner: "You seem angry. Are you mad at me about something?" Then listen to their response and talk with them calmly about the issue.

3. During the next week, please record an incident where you were teased in a hurtful way by another person. How did you respond to the hurtful teasing? _____

_____

_____

_____

Please bring your responses to the questions or items back to your next therapy session to process with your therapist.

SHOW YOUR STRENGTHS

GOALS OF THE EXERCISE

1. Utilize strengths and interests to help take steps toward building peer friendships.
2. Interact socially with peers on a consistent basis without excessive fear or anxiety.
3. Reduce social isolation and excessive shrinking away from others.
4. Increase positive self-statements in social interactions.

ADDITIONAL PROBLEMS FOR WHICH THIS EXERCISE MAY BE MOST USEFUL

- Depression
- Low Self-Esteem
- Separation Anxiety
- Specific Phobia

SUGGESTIONS FOR PROCESSING THIS EXERCISE WITH THE CLIENT

The purpose of this exercise is to help the socially anxious or shy client begin to establish peer friendships by utilizing his/her strengths and interests. First, meet with the client (and parents) to identify specific strengths and interests. Then, instruct the client to share his/her strengths or interests with three different peers before the next therapy session. Emphasize how the client will likely feel less anxious and insecure around his/her peers when he/she utilizes his/her strengths or interests. Next, the client is required to respond to several process questions after each one of his/her social contacts. The client's responses to these questions will allow you to reinforce his/her efforts and/or offer suggestions to improve his/her social skills. Teach the client basic social skills (i.e., greeting others, maintaining good eye contact, smiling). Use role-playing and behavioral rehearsal to help the client develop conversational skills. Encourage the client to make positive statements about himself/herself or the other peer(s).

SHOW YOUR STRENGTHS

The purpose of this exercise is to help you feel less anxious and more comfortable around your peers at school or in the neighborhood. It will also give you the opportunity to have fun and be yourself around your peers, which is important when it comes to making friends. You are asked to share your strengths or interests with three different people before your next therapy session. Sharing your strengths and interests will help you forget about your worries or nervousness when you interact with others. Remember to maintain good eye contact when you are talking to your peers. Be positive! Compliment your peers, and say something good about yourself. Don't forget to smile, laugh, and have fun.

1. Meet with your therapist (and parents) to identify a list of your strengths and interests. This part of the exercise should take place in the therapy session. Identify at least five strengths, talents, or interests. (*Note:* Your strengths, talents, and interests may not necessarily be the same.)

Strengths and Interests

A. _____

B. _____

C. _____

D. _____

E. _____

F. _____

G. _____

2. Share your strengths or interests with three different peers in the next week or before your next therapy session. Remember to use the skills that you have learned in your therapy sessions to feel more comfortable around your peers.

    The following short story is an example of how one girl, named Tracey, used her interest to make a new friend.

    Tracey was excited. She had saved up her allowance money to buy a new stuffed animal—a dog named Bernie. She was playing with Bernie when she remembered that another girl, Amber, who lived down the street, also liked playing with dolls and stuffed animals. Tracey had been working hard on being less shy and making new friends, so she decided to walk down the street and show off Bernie to Amber. Tracey was nervous but she thought that this would be a good way to make a new friend. She walked down the street and knocked on the door. Amber opened the door and said, "Hi." Tracey smiled and said, "Hi, Amber. I just got a new stuffed animal, and I was wondering if you would like to come down to my house and play." Amber replied, "Oh, cool! Bernie is so cute. Let me go upstairs and get my stuffed animals, and I'll come down to your house in a few minutes." Tracey felt even happier now that she could share her stuffed animals with a new friend.

3. Please respond to the following items or questions after each occasion when you shared your strengths or interests. Fill out a separate form for each social contact. (*Note:* Your therapist will give you three copies of this form.) Remember to bring the forms to your next therapy session.

  A. Identify name(s) of peer(s) with whom you shared your strengths or interests.

  _____

  _____

  _____

  B. What strength or interest did you share with your peer(s)? _____

  _____

  _____

  _____

  C. How did you feel about yourself when sharing your strength or interest? _____

  _____

  _____

  _____

  D. How did your peer(s) respond to you when you shared your strength or interest? _____

  _____

  _____

  _____

  _____

  E. What opportunities will you have to share this strength or interest in the future? _____

  _____

  _____

  _____

  _____

EXPRESSIONS OF FEAR THROUGH ART

GOALS OF THE EXERCISE

1. Describe the history and nature of the phobia(s), complete with impact on functioning and attempt to overcome it.
2. Reduce the intensity or degree of anxiety and fearfulness connected to the stimulus object or specific situation.
3. Develop and begin to use effective coping strategies to manage or overcome fears.

ADDITIONAL PROBLEMS FOR WHICH THIS EXERCISE MAY BE MOST USEFUL

- Anxiety
- School Refusal
- Separation Anxiety
- Social Anxiety

SUGGESTIONS FOR PROCESSING THIS EXERCISE WITH THE CLIENT

This assignment is a fun-filled activity that can be used in the early stages of therapy to help the client identify his/her specific fear. The client is asked to draw three separate pictures. The client is first asked to draw a picture of what he/she fears. In the second drawing, the client is asked to identify what he/she fears will happen if he/she is exposed to the stimulus object or specific situation. Finally, the client is asked to draw a picture of himself/herself doing something to master or overcome the fear. The client is also asked to respond to several processing questions. After processing the client's drawings and responses in the follow-up therapy session, the therapist can then assist the client in identifying positive coping strategies that, in turn, can help him/her overcome his/her fearfulness to the specific object or situation.

EXPRESSIONS OF FEAR THROUGH ART

This assignment gives you the chance to use your artistic talents. You will be asked to draw three separate pictures that have to do with your fear. Your drawings will help your therapist better understand your fear. In the end, it is also hoped that you will learn some helpful ways to deal with your fear. Please draw your pictures on a separate sheet of paper and bring them to your next therapy session. You are also asked to answer a few questions after you complete each drawing.

PICTURE #1—Picture of Fearful Object

Please draw a picture of the object, thing, or situation that you fear the most. After finishing the drawing, please respond to these questions:

1. What is your fear? _____
    _____
    _____

2. How long have you had this fear? _____
    _____

3. How strong is your fear? (Please check the appropriate space.)
    ___ mild ___ medium _____ strong _____ very strong

PICTURE #2—Picture of What Will Happen if You Face Your Fear

Next, please draw a picture that shows what bad or harmful thing you think will happen if you come in contact with the feared object, thing, or situation.

1. What bad or harmful thing do you think will happen if you come in contact with the feared object, thing, or situation? _____
    _____
    _____

2. After looking at your picture, what do you think are the chances that the bad or harmful thing will actually come true? (Please check the appropriate space.)
    ___ no chance ___ small chance ___ medium chance ___ high or strong chance

3. What has happened in the past when you came in contact with the feared object, thing, or situation? _____

    _____

    _____

    _____

    _____

PICTURE #3—Conquering Your Fears

Finally, please draw a picture that shows you doing something to overcome or conquer your fear.

1. What can you do to overcome or master your fear? _____

    _____

    _____

    _____

    _____

2. After looking at your picture, what do you think are the chances of you overcoming your fear by using this strategy? (Please check the appropriate space.)

    ___ low ____ medium _____ good ____ very good

3. Have you ever tried this strategy? If so, please state what happened. If you have never used this strategy, then state whether you would be willing to use this strategy or approach in the future.

    _____

    _____

    _____

    _____

4. Who can you turn to for support to help you overcome your fear? _____

    _____

    _____

    _____

    _____

MAURICE FACES HIS FEAR

GOALS OF THE HOMEWORK

1. Verbalize fears and identify the stimulus object or situation that produces anxiety.
2. Reduce phobic avoidance of the specific object or situation, leading to comfort and independence in moving around in a public environment.
3. Learn and implement calming skills to reduce and manage anxiety symptoms.

ADDITIONAL PROBLEMS FOR WHICH THIS EXERCISE MAY BE MOST USEFUL

- Anxiety
- School Refusal
- Separation Anxiety
- Social Anxiety

SUGGESTIONS FOR PROCESSING THIS EXERCISE WITH THE CLIENT

This homework assignment involves the reading of a story about a young monkey, Maurice, who initially is afraid to leave the safety of his home because of his fear of snakes. The parents or caretakers are encouraged to read the story to the client between therapy sessions. Following the story are several process questions that can be asked of the client either at appropriate points in the story or after the entire story has been read. The specific questions are offered as guides to help the client verbalize his/her fears and identify the phobic stimulus object or situation that evokes his/her anxiety. The reader of the story is encouraged to ask other questions that may be appropriate for each particular client. The client should not be pressured into answering any questions that he/she does not feel comfortable in answering. Encourage the parents or caretakers to record the client's responses to the questions in the spaces provided. The responses to the questions will help you and the client to develop coping strategies (e.g., deep breathing, muscle relaxation techniques, positive self-talk, cognitive restructuring, systematic desensitization) to manage his/her anxiety. It is hoped that the client will experience greater motivation to face his/her fears after reading the story and identifying coping strategies to help manage his/her anxiety. The story is written for children approximately 6 to 11 years of age.

MAURICE FACES HIS FEAR
READER'S INSTRUCTIONS

Storytelling can be an effective way to join with the fearful child who experiences strong feelings of anxiety. Before reading "Maurice Faces His Fear" to the child, try to create a relaxed atmosphere. Spend a few minutes talking gently to the child. Feel free to sit on the floor with the child or have the child stretch out on a couch. Familiarize yourself with the story by reading it in advance. This will help you to be more animated or spontaneous in your expressions as you read the story.

The purpose of reading "Maurice Faces His Fear" is to help the child verbalize his/her own fears and identify the specific objects or situations that produce his/her anxiety. It is hoped that by creating a supportive environment, the child will feel comfortable in opening up and talking about his/her fears. After reading the story, you are encouraged to ask the child several questions about his/her fears. With some children it may be beneficial to ask them some of the questions as you read through the story. If the child begins to spontaneously talk about his/her fears, then encourage this.

Following is a list of questions that you may find helpful in allowing the child to identify and discuss his/her fears. These questions are offered as a guide. Please feel free to ask other questions that you feel are more appropriate for each individual child. Do not feel that you have to ask all the questions. Furthermore, it is very important that you be sensitive to how the child responds to the story or questions. Do not force or pressure the child into responding to any questions that he/she may not be willing to answer. Record any noteworthy remarks that the child may make in the spaces provided. This will help the child share his/her fears with the therapist in the next therapy session. The therapist, with your help, can assist the child in finding ways to manage his/her anxiety.

1. What are your fear(s)? _____
   _____
   _____

2. How long have you had this fear? _____
   _____
   _____

3. How did you first develop your fear(s)? What events or situations happened that caused you to have the fear(s)? _____

_____

_____

4. In the beginning of the story, Maurice becomes very anxious and nervous when he tries to leave Rasheeka's Tree. His heart begins to pound, thoughts race through his head, and his breathing becomes short and quick. How do you act when you get scared? _____

_____

_____

5. Maurice realizes how unhappy he is after being teased by two pesky monkeys, Richard and Johnny. He is so afraid to leave Rasheeka's Tree that he does not explore the rest of the rain forest. What do you avoid doing because of your fears? _

_____

_____

_____

6. What things have occurred to make you afraid? _____

_____

_____

_____

7. In the story, Maurice receives help from his grandfather, Rasheeka, and a friendly snake, Roger, to overcome his fears. Who can help you to overcome your fear(s)? ___

_____

_____

_____

8. Maurice, with Rasheeka's encouragement, agrees to face his fear and gradually draw closer and closer to Roger. What have you learned to help decrease your fears? _____

_____

_____

9. In the end, Maurice overcomes his fear and feels free to explore the rain forest. What things would you like to do in the future once you are free of your fears?

_____

_____

MAURICE FACES HIS FEAR

Deep in the heart of the Amazon rain forest lies a very tall tree that towers above all the other trees. Its roots are deeply planted in the earth, and its trunk is strong and wide, supporting the many branches that rise like pillars into the sky. The tree is called Rasheeka's Tree because it was inhabited by Rasheeka, the grandfather of a large family of howler monkeys. Rasheeka was widely respected and he taught his entire family how to hunt and gather food. He taught his grandchildren of the goodness of the rain forest, but at the same time, he warned them of some of the dangers, like the snakes.

One of Rasheeka's grandchildren was a little monkey named Maurice who loved to climb and scamper among the tree's many branches. He listened closely to his grandfather's stories but became very frightened when he heard his grandfather's warnings about the snakes in the rain forest. Maurice became even more afraid when one day he saw a 25-foot-long snake pass under his tree. After that, he told himself that he would never leave Rasheeka's Tree because he did not want to be captured by a hungry snake. Maurice's mother, Rhianna, and father, Manley, were sure that Maurice would overcome his fear as he grew up. They became concerned, however, after Maurice grew up and still refused to leave the safety of the tree. Every time they encouraged Maurice to go out with his cousins and gather food for the relatives, Maurice would shake his head and shout, "No." Rhianna pleaded with her son and promised him that she would give him extra bananas if he ventured away from home. Manley scolded his son and insisted that he gather food along with his cousins.

Although Maurice tried to go with his cousins several times, as soon as his feet touched the ground, he began to panic. He became dizzy and lightheaded; hot flashes shot through his body. Maurice's heart pounded, his breathing became quick, and his hands and feet trembled like palm branches swaying in a tropical storm. Feeling overwhelmed by his own fear and nervousness, Maurice would quickly scurry back up the trunk of Rasheeka's Tree.

Rhianna and Manley went to Rasheeka and asked him to talk to Maurice. Rasheeka gently approached the frightened young monkey, and said, "It's a terrible thing to live in fear. I know that I have warned you about the snakes and you have even seen a large snake, but the chances of you being attacked by a snake are very small, especially if you travel in a group with other monkeys. You will find, Maurice, that you will be happier if you face your fears." Maurice listened to his grandfather and even tried to leave the tree a couple more times. Each time, however, he began to feel nervous and afraid and would scurry up the tree again. Rasheeka sadly nodded his head and said to Rhianna and Manley, "He will not listen to my advice. Maurice will have to find out for himself that he will become a very lonely monkey if he does not overcome his fears."

Time passed and Maurice stopped trying to leave the tree. Each day his cousins would leave without saying a word to Maurice. They searched for delicious berries, fruits, and nuts in other parts of the rain forest. Maurice told himself that he was happy just to stay in his tree.

One day, Maurice was sitting all alone in the tree, keeping a watchful eye out for insects to eat as a midmorning snack. He was minding his own monkey business when all of a sudden—splat! Maurice felt a mooshy, gooshy glob running down his face. He wiped the glob off his face and noticed that it was a rotten, squashed banana. "Oh yuck!" cried Maurice, and then he heard laughter coming from the ground below. He looked down and saw two mischievous monkeys, Richard and Johnny, who lived in a neighboring tree. The two monkeys were rolling on the ground in laughter. They had fired a rotten, squashed banana at Maurice using a hollowed out bamboo pole. They called their weapon a "banana bazooka." Richard and Johnny had a reputation of being very playful monkeys, but Maurice thought they were just plain pesky. Richard and Johnny began firing more rotten, squashed bananas at Maurice. Maurice ducked each time and avoided getting hit. He hollered at the two pests, "Hey, knock it off, or else you'll get it!" Johnny fired back, "Or else what?" "Yeah," said Richard, "what are you going to do? Are you going to come down out of that tree and get us?" Johnny cried out, "If you come down out of that tree, you better watch out for snakes!"

Maurice dropped his head in shame. He knew Richard and Johnny were right, and he knew that he would never leave the tree because he was too afraid. Maurice began to cry and said to himself, "I'm nothing but a misfit monkey. I'll never leave this tree; I'll just live my whole life being afraid. Oh, what a miserable life I'll lead!"

Maurice's cries were overheard by his grandfather, Rasheeka. Rasheeka came to Maurice's side and tried to comfort him. He put his arm around Maurice and said, "Everything will be all right. You just need to face your fears, and in time, you won't be afraid any longer." Maurice continued to cry, "There's no way I'm going to go anywhere near a snake." Rasheeka replied, "I have an idea. I know a friendly snake named Roger. He doesn't bite, and he won't hurt you. I want you to meet Roger, and then maybe you won't be so afraid of snakes." Maurice persisted, "I told you, I'm not going anywhere near a snake." Rasheeka continued, "Well, how about if I bring him to the base of the tree tomorrow and introduce him to you. You can just say hello. After that, you can draw closer and closer to him. That way you will gradually overcome your fear." Maurice whined a little bit, but said, "Okay, I'll try it."

The next day, Rasheeka brought Roger to the base of the tree. Maurice was standing on a big branch, 40 feet up in the air, when he looked down and saw the snake. His head started to spin, he became dizzy, and his heart began to pound. Maurice was breathing very rapidly. Rasheeka looked up into the tree and could see that Maurice was very nervous. He shouted up to Maurice, "Relax. Slow down. You're huffing and puffing like a scared puffer fish trying to get away from a piranha. Take some deep breaths, relax your muscles, and think of some positive thoughts." Maurice did what his grandfather told him to do, and to Maurice's surprise, he started to feel less afraid. After Maurice calmed down, he said, "I think I'm all right." Rasheeka said, "Good.

Tomorrow, we'll try it again, except you'll come down out of the tree, and Roger will stand 30 feet away." Maurice began to whine again and said, "Promise me Roger won't come any closer than 30 feet." Roger joined in at this point and said, "I promise I won't come any closer than 30 feet. You'll find that I'm a friendly snake."

Rasheeka and Roger showed up the next day. Maurice agreed to come down to the base of the tree, while Roger lay 30 feet away. Maurice began to experience the feeling of panic again, but Rasheeka quickly jumped in and told him to practice the skills he learned yesterday. Maurice followed his advice and again found that he could manage his anxiety. Maurice practiced Rasheeka's relaxation techniques with Roger for the next 3 weeks. Slowly, but surely, Maurice drew closer and closer to Roger. He went from standing 30 feet away from Roger to 25, to 20, to 15, to 10, to 5, and then to 2 feet away. Finally, after 3 weeks, Maurice was ready to take the next big step. He agreed to pick up and hold Roger.

The next day arrived. Maurice was nervous, but he was confident that he could deal with it. He climbed down the tree and met Rasheeka and Roger. He chuckled and said, "I'm nervous, but I'm ready to do this." He picked up Roger and felt Roger's cool, scaly skin on his fur. He laughed because it tickled. Maurice held Roger for 15 minutes, and then he let Roger down because Roger wanted to go back to his family. Maurice thanked Rasheeka and Roger for being such good helpers and special friends. Maurice said, "Without your help I would have never come out of the tree, and now I feel ready to explore the rain forest." Rasheeka and Roger cheered for Maurice.

Maurice left Rasheeka's Tree every day after that and journeyed out into the rain forest with his family and friends. His confidence grew with each passing day, and he no longer lived his life in fear. Maurice still felt a little nervousness from time to time, but he realized that was normal. He knew how to manage his fear when it came on. He kept a watchful eye out for any dangerous snakes, such as the boa constrictor, but he was no longer terrified by them, especially after discovering that a howler monkey's howl can be very loud. He learned that his loud, screeching howl could drive away any boa constrictor when he came across one.

Maurice's journeys took him farther and farther away from Rasheeka's Tree each month. One day, Maurice came across a hidden garden of papaya and guava trees. Maurice and the others gathered up a large number of papayas and guavas to bring back home. On the way home, Maurice stopped at Roger's home and shared some of the fruits with him. After arriving home, they shared their delicious treasures with the other monkeys. Maurice even shared a papaya and guava with Richard and Johnny. The two mischievous monkeys agreed not to bother Maurice and his cousins anymore if Maurice agreed to show them the location of the hidden garden. Maurice agreed to show them the garden, but first he made them hand over the banana bazooka.

Later that day, Rasheeka, Maurice's grandfather, approached Maurice and said, "I'm very happy for you, my grandson. You have faced your fears and overcome them. You have shared the treasures of the rain forest with your family, and in doing so, you have discovered the treasure that lies within your heart. The treasure of giving." Maurice smiled and felt good that he was able to help his family.

HOME-BASED READING AND LANGUAGE PROGRAM

GOALS OF THE EXERCISE

1. Improve the expressive and receptive language abilities to level of capability.
2. Improve reading comprehension skills.
3. Parents increase the time spent with the client in activities that build and facilitate speech/language development.
4. Parents or caretakers increase support of and involvement in improving client's expressive and receptive language skills.
5. Feel more comfortable and confident in verbalizing thoughts and opinions.

ADDITIONAL PROBLEMS FOR WHICH THIS EXERCISE MAY BE MOST USEFUL

- Academic Underachievement
- Depression
- Low Self-Esteem
- Social Anxiety

SUGGESTIONS FOR PROCESSING THIS EXERCISE WITH THE CLIENT

In this assignment, the client and parent(s) are assigned the task of reading together several times each week to improve the client's receptive and expressive language skills. Instruct the client to read a story to his/her parents, and then to retell the story in his/her own words. The parents are encouraged to ask several questions that require the client to use his/her language skills. The parents can also read to younger children (first grade or below) or to children who are suspected of having a severe learning disability in the area of reading. Have the child read for approximately 15 minutes, four times per week. The frequency and length of time spent reading can be adjusted to meet the needs of the child. This assignment can also be used with children who have a learning disability in the area of reading comprehension.

HOME-BASED READING AND LANGUAGE PROGRAM
PARENTS' INSTRUCTIONS

This program is designed to be used at home to improve your child's vocabulary and reading skills.

1. Have your child read aloud for approximately 15 minutes, four times per week. The length and frequency of the reading sessions can be adjusted to meet the needs of your child and family. For example, you may decrease the amount of time to 10 minutes for a younger child who has just begun to learn how to read. On the other hand, you may want to increase the frequency or length of the reading sessions for children in the later elementary school grades.

    You have several options as far as how you read along with your child. It is generally recommended that you allow the child to read aloud in your presence. This gives you the opportunity to help him/her pronounce any difficult words or to explain the meaning of any words that he/she does not understand. However, you will obviously have to read for younger children (first grade or below) who have not yet started or have just recently started to learn how to read. For some children, it may be beneficial to take turns reading along with him/her. This option may be particularly helpful with children in the first and second grades. Older children (fifth grade and up) may prefer to read independently before they verbally retell the story.

    Consult with your child's teacher about what books or reading materials are appropriate for his/her reading level. It is recommended that you select books or reading materials that match your child's interests, as well as reading difficulty level, particularly with those children who are not highly interested or motivated to read on their own.

2. After your child has finished reading for the designated period of time, ask him/her to retell the story. The purpose of retelling the story is to improve your child's vocabulary and also to help him/her feel more confident in communicating his/her thoughts. Allow the child to take the lead in retelling the story. However, you are encouraged to ask questions if you feel that the child has left out any important information. The questions will also serve as prompts to help the child verbalize what he/she has read. Following is a list of suggested questions that you may ask the child:

    *   What is the title of the book?
    *   Who are the main characters?

- Where did the story take place?
- In what time period did the story occur?
- How did the story begin?
- What happened next?
- How did the story end?
- What did you like or find interesting about the story?
- What did you dislike about the story?
- What was the moral or lesson of the story?
- Have you experienced anything like what happened in the book or story? If so, please explain.
- Would you recommend this book to other children your age? Why or why not?

3. A reward system can easily be tied into this home-based reading and language program. Reward the child for spending a certain amount of time reading and also for being able to retell the story satisfactorily. Use the following Home-Based Reading and Language Program Contract to clearly define how long and how often the child must read before he/she receives the reward. Use the following Reading Log to record the title of the book and the time spent reading it. Post the contract and reading log in a prominent or visible place in the home (such as the refrigerator or on a bulletin board in the child's room). Following is a list of potential rewards:
    - Purchase a book (by child's favorite author)
    - Rent or go see a movie
    - Allow extra time to play video games or use computer
    - Extended bedtime
    - One-on-one time with mother or father in an agreed-upon play activity
    - Allow child to invite friend over to spend the night at your house
    - Help to prepare a favorite meal
    - Snacks
    - Small toys
    - Tokens or stickers that can be exchanged for toys, prizes, or privileges

HOME-BASED READING AND LANGUAGE PROGRAM CONTRACT

If _____ spends _____ per _____ reading and is able to re-
   (Child's name)   (Time spent)   (Day or week)

tell the story to a satisfactory degree, then _____ will receive the follow-
                        (Child's name)

ing reward:

_____

_____

_____

_____

_____

_____

_____

_____

_____   _____
Signature of Child   Signature of Parent

_____   _____
Signature of Parent   Signature of Teacher or Therapist

READING LOG

Please record the date, title of book, and time spent reading for the day. Ask your parents to initial the sheet each day.

Date	Book Title	Time Read (in minutes)	Parent's Initials

SHAUNA'S SONG

GOALS OF THE EXERCISE

1. Develop an awareness and acceptance of speech/language problems so that there is consistent participation in discussions in the peer group, school, or social settings.
2. Decrease level of anxiety associated with speech/language problems.
3. Identify strengths that can be used to help gain acceptance in peer group.

ADDITIONAL PROBLEMS FOR WHICH THIS EXERCISE MAY BE MOST USEFUL

- Academic Underachievement
- Intellectual Development Disorder
- Low Self-Esteem

SUGGESTIONS FOR PROCESSING THIS EXERCISE WITH THE CLIENT

The story "Shauna's Song" is specifically written for the child who is experiencing difficulty coping emotionally with his/her speech/language problems. The parents or caretakers are encouraged to read this story to the child between therapy sessions. After reading the story, the parents or caretakers ask the child several process questions. It is hoped that the story and process questions will lead to a discussion about how the child copes with his/her speech/language problems. The specific questions are offered as guides to help the child verbalize his/her thoughts, feelings, or insecurities. The parents are encouraged to ask other questions that may be more appropriate for each individual child. It is not necessary that all the questions on the form be asked. Instruct the parents to record any noteworthy remarks made by the child and then to bring his/her responses to the next therapy session. The responses can help you identify more effective coping strategies (e.g., positive self-talk, cognitive restructuring, assertiveness training, relaxation techniques) to help the client deal with his/her insecurities or any teasing that the client may receive. The story is designed for children approximately 5 to 11 years of age. The story can also be used with children who experience problems with low self-esteem. (The process questions would have to be changed for such clients.)

SHAUNA'S SONG
READER'S INSTRUCTIONS

"Shauna's Song" is about a young songbird who experiences feelings of sadness and insecurity because she is teased by the other songbirds about her squeaky voice. Shauna withdraws, becomes very quiet, and eventually leaves home. But an unlikely friend helps Shauna discover her own talents, which she uses to help her deal with her squeaky voice.

1. "Shauna's Song" is a story written for children who experience feelings of low self-esteem and insecurity about their speech or language problems. Storytelling can be used as an effective intervention to get a child to open up and talk about his/her problems. Before reading "Shauna's Song" to the child, try to create a relaxed atmosphere. Spend a few minutes talking gently with the child. Feel free to sit on the floor with the child or have the child stretch out on the couch. Familiarize yourself with the story by reading it in advance. This will help you to be more animated or spontaneous in your expressions as you read the story.

2. The purpose of reading "Shauna's Song" is to help the child talk about his/her speech or language problems. Some children cope with their speech or language problems by withdrawing and becoming very quiet. They may be reluctant to say anything because they are worried about being teased by their peers or afraid of being seen as dumb or stupid. They may also remain quiet because they have a hard time finding the right words to express themselves. Other children react with frustration or anger when they feel insecure about their speech or language problems. They may disrupt the class with negative attention-seeking behaviors or by becoming verbally or physically aggressive. It is hoped that by talking about the child's speech or language problems, he/she will gain an acceptance of his/her problems, take steps to improve his/her speech or language skills, and feel good about himself/herself for the special talents or strengths that he/she possesses. You can help the child talk about his/her language problems by creating a supportive environment where you offer a listening ear and empathetic tone of voice.

    After reading the story, ask the child several process questions about his/her speech or language problems. Following is a list of questions that you may find helpful. These questions are offered as a guide. Feel free to ask other questions that you feel are more appropriate for each individual child. Be flexible in asking the questions—do not feel that you have to ask all of the questions. Do not force or pressure the child into responding to any questions that he/she does not want to answer. Also, with some children, you may find it beneficial to ask some of the questions as you read the story.

Record any noteworthy remarks that the child makes in response to the questions in the following spaces. The therapist will be able to process this information with the child at the next therapy session. The therapist, with your assistance, can then help the child find more effective ways to deal with his/her insecurities about the speech or language problems.

1. In the story, Shauna is teased by the other songbirds because of her squeaky voice. What speech or language problems do you have? _____

   _____

   _____

   _____

2. What type of help or services do you presently receive for your speech or language problem? _____

   _____

   _____

3. How do you deal with your speech or language problem around your family, friends, or peers? _____

   _____

   _____

   _____

   _____

4. How do your family members, friends, or peers accept your speech or language problem? _____

   _____

   _____

   _____

   _____

   _____

5. In the story, Shauna responds to the teasing by the other songbirds by becoming very quiet and leaving her home. Have you ever been teased by others because of your speech or language problem? If so, please explain. _____

   _____

   _____

   _____

   _____

6. Some children respond to teasing or their frustrations about their speech or language problems by acting up, becoming silly, or getting angry. Have you ever acted up in a silly manner or become very angry when teased or frustrated about your speech or language problem? If so, please explain. _____

_____

_____

_____

_____

7. Shauna received friendly advice and encouragement from a hawk named Skylar. Whom can you turn to for support and encouragement when you feel sad, upset, or frustrated about your speech or language problem? _____

_____

_____

_____

8. Shauna listens to Skylar's advice and returns home. She discovers that her special talents are her willingness to share and show kindness to others. What are your special talents or strengths? List at least three of them in the following space. _____

_____

_____

_____

_____

_____

9. In the end, Shauna is accepted by the other songbirds. They realize she has a very important message to send. What important things do you have to say to your family members, friends, or peers? _____

_____

_____

_____

_____

SHAUNA'S SONG

If you and your family are looking for a fun and relaxing place to visit, then y'all should come to East Tennessee and the Great Smokey Mountains National Park. The Smokies are one of the most beautiful and scenic places on earth. There are miles of trails to hike, and you never know what creature you'll meet around the next bend. When you get tired from all that hiking, just take your shoes off, and wade through a refreshing mountain stream. The Smokies are a peaceful place, especially during the early morning hours when the sun comes up through the low-lying clouds. The quiet calm of the early morning hours naturally seems to put your soul at ease. Perhaps that's one of the reasons the national park attracts so many different visitors each year.

Now, when your family is traveling by car through the foothills and small towns leading to the Smokies, roll down your window and listen for the sounds of the area. Don't be surprised if the quiet calm is broken by the sounds of dueling banjos. The hills seem to come alive when you hear banjos playing. The folks of East Tennessee take their music seriously, especially bluegrass music. When two banjo pickers get together to challenge each other and test their skills, everything else in a small town comes to a halt. The townsfolk quit doing whatever they are doing, whether it's whittling or working, and listen to the sound of the dueling banjos. Nothing gets any hotter, not even the weather during the dog days of August, than when two banjo players are trying to outdo one another.

It's not common knowledge, but some of the songbirds of East Tennessee also have a contest to see who can sing the prettiest song. The foothills of the Smokies are blessed with a variety of song birds—the mockingbird, whippoorwill, and bobwhite, among others. Their songs echo through the woods and proclaim the wonders of creation. The whippoorwills and bobwhites, just like the local people, have a friendly competition to see who can produce the sweetest sounds. The whippoorwill announces its presence by calling out its name in a beautiful melody, "Whippoorwill, whippoorwill." The bobwhites respond by singing, "Bobwhite, bobwhite, bobwhite." The whippoorwills and bobwhites take great pride in their voices and will sing for hours upon hours.

Our story takes place in the Smokey Mountain foothills. Shauna, a young whippoorwill, grew up listening to the beautiful music of her kin. Each day, she listened to the music of the forest, and she dreamed of becoming one of the best songbirds around. But, oh, poor Shauna! It quickly became apparent that she was not blessed with a good voice. She tried so hard to produce the beautiful sound of "whippoorwill, whippoorwill," but her song sounded more like a squeaky version of "wop bob a do bop, wop bop a do bop." Shauna tried, but she just couldn't get it right.

At first, her cousins and neighbors in the forest just laughed and chuckled when they heard Shauna sing, "Wop bop a do bop, wop bop a do bop." They would pat Shauna on the back with their wings and tell her to keep trying. They thought Shauna was cute when she was very young, but as she grew up and her voice didn't change, they began to wonder what was wrong with her voice. Some whippoorwills tried to be helpful and suggested that Shauna try their home remedies to help solve the problem. One of her cousins, Breanne, suggested that she eat ten nightcrawlers each day, but that just gave Shauna a bellyache. Another cousin, Kelsey, told Shauna to try flying upside-down while singing for a full hour each day. That remedy didn't work either. It just gave Shauna a headache.

The whippoorwills offered up all kinds of solutions, but each time Shauna just ended up singing out in her squeaky voice, "Wop bop a do bop, wop bop a do bop." By now, they were growing tired of trying to help Shauna. They were getting irritated at having to listen to her squeaky, unsoothing voice. Some of the whippoorwills shouted out in anger, "Be quiet" or "Pipe down." They called Shauna an embarrassment to the whippoorwills and continuously teased and made fun of her by telling her that she sounded more like a sick turkey. Their teasing hurt Shauna, and she became very quiet. She stopped singing so as not to bother the other songbirds. She felt even more hurt when none of the other whippoorwills came and asked her to join in any air games. In her sadness, she decided to fly away and find a new home where songbirds would accept her for who she was. Shauna soared high into the sky, looking for the right home. Without realizing it, Shauna flew so high that she could barely make out the trees on the ground below her. She felt a little afraid, and noticed she was surrounded by a huge shadow. Looking up, Shauna expected to see a cloud, but instead she was greeted by a red-tailed hawk, a bird of prey. Shauna thought that she was about to become a midmorning snack for the red-tailed hawk. Fortunately, the hawk was not hungry and curiously asked, "Say, little songbird, what are you doing up here so high where only the hawks and eagles soar?"

Shauna answered in her squeaky voice, "I am flying away from home. I can't sing very well, and nobody wants to listen to a songbird who can't sing." The red-tailed hawk, named Skylar, said in return, "Well, up here is no place for you. You'll only be food for the other birds of prey. I suggest that you go back home." Shauna replied, "But they'll only make fun of me or become irritated with me because of my squeaky voice. Or worse yet, they'll just ignore me."

Skylar wisely answered, "They may make fun of you, but you'll just have to show them that you have your own special talents. In time they will learn to like you for who you are." Shauna commented sadly, "I'm not good at anything." Skylar continued, "Oh, I'm sure that you're good at something. All creatures, of the land or air, have some talent that makes them special. Why, look at those ants down there on that big hill. They are working very hard to build a strong anthill. They are smart because they know that they need to build a strong home to survive the bad storms here in Tennessee." Shauna responded in amazement, "Wow, you can see ants from all the way up here! That's amazing! I can see that your special talent is that you have great eyes.

You must be able to see everything." Skylar chuckled and said, "Yes, I suppose that's what makes us hawks special. We can see things from very far off. Now, I suggest that you go home and discover what you can do well. Perhaps you'll be a great nest builder just like those ants. I'll lead you back home so you are not attacked by another hawk or eagle."

Shauna agreed to go back home. She thanked Skylar for his wisdom. After returning home, she stopped by the anthill to inspect their work. She asked them why they were building such a big anthill, and one of the ants said, "We're making it strong because the signs of nature all show that there are going to be some really big storms in a few weeks. We don't want to be unprepared."

Shauna decided to take their advice. She got busy right away, building a strong and sturdy nest that would keep her safe during the storms. She flew around gathering leaves, sticks, and twigs. She listened to the other whippoorwills sing out in their beautiful voices as she worked. While the other birds were busy admiring their own voices, Shauna kept on working. She also gathered up food supplies in case a really big storm came along. Some of the younger whippoorwills noticed how hard Shauna was working and began to tease her, "Well, we guess that you can't sing like a whippoorwill, so you've go to work hard like the sparrows do." Shauna ignored their teasing and just kept working.

One morning, Shauna woke up to the sound of rumbling thunder. She peeked out of her nest on the ground and saw that some dark storm clouds had rolled in. There was an uncomfortable quiet for a few minutes, but then the quiet was interrupted by a bolt of lightning that streaked across the sky. The rain came and the wind blew and began to howl. The earth shook when the thunder rumbled, but Shauna's nest was built so strong that it didn't shake at all. Unfortunately, the same could not be said for the other whippoorwills. They had not built their nests very strong, and the wind easily destroyed their nests. Shauna could hear many of the other whippoorwills crying out in their sad voices, "Help! Help! Help!"

Shauna heard their cries and immediately left the safety of her own nest and went to help them. Shauna flew through the rainy forest crying out, "Wop bop a do bop, wop bop a do bop! Come with me. You'll be safe in my nest." The whippoorwills now rejoiced when they heard Shauna's squeaky voice. They followed her into the safety of her nest. While the storm raged on, Shauna continued to rescue other birds; in 1 day, she rescued 25 other birds. Once she was inside her nest, Shauna could see that the other birds were frightened, wet, and hungry. She brought out her stored food and shared it with them.

Finally, the storm ended. Shauna was the first to peek her head out of her nest. She looked around and saw all of the damage from the storm. Many branches had fallen to the ground. Shauna's nest was the only one that remained. The other whippoorwills were sad that their nests were destroyed, but they were happy they were safe. No one was even hungry.

The whippoorwills left Shauna's nest one by one. They rested in the branches of a large maple tree. One of the songbirds, Lynn Elaine, said "I have to admit, Shauna, that I used to become annoyed when I heard you calling out 'wop bop a do bop,' but I sure was glad to hear your voice during the storm. You've been so kind in opening up your home to all of us. Thank you so much." Another bird, Andrew, chirped in, "I have to admit that I was one of the birds making fun of you, Shauna. I feel bad about that now. I was too busy teasing you and didn't notice how kind you are. You have a big heart. Your kindness makes you a very special whippoorwill."

Shauna humbly accepted their thanks. Inside, she felt good that she was able to help. She recognized that her special talents were helping others and showing kindness. Shauna continued to show her kindness for the rest of the day. She worked busily beside the other songbirds, helping them to rebuild their nests. She flew here and there, collecting leaves, twigs, and sticks. She gave expert advice on how to build a really strong nest. The other songbirds thanked her for her advice and willingness to help.

After all of the nests were rebuilt, all of the whippoorwills met in the middle of the forest to hold a meeting. They worked out some plans in the event that another bad storm occurred. They all agreed that the next time a terrible storm approached their hill, Shauna would alert everyone by crying out, "Wop bop a do bop, wop bop a do bop." Shauna was no longer laughed at by the other whippoorwills because of her squeaky voice. Rather, she was now respected and admired.

Now, if you are driving through the foothills of East Tennessee on the way to the Smokey Mountains, roll down your window, listen to the sounds of dueling banjos and the beautiful melody of the songbirds. But, y'all better be alert if you hear the sound of "Wop bop a do bop."

TELL ALL ABOUT IT

GOALS OF THE EXERCISE

1. Improve the expressive and receptive language abilities to the level of capability.
2. Parents increase the time spent with the client in activities that build and facilitate speech/language development.
3. Feel more comfortable and confident in expressing his/her thoughts and feelings.
4. Parents increase praise and positive reinforcement of the child in regard to his/her language development.

ADDITIONAL PROBLEMS FOR WHICH THIS EXERCISE MAY BE MOST USEFUL

- Academic Underachievement
- Depression
- Low Self-Esteem
- Social Anxiety

SUGGESTIONS FOR PROCESSING THIS EXERCISE WITH THE CLIENT

In this exercise, the child and the parents are given the directive of going on a weekly outing or engaging in a joint activity. After the outing or activity, the client is required to retell his/her experience. Instruct the parents to allow the client to take the lead in sharing his/her thoughts and feelings. However, the parents can ask questions or prompt the child if he/she is too brief in verbalizing his/her thoughts and feelings. The exercise seeks to help the child feel more comfortable and confident in communicating his/her thoughts and feelings. Younger children can also be encouraged to verbally share their experiences at school (e.g., show and tell).

TELL ALL ABOUT IT

The purpose of this assignment is to help you feel more comfortable and confident in speaking to others, while also having fun. In this assignment, you are asked to go on a weekly outing or to spend time with your family in some activity. Then you are asked to retell your experience to your parents. Pretend that you are an artist as you retell your story, and instead of using paintbrushes, you can use your words to paint a picture of what you did.

1. The first step in this exercise is for you to meet with your parents and family members to decide what activity or outing you want to go on during the next week. The activity or outing should last for at least 1 hour. There are a number of different activities that you can do or places that you can go. If your family is unable to come up with any ideas on what to do, then here are some suggestions:
    *   Go to movie or watch a video together
    *   Take a hike in the woods
    *   Visit a museum on natural history
    *   Go to a children's museum
    *   Tour a factory in local community
    *   Attend a sporting event, play, or concert
    *   Go to a parade or city festival
    *   Visit an historical site in the community
    *   Travel to a new place of interest in the car
    *   Go to a puppet show or ballet
    *   Take a bike ride to a new area
    *   Go rollerblading
    *   Take a walk in the neighborhood and identify all cars 10 years old or older
    (*Note to parents:* Allow your child and other siblings to take the lead in deciding what to do. Establish boundaries or limits as far as cost and distance are concerned.)

2. After the activity or outing has been completed, meet with your parents and retell your experiences from start to finish. Take the lead in sharing your thoughts and feelings about your experiences. Following is a list of questions that your parents may ask to help you express your thoughts and feelings. Your parents are encouraged to ask other questions that they feel may be appropriate for your experiences.
    (*Note to parents:* Encourage child to retell the experience from start to finish. Prompt the child by asking what happened next.)

- What did you like most about the outing or activity?
- What did you dislike about the activity or experience?
- What new or interesting things did you experience?
- What did you learn during your activity or outing?
- Would you like to do this activity or go on this outing again? Why or why not?
- What would you do differently?

3. Describing your experiences will give you the chance to learn the meaning of some new words. Pay attention to some new words or key terms as you go through your experiences. Then identify three new words or key terms that you learned during your activity or outing. List the three words in the appropriate spaces, and then either define the words or use them in sentences. Use a dictionary, if needed. If you do not remember hearing any new words, then identify three key terms that relate to your activity or outing; either define the terms or use them in sentences.

First new word:

_____

Define the word or use it in a sentence.

_____

_____

_____

Second new word:

_____

Define the word or use it in a sentence.

_____

_____

_____

Third new word:

_____

Define the word or use it in a sentence.

_____

_____

_____

APPENDIX A:
ALTERNATE ASSIGNMENTS FOR PRESENTING PROBLEMS

ACADEMIC UNDERACHIEVEMENT

Attention-Deficit Hyperactivity Disorder (ADHD) — Getting It Done

Intellectual Development Disorder — Activities of Daily Living Program

Intellectual Development Disorder — A Sense of Belonging

Low Self-Esteem — Learn From Your Mistakes

Medical Condition — Dealing With Childhood Asthma

School Refusal — A Pleasant Journey

School Refusal — Letter of Encouragement

Speech/Language Disorders — Home-Based Reading and Language Program

Speech/Language Disorders — Shauna's Song

Speech/Language Disorders — Tell All About It

ADOPTION

Attachment Disorder — Attachment Survey

Blended Family — Blended Family Sentence Completion

Blended Family — Interviewing My New Family Member

ANGER CONTROL PROBLEMS

Attention-Deficit Hyperactivity Disorder (ADHD) — Problem-Solving Exercise

Bullying/Intimidation Perpetrator — Apology Letter for Bullying

Bullying/Intimidation Perpetrator — Bullying Incident Report

Conduct Disorder/Delinquency — Building Empathy

Conduct Disorder/Delinquency — Childhood Patterns of Stealing

Conduct Disorder/Delinquency — Risk Factors Leading to Child Behavior Problems

Depression — Childhood Depression Survey

Depression — Surface Behavior/Inner Feelings

Social Anxiety — Learn to Be Assertive

ANXIETY

Academic Underachievement	Positive Self-Statements
Conduct Disorder/Delinquency	Concerns About Parent's Drug or Alcohol Problem
Depression	Replace Negative Thoughts With Positive Self-Talk
Depression	Three Ways to Change the World
Divorce Reaction	Feelings and Faces Game
Divorce Reaction	My Thoughts and Feelings About My Parents' Divorce
Fire Setting	When a Fire Has No Fuel
Grief/Loss Unresolved	Create a Memory Album
Grief/Loss Unresolved	Grief Letter
Grief/Loss Unresolved	Petey's Journey Through Sadness
Low Self-Esteem	Dixie Overcomes Her Fears
Low Self-Esteem	Learn From Your Mistakes
Low Self-Esteem	Symbols of Self-Worth
Low Self-Esteem	Three Ways to Change Yourself
Low Self-Esteem	Three Wishes Game
Obsessive-Compulsive Disorder (OCD)	Concerns, Feelings, and Hopes About OCD
Obsessive-Compulsive Disorder (OCD)	Refocusing
Obsessive-Compulsive Disorder (OCD)	Ritual Exposure and Response Prevention
Overweight/Obesity	Increasing My Physical Activity
Overweight/Obesity	My Eating and Exercise Journal
School Refusal	A Pleasant Journey
Separation Anxiety	Explore Your World
Social Anxiety	Greeting Peers
Social Anxiety	Learn to Be Assertive
Specific Phobia	Expressions of Fear Through Art
Specific Phobia	Maurice Faces His Fear

REACTIVE ATTACHMENT/DISINHIBITED SOCIAL ENGAGEMENT DISORDER

Autism Spectrum Disorder	Initial Reaction to Diagnosis of Autism
Autism Spectrum Disorder	Reaction to Change and Excessive Stimulation
Blended Family	Interviewing My New Family Member

ATTENTION-DEFICIT/HYPERACTIVITY DISORDER (ADHD)

Academic Underachievement	Establish a Homework Routine
Academic Underachievement	Reading Adventure
Anger Control Problems	Anger Control
Autism Spectrum Disorder	Reaction to Change and Excessive Stimulation
Conduct Disorder/Delinquency	Childhood Patterns of Stealing
Enuresis/Encopresis	Bladder Retention Training Program
Enuresis/Encopresis	Dry Bed Training Program
Fire Setting	Fireproofing Your Home and Family
Low Self-Esteem	Three Ways to Change Yourself
Lying/Manipulative	Bad Choice—Lying to Cover Up Another Lie
Lying/Manipulative	The Value of Honesty
Lying/Manipulative	Truthful/Lying Incident Reports
Medical Condition	Gaining Acceptance of Physical Handicap or Illness
Oppositional Defiant	Filing a Complaint
Oppositional Defiant	Share a Family Meal
Oppositional Defiant	Switching From Defense to Offense
Parenting	Being a Consistent Parent
Parenting	Picking Your Battles
Peer/Sibling Conflict	Negotiating a Peace Treaty

AUTISM SPECTRUM DISORDER

Attention-Deficit Hyperactivity Disorder (ADHD)	Social Skills Exercise
Intellectual Development Disorder	Activities of Daily Living Program
Intellectual Development Disorder	A Sense of Belonging
Medical Condition	Gaining Acceptance of Physical Handicap or Illness

BLENDED FAMILY

Adoption	Some Things I Would Like You to Know About Me
Divorce Reaction	Feelings and Faces Game
Divorce Reaction	My Thoughts and Feelings About My Parents' Divorce
Oppositional Defiant	Share a Family Meal

BULLYING/INTIMIDATION PERPETRATOR

Anger Control Problems	The Lesson of Salmon Rock...Fighting Leads to Loneliness
Conduct Disorder/Delinquency	Building Empathy
Disruptive/Attention-Seeking	Finding Ways to Get Positive Attention
Disruptive/Attention-Seeking	Reasons for Negative Attention-Seeking Behaviors

CONDUCT DISORDER/DELINQUENCY

Anger Control Problems	Anger Control
Anger Control Problems	Child Anger Checklist
Attention-Deficit Hyperactivity Disorder (ADHD)	Getting It Done
Attention-Deficit Hyperactivity Disorder (ADHD)	Problem-Solving Exercise
Attention-Deficit Hyperactivity Disorder (ADHD)	Social Skills Exercise
Bullying/Intimidation Perpetrator	Apology Letter for Bullying
Depression	Surface Behavior/Inner Feelings
Fire Setting	Fireproofing Your Home and Family
Low Self-Esteem	Three Ways to Change Yourself
Low Self-Esteem	Three Wishes Game
Lying/Manipulative	Bad Choice—Lying to Cover Up Another Lie
Lying/Manipulative	The Value of Honesty
Lying/Manipulative	Truthful/Lying Incident Reports
Oppositional Defiant	Filing a Complaint
Oppositional Defiant	Share a Family Meal
Oppositional Defiant	Switching From Defense to Offense
Parenting	Being a Consistent Parent
Peer/Sibling Conflict	Negotiating a Peace Treaty

DEPRESSION

Academic Underachievement	Positive Self-Statements
Anxiety	Worry Time
Attention-Deficit Hyperactivity Disorder (ADHD)	Problem-Solving Exercise
Bullying/Intimidation Perpetrator	Bullying Incident Report
Divorce Reaction	Feelings and Faces Game

Divorce Reaction	My Thoughts and Feelings About My Parents' Divorce
Gender Identity Disorder	One-on-One
Grief/Loss Unresolved	Create a Memory Album
Grief/Loss Unresolved	Grief Letter
Grief/Loss Unresolved	Petey's Journey Through Sadness
Intellectual Development Disorder	Activities of Daily Living Program
Intellectual Development Disorder	A Sense of Belonging
Low Self-Esteem	Learn From Your Mistakes
Low Self-Esteem	Symbols of Self-Worth
Low Self-Esteem	Three Ways to Change Yourself
Low Self-Esteem	Three Wishes Game
Overweight/Obesity	Developing and Implementing a Healthier Diet
Overweight/Obesity	Increasing My Physical Activity
Overweight/Obesity	My Eating and Exercise Journal
Physical/Emotional Abuse Victim	Letter of Empowerment
Separation Anxiety	Explore Your World
Sexual Abuse Victim	You Are Not Alone
Sleep Disturbance	Childhood Sleep Problems
Social Anxiety	Greeting Peers
Social Anxiety	Show Your Strengths
Speech/Language Disorders	Home-Based Reading and Language Program
Speech/Language Disorders	Tell All About It

DISRUPTIVE/ATTENTION-SEEKING

Anger Control Problems	Child Anger Checklist
Conduct Disorder/Delinquency	Concerns About Parent's Drug or Alcohol Problem
Conduct Disorder/Delinquency	Risk Factors Leading to Child Behavior Problems
Lying/Manipulative	Bad Choice—Lying to Cover Up Another Lie
Lying/Manipulative	Truthful/Lying Incident Reports

DIVORCE REACTION

Blended Family	Blended Family Sentence Completion
Blended Family	Thoughts and Feelings About Parent's Live-In Partner
Depression	Childhood Depression Survey

| Depression | Surface Behavior/Inner Feelings |
| Posttraumatic Stress Disorder (PTSD) | PTSD Incident Report |

ENURESIS/ENCOPRESIS

| Low Self-Esteem | Dixie Overcomes Her Fears |
| Sleep Disturbance | Childhood Sleep Problems |

FIRE SETTING

Anger Control Problems	Anger Control
Conduct Disorder/Delinquency	Risk Factors Leading to Child Behavior Problems
Enuresis/Encopresis	Bladder Retention Training Program
Enuresis/Encopresis	Dry Bed Training Program

GENDER DYSPHORIA

| Disruptive/Attention-Seeking | Finding Ways to Get Positive Attention |
| Low Self-Esteem | Three Ways to Change Yourself |

GRIEF/LOSS UNRESOLVED

Anger Control Problems	The Lesson of Salmon Rock . . . Fighting Leads to Loneliness
Depression	Childhood Depression Survey
Divorce Reaction	Feelings and Faces Game
Divorce Reaction	My Thoughts and Feelings About My Parents' Divorce
Fire Setting	When a Fire Has No Fuel
Posttraumatic Stress Disorder (PTSD)	PTSD Incident Report
Sexual Abuse Victim	My Story
Sexual Abuse Victim	You Are Not Alone

INTELLECTUAL DEVELOPMENTAL DISORDER

Academic Underachievement	Reading Adventure
Autism Spectrum Disorder	Initial Reaction to Diagnosis of Autism
Autism Spectrum Disorder	Reaction to Change and Excessive Stimulation
Speech/Language Disorders	Shauna's Song

LOW SELF-ESTEEM

Academic Underachievement	Positive Self-Statements
Academic Underachievement	Reading Adventure
Adoption	Some Things I Would Like You to Know About Me
Anxiety	Worry Time
Attention-Deficit Hyperactivity Disorder (ADHD)	Getting It Done
Depression	Childhood Depression Survey
Depression	Replace Negative Thoughts With Positive Self-Talk
Depression	Three Ways to Change the World
Enuresis/Encopresis	Bladder Retention Training Program
Enuresis/Encopresis	Bowel Control Training Program
Enuresis/Encopresis	Dry Bed Training Program
Gender Identity Disorder	I Want to Be Like . . .
Gender Identity Disorder	One-on-One
Grief/Loss Unresolved	Create a Memory Album
Grief/Loss Unresolved	Petey's Journey Through Sadness
Intellectual Development Disorder	A Sense of Belonging
Overweight/Obesity	Developing and Implementing a Healthier Diet
Overweight/Obesity	Increasing My Physical Activity
Peer/Sibling Conflict	Joseph, His "Amazing Technicolor Coat," and More
Physical/Emotional Abuse Victim	My Thoughts and Feelings
Sexual Abuse Victim	My Story
Social Anxiety	Greeting Peers
Social Anxiety	Learn to Be Assertive
Social Anxiety	Show Your Strengths
Speech/Language Disorders	Home-Based Reading and Language Program
Speech/Language Disorders	Shauna's Song
Speech/Language Disorders	Tell All About It

LYING/MANIPULATIVE

Conduct Disorder/Delinquency	Building Empathy
Conduct Disorder/Delinquency	Childhood Patterns of Stealing
Conduct Disorder/Delinquency	Concerns About Parent's Drug or Alcohol Problem

| Disruptive/Attention-Seeking | Finding Ways to Get Positive Attention |
| Disruptive/Attention-Seeking | Reasons for Negative Attention-Seeking Behaviors |

MEDICAL CONDITION

Overweight/Obesity	Increasing My Physical Activity
Overweight/Obesity	My Eating and Exercise Journal
Sleep Disturbance	Childhood Sleep Problems

OBSESSIVE-COMPULSIVE DISORDER (OCD)

| Anxiety | An Anxious Story |
| Depression | Surface Behavior/Inner Feelings |

OPPOSITIONAL DEFIANT

Academic Underachievement	Establish a Homework Routine
Anger Control Problems	Anger Control
Anger Control Problems	Child Anger Checklist
Anger Control Problems	The Lesson of Salmon Rock . . . Fighting Leads to Loneliness
Attention-Deficit Hyperactivity Disorder (ADHD)	Getting It Done
Attention-Deficit Hyperactivity Disorder (ADHD)	Problem-Solving Exercise
Attention-Deficit Hyperactivity Disorder (ADHD)	Social Skills Exercise
Bullying/Intimidation Perpetrator	Bullying Incident Report
Conduct Disorder/Delinquency	Building Empathy
Conduct Disorder/Delinquency	Childhood Patterns of Stealing
Conduct Disorder/Delinquency	Concerns About Parent's Drug or Alcohol Problem
Conduct Disorder/Delinquency	Risk Factors Leading to Child Behavior Problems
Depression	Surface Behavior/Inner Feelings
Disruptive/Attention-Seeking	Finding Ways to Get Positive Attention
Disruptive/Attention-Seeking	Reasons for Negative Attention-Seeking Behaviors
Enuresis/Encopresis	Bowel Control Training Program

Fire Setting	Fireproofing Your Home and Family
Intellectual Development Disorder	Activities of Daily Living Program
Low Self-Esteem	Three Wishes Game
Lying/Manipulative	Bad Choice—Lying to Cover Up Another Lie
Lying/Manipulative	The Value of Honesty
Lying/Manipulative	Truthful/Lying Incident Reports
Parenting	Being a Consistent Parent
Parenting	Picking Your Battles
Peer/Sibling Conflict	Joseph, His "Amazing Technicolor Coat," and More
Peer/Sibling Conflict	Negotiating a Peace Treaty
Physical/Emotional Abuse Victim	Letter of Empowerment
Physical/Emotional Abuse Victim	My Thoughts and Feelings

OVERWEIGHT/OBESITY

Low Self-Esteem	Three Ways to Change Yourself

PARENTING

Blended Family	Thoughts and Feelings About Parent's Live-In Partner

PEER/SIBLING CONFLICT

Attention-Deficit Hyperactivity Disorder (ADHD)	Social Skills Exercise
Blended Family	Blended Family Sentence Completion
Blended Family	Thoughts and Feelings About Parent's Live-In Partner
Bullying/Intimidation Perpetrator	Apology Letter for Bullying
Disruptive/Attention-Seeking	Finding Ways to Get Positive Attention
Disruptive/Attention-Seeking	Reasons for Negative Attention-Seeking Behaviors
Fire Setting	When a Fire Has No Fuel
Lying/Manipulative	The Value of Honesty
Oppositional Defiant	Filing a Complaint
Oppositional Defiant	If I Could Run My Family
Oppositional Defiant	Share a Family Meal
Oppositional Defiant	Switching From Defense to Offense

PHYSICAL/EMOTIONAL ABUSE VICTIM

Anxiety	Deep Breathing Exercise
Attachment Disorder	Building Relationships
Depression	Three Ways to Change the World
Enuresis/Encopresis	Bowel Control Training Program
Peer/Sibling Conflict	Joseph, His "Amazing Technicolor Coat," and More
Posttraumatic Stress Disorder (PTSD)	Finding My Triggers
Posttraumatic Stress Disorder (PTSD)	PTSD Incident Report
Sexual Abuse Victim	My Story
Sexual Abuse Victim	You Are Not Alone
Sleep Disturbance	Reduce Nighttime Fears

POSTTRAUMATIC STRESS DISORDER (PTSD)

Anger Control Problems	Child Anger Checklist
Anxiety	Deep Breathing Exercise
Attachment Disorder	Attachment Survey
Overweight/Obesity	Developing and Implementing a Healthier Diet
Physical/Emotional Abuse Victim	Letter of Empowerment
Physical/Emotional Abuse Victim	My Thoughts and Feelings
Sleep Disturbance	Childhood Sleep Problems

SCHOOL REFUSAL

Academic Underachievement	Positive Self-Statements
Anxiety	An Anxious Story
Gender Identity Disorder	One-on-One
Oppositional Defiant	If I Could Run My Family
Separation Anxiety	Explore Your World
Separation Anxiety	Parents' Time Away
Sleep Disturbance	Reduce Nighttime Fears
Specific Phobia	Expressions of Fear Through Art
Specific Phobia	Maurice Faces His Fear

SEPARATION ANXIETY

Anxiety	An Anxious Story
Anxiety	Deep Breathing Exercise

Anxiety	Finding and Losing Your Anxiety
Anxiety	Worry Time
Depression	Replace Negative Thoughts With Positive Self-Talk
Gender Identity Disorder	I Want to Be Like …
Gender Identity Disorder	One-on-One
Grief/Loss Unresolved	Create a Memory Album
Grief/Loss Unresolved	Petey's Journey Through Sadness
Low Self-Esteem	Dixie Overcomes Her Fears
Low Self-Esteem	Symbols of Self-Worth
Obsessive-Compulsive Disorder (OCD)	Refocusing
Obsessive-Compulsive Disorder (OCD)	Ritual Exposure and Response Prevention
Posttraumatic Stress Disorder (PTSD)	Finding My Triggers
School Refusal	A Pleasant Journey
School Refusal	Letter of Encouragement
School Refusal	School Fear Reduction
Sleep Disturbance	Childhood Sleep Problems
Sleep Disturbance	Reduce Nighttime Fears
Social Anxiety	Show Your Strengths
Specific Phobia	Expressions of Fear Through Art
Specific Phobia	Maurice Faces His Fear

SEXUAL ABUSE VICTIM

Anxiety	Deep Breathing Exercise
Attachment Disorder	Building Relationships
Depression	Three Ways to Change the World
Enuresis/Encopresis	Bowel Control Training Program
Fire Setting	When a Fire Has No Fuel
Oppositional Defiant	If I Could Run My Family
Physical/Emotional Abuse Victim	Letter of Empowerment
Physical/Emotional Abuse Victim	My Thoughts and Feelings
Posttraumatic Stress Disorder (PTSD)	Finding My Triggers
Posttraumatic Stress Disorder (PTSD)	PTSD Incident Report
Sleep Disturbance	Reduce Nighttime Fears

SLEEP DISTURBANCE

Posttraumatic Stress Disorder (PTSD)	Finding My Triggers
Sexual Abuse Victim	You Are Not Alone

SOCIAL ANXIETY

Anxiety	An Anxious Story
Anxiety	Deep Breathing Exercise
Anxiety	Finding and Losing Your Anxiety
Attention-Deficit Hyperactivity Disorder (ADHD)	Social Skills Exercise
Blended Family	Interviewing My New Family Member
Depression	Replace Negative Thoughts With Positive Self-Talk
Gender Identity Disorder	I Want to Be Like ...
Low Self-Esteem	Dixie Overcomes Her Fears
Low Self-Esteem	Learn From Your Mistakes
Low Self-Esteem	Symbols of Self-Worth
Medical Condition	Gaining Acceptance of Physical Handicap or Illness
School Refusal	A Pleasant Journey
School Refusal	Letter of Encouragement
School Refusal	School Fear Reduction
Separation Anxiety	Explore Your World
Separation Anxiety	Parents' Time Away
Specific Phobia	Expressions of Fear Through Art
Specific Phobia	Maurice Faces His Fear
Speech/Language Disorders	Home-Based Reading and Language Program
Speech/Language Disorders	Tell All About It

SPECIFIC PHOBIA

Anxiety	An Anxious Story
Anxiety	Deep Breathing Exercise
Anxiety	Finding and Losing Your Anxiety
Anxiety	Worry Time
Low Self-Esteem	Dixie Overcomes Her Fears
Obsessive-Compulsive Disorder (OCD)	Concerns, Feelings, and Hopes About OCD

Obsessive-Compulsive Disorder (OCD)	Refocusing
Obsessive-Compulsive Disorder (OCD)	Ritual Exposure and Response Prevention
School Refusal	A Pleasant Journey
School Refusal	Letter of Encouragement
School Refusal	School Fear Reduction
Separation Anxiety	Explore Your World
Social Anxiety	Show Your Strengths

SPEECH/LANGUAGE DISORDERS

Academic Underachievement	Reading Adventure
Intellectual Development Disorder	A Sense of Belonging
Medical Condition	Dealing With Childhood Asthma
Medical Condition	Gaining Acceptance of Physical Handicap or Illness

APPENDIX B:
ALPHABETICAL INDEX OF EXERCISES

ABOUT THE DOWNLOADABLE ASSIGNMENTS

Thank you for choosing the Wiley Practice*Planners*® series. *Child Psychotherapy Homework Planner*, Fifth Edition's website includes all the book's exercises in Word format for your convenience.

To access the assignments, please follow these steps:

Step 1 Go to www.wiley.com/go/hwpassignments

Step 2 Enter your email address, the password provided below, and click "submit"
Password: child2015

Step 3 Select and download the listed exercises

If you need any assistance, please contact Wiley Customer Care 800-762-2974 (U.S.), 317-572-3994 (International) or visit www.wiley.com.